Scripture Backgrounds

FOR THE Sunday Lectionary

A RESOURCE FOR HOMILISTS

YEAR A

Mary A. Ehle

Peg Ekerdt

Jean Marie Hiesberger

Biagio Mazza

Mary M. McGlone, CSJ

Abbot Gregory J. Polan, OSB

Denise Simeone

George Smiga

Paul Turner

LITURGY
TRAINING
PUBLICATIONS

Nihil Obstat
Very Reverend Daniel A. Smilanic, JCD
Vicar for Canonical Services
Archdiocese of Chicago
May 9, 2016

Imprimatur
Very Reverend Ronald A. Hicks
Vicar General
Archdiocese of Chicago
May 9, 2016

SCRIPTURE BACKGROUNDS FOR THE SUNDAY LECTIONARY, YEAR A: A RESOURCE FOR HOMILISTS. © 2016 Archdiocese of Chicago: Liturgy Training Publications, 3949 South Racine Avenue, Chicago, IL 60609; 1-800-933-1800, fax 1-800-933-7094, e-mail orders@ltp.org. All rights reserved. See our website at www.LTP.org.

Cover and interior art by Steve Musgrave.

20 19 18 17 16   1 2 3 4 5

Printed in the United States of America.

Library of Congress Control Number: 2016946400

ISBN: 978-1-61671-312-6

SBSLA

For the Christian, Jesus' fulfillment of the Old Testament attributes the utmost importance to the truth of the Jewish Scriptures. Of course, the supreme reader of the Old Testament is Christ himself, who applied to his own life, Death, and Resurrection all that the Scriptures had promised (Luke 24:27). It is through this rich relationship between the Old and the New Testaments, in all of their various interrelated images and types, that the homilist is able to proclaim to the faithful the one supreme mystery of faith that is Jesus Christ.

Preaching the Mystery of Faith: The Sunday Homily
United States Conference of Catholic Bishops

Contents

Advent

Once again, we enter Advent. Most of us recognize this as the time during which we prepare for Christmas. The hectic pace of our lives seems to increase rapidly each year, especially with the passing of the Thanksgiving holiday. Yet, the liturgical year gifts us with the opportunity to slow down and reflect on the significance of what and whom we will celebrate on Christmas and throughout Christmas Time. This opportunity is the time of Advent, which includes the four Sundays and the weekdays in between those Sundays until Evening Prayer I of Christmas, prayed on Christmas Eve.

Advent has three dimensions. It is the season to prepare for Christmas when we remember Christ's first coming long ago, celebrate Christ in our hearts today, and wait in joyful expectation as we ponder our belief in Christ's Second Coming in glory at the end of time. These three dimensions are what we prepare to celebrate in the Church's liturgies of Christmas Time and in our lives.

FIRST READINGS

The First Readings during Advent are from the Old Testament and are prophecies about the Messiah and the messianic age. For three of the four Sundays of Advent, the First Reading is from the Book of the prophet Isaiah, although from different parts of this book. On all four Sundays, the First Reading sets the stage for the Gospel, which identifies Jesus as the one who fulfills the prophecies of the Messiah. Jesus, born of a virgin and named Emmanuel, is the Lord's sign of salvation for his people.

RESPONSORIAL PSALMS

The new liturgical year begins on the First Sunday of Advent with the same Responsorial Psalm that was sung on the Solemnity of Jesus Christ, King of the Universe to conclude the previous liturgical year, Year C. Psalm 122 encourages us to go rejoicing to the Lord's house. The psalms for the Second and Third Sundays of Advent speak of the Lord's justice and his coming to save us, respectively (Psalms 72 and 146). On the Fourth Sunday of Advent, Psalm 24 bookends that of the First Sunday as it, like the psalm on the First Sunday, speaks of "entering." It calls us to let the Lord enter, because he is the King of Glory.

SECOND READINGS

On three of the four Sundays of Advent in Year A, the Second Reading comes from Paul's Letter to the Romans. On the other Sunday, the Third Sunday of Advent, the Second Reading is from the Letter of James. The exhortations to awake from sleep, to welcome one another as Christ welcomes us, to be patient until the coming of the Lord, and to be obedient and firm in our faith in the Son of God are the common Advent themes of the Second Readings.

GOSPEL READINGS

As we begin the new liturgical year with the First Sunday of Advent, we also move into Year A of the Lectionary cycle of readings. In Year A, the Gospel according to Matthew is the primary account of the Gospel proclaimed in the Sunday liturgy. The Gospel readings from Matthew introduce us to Jesus who is Emmanuel—God-with-us—who comes to instruct his disciples and us today about what it means to be his followers.

During Advent of each of the three years of the Lectionary cycle of readings, the Gospel reading has a particular theme related to the meaning of the season. The Gospel on the First Sunday of Advent speaks of the Lord's coming at the end of time. This year, Year A, the Gospel on the first Sunday of Advent has Jesus teaching his disciples about staying awake for the coming day of the Lord. On the Second and Third Sundays of Advent, the Gospel reading involves John the Baptist. In particular, the Gospel readings for these Sundays in Year A, the year of Matthew, are about John the Baptist's call to repentance and Jesus' own affirmation of John as the messenger who prepared the way for him, and the followers of John querying Jesus as to whether or not he is the one who is to come. The Gospel proclaimed on the Fourth Sunday of Advent each year always focuses on an event that immediately precedes the Lord's birth. In Year A, the Gospel on this Sunday involves Joseph, Jesus' foster father, who appears infrequently in the Gospel readings proclaimed during the Church's liturgies. The Gospel is an intensely personal interaction between Joseph and an angel, who appears to him in a dream, asking him to take Mary into his home because the child she bears has been conceived through the Holy Spirit.

ISAIAH 2:1–5 Isaiah was a prophet in the eighth century BC. Chapter 2 is part of a collection of oracles against Jerusalem and the southern kingdom of Judah for their apostasy. The northern kingdom of Israel along with its capital, Samaria, was conquered by the Assyrians in 733 BC and was later destroyed in 722 BC. In the prophet Isaiah's time, King Hezekiah demolished the idolatry practiced on the "high places" (2 Kings 18:4) and tried to centralize worship in Jerusalem. Isaiah sees a time in the future when all nations shall stream to the Holy City to receive instruction from the Lord. It will be a time of world peace when people "beat their swords into plowshares and their spears into pruning hooks" (v. 4). All peoples will be attracted to the true worship offered by God on Mount Zion.

PSALM 122:1–2, 3–4, 4–5, 6–7, 8–9 Psalm 122 is a psalm of ascent, sung by pilgrims as they reached the gates of Jerusalem. According to God's decree, the tribes were to go up to the Holy City three times a year for the pilgrimage feasts of Passover, Pentecost, and Tabernacles. As they gathered for worship, the pilgrims prayed in thanksgiving for God's protection on their journey and for the peace and prosperity of Jerusalem. The city had been the religious and political capital of Israel from the time of David. Prayer for Jerusalem was a prayer for the good of the whole nation. In time, Jerusalem became the symbol of the Church, the New Jerusalem.

ROMANS 13:11–14 Paul stresses the urgency of the time. He declares that salvation is near and urges that "it is now the moment for you to wake from sleep" (v. 11). He and the early Church expected the Second Coming of Christ at any moment; they were to live ready for it to happen.

Paul's words in the last verses of this passage brought St. Augustine to conversion, as he describes in his autobiographical work *Confessions*. Augustine was walking in the garden, distressed because of his failure to live a life in Christ. Suddenly, he heard a child's voice saying, "Take and read; take and read." He snatched up a volume of Paul's writings and read the first passage on which his eyes fell: "The night is advanced, the day is at hand" (v. 12). Like Paul, Augustine shed his former way of life and "put on the

CONNECTIONS TO CHURCH TEACHING AND TRADITION

- During Advent the Church presents the ancient expectancy of the Messiah and his coming in the flesh in the Incarnation. It is a season of preparation, worship, and service (CCC, 524).

- In Advent we await Christ's Second Coming at the end of time, described as "eschatological," which can happen at any moment (CCC, 673, 840, 2853).

- We pray for and anticipate God's promise of peace and justice in the world. Peace is God's gift, the fruit of the Holy Spirit and charity, the foundation of the common good (CCC, 736, 1828–1832, 1909).

Lord Jesus Christ" (v. 14). Now is the time for all Christians to wake and live in the light of the new life they have received in Jesus Christ.

MATTHEW 24:37–44 Chapters 24–25 form the fifth and final discourse in the Gospel according to Matthew. Jesus speaks both of the destruction of Jerusalem by the Romans in AD 70 and of his coming at the end of time. The early Christians eagerly anticipated the Second Coming, and they longed for the liberation from suffering that he would bring.

Jesus does not give them a timetable, but says that they will see warning signs of his return. He points to the fig tree and tells them to learn its lesson (v. 32). If a person can tell when summer is near by the signs of nature, so, too, the signs of the times will indicate when Christ is near. Yet no one knows the time of his coming, not the angels, not even Jesus himself. The exact time of his return is known to none but God. It is futile for Jesus' disciples to speculate; their duty is to prepare and to watch.

Jesus warns them that his coming will be similar to Noah's day. When "God saw that the earth was corrupt," God determined to "bring a flood of waters on the earth" (Genesis 6:12, 17). The perverse and lawless people had no concern about the future until it was too late and "the flood came and carried them all away" (Matthew 24:39). Noah was "a righteous man and blameless in his generation" (Genesis 6:9). Because he listened to God's warning, he and his family were saved from destruction. So, too, at the time of Christ's coming, men and women will be preoccupied with their ordinary activities. Those who are prepared for his arrival will be taken into God's Kingdom. Those who are unready will be left in their own sin. Jesus' followers must be vigilant for his return whenever it may occur.

Second Sunday of Advent
Justice Shall Flourish

ISAIAH 11:1–10 Isaiah paints the possibility of a reign of justice and faithfulness where the spirit of wisdom and harmony will sprout and grow. The Israelites could imagine all the signs of a new springtime sprouting forth almost instantly, like seeing a flower bloom in time-lapse photography. In the previous chapter, Isaiah used natural images to tell of the destruction of unfaithful kings: "Behold, the Lord, the Lord of hosts, / lops off the boughs with terrible violence; / The tall of stature are felled, / and the lofty ones brought low; / The forest thickets are felled with the axe, / and Lebanon in its splendor falls" (Isaiah 10:33–34). Isaiah brings to life the qualities a king was supposed to have and demonstrates what would happen under such a king's reign. Isaiah's description of the world that we hope for is reminiscent of the Garden of Eden.

Isaiah's listeners hoped for a political king to make this kingdom of God possible. But Israel must remain firmly rooted in God, confident in their hope for such a Messiah. As such, believers have found in this passage a deeper meaning that has been revealed through the coming of Jesus Christ. Jesus Christ, the Messiah, the sign of God's fidelity to his people, is the fulfillment of Isaiah's prophecy.

PSALM 72:1–2, 7–8, 12–13, 17 (SEE 7) A perfect world where justice and peace and abundance will flourish forever. This sounds incredible and perhaps even impossible, yet Psalm 72 imagines just such a world. All people—especially the poor, the afflicted, and the lowly—will be rescued and saved. All will have what they need, and because of this, justice will flourish and peace will reign.

This royal psalm prays for blessings upon the reign of the anointed king. In an ideal world, this king, who as God's representative was to care for the weaker members of the community, was also to govern with justice and release God's blessings upon his people. But earthly kings fell short of this work, and when the rule of kings ended in the sixth century BC, God's people continued to hope for this kind of intervention. They believed in the possibility of God's kingdom of peace and justice and expressed it in their hope for the coming of a Messiah. This Advent, we, too, can pray this psalm in longing for a world that will bring about God's reign, full of the fruits of justice and peace. As we pray, we

- "Many Jews and even certain Gentiles who shared their hope recognized in Jesus the fundamental attributes of the messianic 'Son of David,' promised by God to Israel (cf. Matthew 2:2; 9:27; 12:23; 15:22; 20:30; 21:9, 15)" (CCC, 439).

- "Love of preference for the poor, and the decisions which it inspires in us, cannot but embrace the immense multitudes of the hungry, the needy, the homeless, those without medical care and, above all, those without hope of a better future" (SRS, 42).

- "Action on behalf of justice and participation in the transformation of the world fully appear to us as a constitutive dimension of the preaching of the Gospel, or, in other words, of the Church's mission for the redemption of the human race and its liberation from every oppressive situation" (JM, 6).

prepare ourselves to do our part that justice and peace might flourish.

ROMANS 15:4–9 In his letter to the Romans, Paul makes it clear that there are no special rights to salvation that come with being either a Jew or Gentile. Rather, the righteous are saved because Jesus Christ died and rose for all, Jew and Gentile alike. God's action in Christ has brought salvation. For Paul, followers of the Messiah are called to respond to his call by the way they live. In these verses, which are part of Paul's response to an argument begun in chapter 14, he advises his listeners to think in harmony, praise God in one voice, and welcome others as Christ did. Despite conflict, tensions, or divisions, believers must act like Christ because they have been shown mercy, grace, and salvation by God's astounding action in Christ.

MATTHEW 3:1–12 We may wonder why Matthew spends so much time describing John the Baptist's strange clothes and odd diet. By describing his camel-hair clothing and leather belt, Matthew links John to prophets before him, such as Elijah and Samuel, who preached against injustice and called for social transformation. John's clothing indicates that he, too, will preach about the coming of a reign of justice and the need to reform one's life and heart. Repentance is a necessary part of baptism, and producing good fruits demonstrates a repentant heart.

In Luke's version of this scene, the Baptist speaks to the multitudes, but in Matthew, John directs his words to the Pharisees and Sadducees, the religious leaders of his time. His point seems to challenge them with the question, What made you think you could escape this call to produce good fruit? They cannot claim that their religious superiority or legacy exempts them from this condition of repentance. Perhaps this is a good question for us to ask ourselves as believers this Advent. We can claim nothing in the face of God's judgment except how we have changed our lives, believed in the Messiah, and helped build up the kingdom of God.

The Lord Comes to Save

ISAIAH 35:1–6A, 10 On this Third Sunday of Advent, also called Gaudete (Rejoice) Sunday, Isaiah speaks of great joy in the realization that our loving God comes to restore and save us. Isaiah speaks of the anticipated return of the people from exile through God's mighty hand. God's saving actions will be evident in both the natural and the human world. All of nature will exult and rejoice. The desert, the parched land, and the steppe all will bloom abundantly and burst into joyful song. The fertile and life-giving qualities of the most enviable lands will be theirs.

All the weak, those without hope, and those who fear God's abandonment, are challenged to "be strong, fear not," for "[God] comes to save you" (v. 4). The blind, the deaf, the lame, and the mute will be healed of their infirmities and will experience God's great care. All that is debilitated, limited, and without life will be restored and renewed. Those returning home from exile will experience God's life-giving and restoring work. God has willingly paid the ransom for their return. Restored and renewed in hope and spirit, they "will enter Zion singing" and "sorrow and mourning will flee" (35:10). Christians understand and experience Christ's coming to renew and restore all humanity in this same rich fashion of joy and renewed life.

PSALM 146:6–7, 8–9, 9–10 (SEE ISAIAH 35:4) The psalm's refrain repeats and continues Isaiah's focus of renewal and restoration by calling upon the Lord to "come and save us." Assured of God's affirmative response, the psalmist breaks into praise of the Lord who "keeps faith forever" (v. 6). God's continued care and enduring love are manifested in very concrete and specific terms. The oppressed, the hungry, and the captives have their needs met. The blind are given sight and the "bowed down" are raised up (v. 8). Working for justice is especially endearing to God, who "protects strangers" and sustains "the fatherless and the widow," while the "way of the wicked" is thwarted (v. 9). Thus "the Lord shall reign forever" (v. 10). God's saving work among us becomes the model of how we are called to deal with one another.

JAMES 5:7–10 James' advice to his community stresses the need for patience whenever anxiety and fear surface

CONNECTIONS TO CHURCH TEACHING AND TRADITION

- "Jesus accompanies his words with many 'mighty works and wonders and signs,' which manifest that the kingdom is present in him and attest that he was the promised Messiah[1]" (CCC, 547).

- "The signs worked by Jesus . . . invite belief in him.[2] . . . So miracles strengthen faith in the One who does his Father's works; they bear witness that he is the Son of God.[3] But his miracles can also be occasions for 'offense'[4]" (CCC, 548).

- "By freeing some individuals from the earthly evils of hunger, injustice, illness, and death,[5] Jesus performed messianic signs. Nevertheless he did not come to abolish all evils here below,[6] but to free men from the gravest slavery, sin" (CCC, 549).

---

1 Acts 2:22; cf. Luke 7:18–23.

2 Cf. Jn 5:36; 10:25, 38.

3 Cf. Jn 10:31–38.

4 Mt 11:16.

5 Cf. Jn 6:5–15; Lk 19:8; Mt 11:5.

6 Cf. Lk 12:13–14; Jn 18:36.

because of delayed expectations. The Lord has come to save us and upon his return, all will be brought to fulfillment. In the meantime, we are to live life in the concrete, facing the challenges of living together in community and the impulse to complain and judge, along with misunderstanding and possible persecution by others for our beliefs. Throughout these challenges James counsels patience, for "the coming of the Lord is at hand" (v. 8).

Just as the farmer patiently waits for rain in hope of a fruitful harvest, so we are to wait for the Lord in hope of complete fulfillment. We are challenged to be patient, make our hearts firm, and resist the temptation to judge others. James offers the prophets as models of "hardship and patience" (v. 10). They remained faithful during the many difficulties they encountered for speaking "in the name of the Lord" (v. 10), and we are to be patient in our hardships for the Lord, too. Advent, the season of joyful anticipation of the Lord's return, helps us cultivate patience as we strive to carry on the Lord's work until he comes again.

MATTHEW 11:2–11 This dialogue between Jesus and John the Baptist's disciples reveals Matthew's theological affirmation that in Jesus, God's saving action is now being accomplished. In response to John's inquiry concerning "the one who is to come" (v. 3), namely, the Messiah, Jesus responds by pointing to all the signs that the Scripture specified as indicators of the presence of the Messiah: concern for the poor and all those who are in need of God's healing touch.

This somewhat different messianic concept from the one anticipated has Jesus conclude his response by asserting, "Blessed is the one who takes no offense at me" (v. 6). The messianic times are full of God's saving actions on behalf of the poor and needy, and not displays of military might. This neglected messianic image would cause some to take offense at Jesus and challenge his messianic claims.

Jesus praises John as a prophet who prepared for his coming as Messiah. Jesus also affirms, though, that those who accept him as the Messiah and carry on his work will do greater things than John. The power of God's saving action will be evident in all those who choose to model themselves on Jesus' messianic mission.

- "God blesses those who come to the aid of the poor and rebukes those who turn away from them. . . . It is by what they have done for the poor that Jesus Christ will recognize his chosen ones.[7] When 'the poor have the good news preached to them,' it is the sign of Christ's presence[8]" (CCC, 2443).

---

7 Cf. Mt 25:31–36.
8 Mt 11:5; cf. Lk 4:18.

Promise Is Given Birth

ISAIAH 7:10–14 In 736 BC, Assyria is threatening to take over the whole region. Some counsel the king, Ahaz, to join in a coalition against Assyria, while others, most notably Isaiah, tell him to lay low. It would be better for him and for Judah not to do a thing. Ahaz himself is leaning toward conciliation with Assyria in hopes of saving himself and his country.

Through Isaiah, God offers Ahaz a sign of hope, but Ahaz is not sure he wants one. In a false show of piety, he refuses the offer. God, however, is not dissuaded that easily. God tells Ahaz that Jerusalem shall be saved. The threat he fears shall be averted, and the sign of this hope is the birth of a child. This child, Isaiah says, will be God's concrete sign of compassion, for through the child, Ahaz's line will continue in spite of the Assyrian threat.

No wonder the Church associates this passage with the birth of Jesus. Just as the birth of Emmanuel was a sign of promise to Ahaz, the birth of Jesus is a concrete sign of God's compassion for the world.

PSALM 24:1–2, 3–4, 5–6 (7C, 10B) Psalm 24 was originally composed as a processional liturgy and was used as such for years in the Second Temple, sung antiphonally by priest and people. It celebrates the entrance of the Ark, which represented the presence of God, into the Temple. The most striking feature of this psalm is the connection it makes between ethical behavior and worship.

This psalm celebrates the entrance of the promised child, God's Own Begotten, into this earthly tabernacle to be with us and dwell among us.

ROMANS 1:1–7 Paul never visited the Church in Rome, so he begins his letter with a whirlwind summary of his Gospel. He describes himself as a personal slave of Christ. He then launches into a long exposition on who Christ is and what that means to the world in general and to the believers in Rome in particular. Paul's readers, no doubt, would have recognized at least part of this, for Paul deliberately wove familiar traditions into his own interpretation of the Gospel.

CONNECTIONS TO CHURCH TEACHING AND TRADITION

- Jesus Christ is the incarnate love of God (DCE, 12).

- Mary is Mother of the Church and the model for us all (NDC, 74).

- Mary shows us what love is, its origin, and constantly renewed power (DCE, 42).

- Mary submitted to God's will to conceive by the Holy Spirit (LG, 55–56; CCC, 484–507, esp. 484–486 and 494).

Although it is clear that the birth of the Christ child is not nearly as important to Paul as the life of the man Jesus, Paul makes several points that befit our celebration of Advent. First, he reminds us that the promise fulfilled in the coming of Christ is the culmination of an age-old hope first sounded by the prophets. Second, by emphasizing the Spirit and the power of God at work in Jesus, Paul points us to the larger implications of the child of promise we await this Advent. He reminds us that the coming of Christ involves not just his birth but his life, Death, and Resurrection as well.

MATTHEW 1:18–24 To appreciate this reading on its own terms, we must first separate it from the more familiar account in Luke. Here, Joseph is the primary player, not Mary. As the head of the household, Joseph is the one who receives the annunciation. There are no shepherds, no angels (except the one in the dream), and no trips to Bethlehem.

Once Matthew's and Luke's accounts are distinguished, one can see that they address similar issues but with different approaches. The Messiah was expected to be a descendant of King David, but Jesus' only claim to the Davidic line was through Joseph, who was not his natural father. While Luke sidesteps the issue by emphasizing Mary, Matthew's account shows that it was God's will that Joseph be regarded as Jesus' legitimate, if adoptive, father.

Likewise, both evangelists knew the Messiah was supposed to be from Bethlehem. Jesus, however, was from Nazareth. Luke's version has Jesus born while his parents are visiting Bethlehem, but in Matthew, the Holy Family already lives in Bethlehem and moves to Nazareth later.

Most of all, both Luke and Matthew want to emphasize that even though it seems that Jesus was born illegitimately, his birth was God's doing and thus quite legitimate, even purposeful. Matthew's account gives us still another important insight into the birth we await this Advent: it did not happen according to human convention. Indeed, it broke many of those human conventions that God's will might become manifest.

Christmas Time

Advent leads us to the joy of Christmas Time. For Catholics, Christmas is more than just one day; it is an entire period of liturgical time. The duration of Christmas Time demonstrates how sacred the memorial of Christ's birth and the early manifestations of the Savior of the World are to believers. Next to the yearly celebration of the Paschal Mystery during the Sacred Paschal Triduum and Easter Time, these are the days the Church holds most sacred. Christmas Time goes from Evening Prayer I of Christmas until the Sunday after Epiphany, the Feast of the Baptism of the Lord. During these days, we celebrate all that we have prepared for during Advent. The lights in the church are bright to reflect the brightness of the Lord's glory shining throughout the world. Through his birth, life, Death, and Resurrection, he has once and for all overcome the darkness.

After the liturgies for the Nativity of the Lord (Christmas), the Church celebrates the Feast of the Holy Family. The purpose of this feast is to encourage families to live out their faith. On the eighth day of the octave of Christmas, January 1, the Church celebrates the Solemnity of Mary, the Holy Mother of God. This title is the oldest title given to Mary by the Church. She is the image of the Church and the model of discipleship and holiness. This is also the day on which the Church celebrates the naming of Jesus; hence its association with circumcision, which was traditionally celebrated eight days after the birth of a Jewish male child.

The next solemnity celebrated during Christmas Time is the Epiphany of the Lord. Most Catholics are familiar with this day as the time when the three wise men, or Magi, follow the star and visit Jesus, bringing him gifts as a sign of homage to him. Epiphany, which means "manifestation," also offers us an opportunity to reflect deeply on the mystery of the Incarnation. Jesus, in his coming as man, manifested God to us. He was, is, and forever will be Emmanuel—God-with-us—our Savior and the Savior of the World. For this, we praise and honor him.

Christmas Time concludes with the celebration of yet another manifestation feast: the Feast of the Baptism of the Lord. During the event of Jesus' baptism, proclaimed this year from Matthew's account of the Gospel, the Spirit of God descends on Jesus, and a voice from heaven identifies him as "my beloved Son, with whom I am well pleased" (Matthew 3:17). Jesus' identity as the Son of God and Messiah is made known in this event. Moreover, just as Jesus' baptism marks the beginning of his public ministry, our Baptism marks the beginning of our life in the world as his disciples.

FIRST READINGS

As Advent ends and Christmas Time begins, we continue to hear often from the prophet Isaiah. His proclamation of salvation—the truth that the Lord does not forsake his people and that the Lord redeems—resounds in beautiful, poetic language. On the Feast of the Holy Family, we hear instructions from the Book of Sirach about how children are to honor and care for their mothers and fathers. Then, on the Solemnity of the Epiphany, Isaiah's exhortation to Jerusalem to rise up in splendor calls us, as recipients of the Lord's salvation, to let our own light shine today. By our example, we, like Jerusalem, reflect the Lord's glory so that other nations and peoples will walk by our light. Fittingly, on the Feast of the Baptism of the Lord, the First Reading is one of the four servant songs from Isaiah. This song speaks of the Lord's chosen servant and is appropriately paired with the Gospel reading of Jesus' baptism by John in the Jordan.

RESPONSORIAL PSALMS

During Christmas Time, the Responsorial Psalms emphasize the light, salvation, and saving power of the Lord. The psalm speaks of those who walk in the Lord's ways as blessed on the Feast of the Holy Family; the Solemnity of Mary, the Holy Mother of God; and the Feast of the Baptism of the Lord. On the latter two feasts, the psalm professes that the Lord will bless his people with peace and offers the Israelites' and our prayers for God to bless us in mercy.

SECOND READINGS

The Second Readings during Christmas Time are the same for all three years of the Lectionary cycle of readings except on the Feasts of the Holy Family and Baptism of the Lord. On both of these days, however, the reading from Year A can be proclaimed in all three years of the Lectionary cycle of readings. The Second Readings for the four Christmas Masses proclaim how God has fully spoken to us through his Son, to whom we are to bear witness as the Apostle Paul did. On the ensuing feasts and solemnities of Christmas Time, the Second Readings come from Colossians, Galatians, Ephesians, and Acts. In turn, they speak of the virtues of family life, God's Son born of a woman, the sharing of Gentiles and all who believe in the promise of the Gospel, and Peter's testimony to how God anointed Jesus with the Holy Spirit.

GOSPEL READINGS

The Solemnity of the Nativity of the Lord (Christmas), which marks the beginning of Christmas Time, has four distinct sets of readings, which are the same for each of the three years of the Lectionary cycle of readings. Each Gospel account assigned to a specific Christmas Mass reflects a particular dimension of the Incarnation—the event of God becoming human in Jesus. The Gospel for the Christmas Vigil, the genealogy in Matthew, recalls Jesus' ancestry. During the Christmas Mass during the night, the Gospel reading is Luke's beloved account of the angels announcing the birth of Jesus in Bethlehem. The Gospel for the Mass at dawn is Luke's description of the shepherds finding Mary, Joseph, and the infant lying in the manger. In this Gospel, we hear of Mary's reflective nature and the shepherds' ecstasy as they return home in awe, praising God because of what they saw. During the fourth Mass of the solemnity, the Mass during the day, the Gospel is a selection from the prologue of John. This passage, deeply theological in character, proclaims the profound truth that the Word became flesh and made his dwelling among us. We hear that the glory of the Word shines in the darkness, never allowing the darkness to overcome it.

As Christmas Time moves forward with the Feast of the Holy Family, the Gospel is about Jesus' childhood. Again this year, the central character is Joseph, who for the second time encounters an angel advising him to journey with Mary and Jesus to a place of safety lest the child be harmed because of Herod's vengeful ways.

The Gospel on the Solemnity of the Epiphany of the Lord is the same in each of the three years and is a time-honored narrative of the Magi following the star to find Jesus and pay him homage. On the Feast of the Baptism of the Lord, the final feast of Christmas Time, the Gospel each year is one of the three synoptic accounts of Jesus' baptism by John in the Jordan. Matthew's account, proclaimed in Year A, emphasizes Jesus as the fulfillment of God's plan for the salvation of humanity.

Jesus' Birth Reveals God's Love for Us

ISAIAH 62:1–5 Isaiah seems to be the Church's favorite prophet, primarily because so much of the Book of Isaiah sheds light on the mystery of Jesus and how salvation history comes to completion in him. This reading comes from "Third Isaiah," the section of the book dealing with how the returned exiles should build up their city and become a renewed people of God. While that is a human task, it is rooted in God and God's great love for the people. Israel's very identity springs from her relationship with God, her Builder. When we read this passage as a reflection on the Incarnation, it reminds us of the thousands of years and multitudinous ways in which God has loved us. Because we are God's delight, yes, even the people to whom God is espoused, we are called and given the grace to be living witnesses to God's great love.

PSALM 89:4–5, 16–17, 27, 29 (2A) *Forever* is a key word in this psalm. "Forever I will sing the goodness of the Lord," the antiphon says. We pledge to sing of God's goodness forever precisely because God's faithfulness is forever. Knowing that, we rejoice in the very name of God, not the unpronounceable name revealed to Moses, but relational names: Father, God, Rock, Savior. First, we know God as our Father, the one who brings us into being and watches over us. Then, we use that theological term, God, which proclaims our devotion. God our Rock is that faithful one whose goodness will never fail, even when we do (see Psalm 89:31–38). Knowing that we do fail, God is also our Savior, always ready to lead us to become again the people we were made to be.

ACTS 13:16–17, 22–25 The Church has chosen this homily by St. Paul for our Christmas celebration to recall salvation history from the time of Moses through Jesus. Paul is careful to point out the continuity of God's action on behalf of the people of Israel in both their good times and their infidelity. The central proclamation is that God gave Jesus to Israel as a Savior in the line of David. Paul's main interest is to help people see that Jesus is God's sign of love, sent to Israel as their savior.

CONNECTIONS TO CHURCH TEACHING AND TRADITION

- "Genuine forms of popular religiosity are incarnate, since they are born of the incarnation of Christian faith in popular culture. . . . They entail a personal relationship . . . with God, with Christ, with Mary, with the saints. These devotions are fleshy, they have a face. They are capable of fostering relationships and not just enabling escapism . . . or . . . a 'theology of prosperity' . . . which are nothing more than a form of self-centeredness" (EG, 90).

- "The divine name, 'I Am' or 'He Is,' expresses God's faithfulness: despite the faithlessness of men's sin and the punishment it deserves, he keeps 'steadfast love for thousands'[1]" (CCC, 211).

- "The Eucharist is at the root of every form of holiness, and each of us is called to the fullness of life in the Holy Spirit" (SCA, 94).

---

1 Exodus 34:7.

MATTHEW 1:1–25 (OR MATTHEW 1:18–25) The longer form of this Gospel includes Matthew's rendering of Jesus' genealogy. This list of fathers and sons, punctuated by the names of a few key women, offers another journey through salvation history. Whereas Luke traces Jesus' genealogy back to Adam, Matthew concentrates on the people of Israel, beginning with Abraham, the father of the people, the one through whom all the nations would find blessing.

While the names mentioned here may mean little to us, they all rang a bell for Israelites who knew and cherished their history. In mentioning women as Jesus' ancestors, Matthew breaks tradition and keeps his readers aware that God acts not just in the expected way, but through surprising people and events, often the ones least likely, by human standards, to be expected to play a part in God's eternal plan.

Matthew introduces this reading as a genealogy (1:1), or more literally, the genesis of Jesus Christ, the son of David, the son of Abraham. This provides a large horizon for the Nativity account that follows it. Although the Nativity is the reason for it all, Matthew has framed the opening of his Gospel from the widest perspective possible. This serves as an introduction to Matthew's work as a whole with its efforts to help the readers develop a long and broad vision of the historical person, Jesus, who is the Christ, God's anointed one, and the son of the deepest traditions of Israel.

The short form of the Gospel focuses on Joseph's role in the life of Jesus, the Christ. We are told that Joseph was righteous, an example of the best Israel had to offer. Like his ancient namesake, he understood God's message through dreams. Although what the angel told him was thoroughly unexpected, Joseph took in the key to the message "Do not be afraid" (v. 20). The angel also reassured him that this unusual turn of events fulfilled an ancient prophecy and that the child to be born was to be Emmanuel. Thus, all of Joseph's concerns, all that seemed impossible to understand, could make sense through knowing and believing in that name. Jesus would be Emmanuel.

The Nativity of the Lord (Christmas), Mass during the Night
There Is Nothing to Fear, God Is with Us

ISAIAH 9:1–6 When hearing this reading, some will undoubtedly recall the words sung in George Frederic Handel's *Messiah*, a tribute to the evangelizing power of music. The words are Isaiah's, somewhat influenced by other cultures' descriptions of an ideal ruler. The historical circumstances surrounding this composition, however, were far from ideal: the people were undergoing deportation and enslavement. The only way for them to describe themselves was as living in a land of gloom. The horror of their abject darkness included their captors' brutality, which involved putting out the eyes of some of them, both as a warning and as a way to debilitate and humiliate would-be leaders.

When Isaiah speaks of light, he is not talking about the decorations that offset the dark of winter in December in the northern hemisphere. For Isaiah, light is a symbol of desperately needed salvation and liberation. The light is coming from God in person and in a person, a child to be born who would deliver the people. In Isaiah's day, that presaged a king. But no king lived up to the promise. Rather than abandon hope, the people came to understand the prophecy as referring to a Messiah to come. For the early Church, the prophecy fit the person of Jesus perfectly, who came offering light and liberation.

PSALM 96:1–2, 2–3, 11–12, 13 (LUKE 2:11) This psalm, so appropriate for Christmas, sings out a core message of the Psalter: Rejoice, for God reigns! The song celebrates and recalls Israel's many experiences of rescue. For us it sings the joy of the Nativity and invites us to ask how the Good News of Christ's birth sheds new light on our lives today. When we strive to let our daily lives be permeated with Christ's presence, we will know how to "announce his salvation, day after day" (v. 2).

TITUS 2:11–14 This short reading reminds us that the coming of Christ at Christmas was only the beginning. The Epiphany has happened; God has appeared definitively in our history. As a result, Christ's presence enables us to live a new way. Even more, we look toward that future when Isaiah's prophecy of peace will come true; not only will there be peace, but every person will know the love of God

CONNECTIONS TO CHURCH TEACHING AND TRADITION

- "It is vitally important for the Church today to go forth and preach the Gospel to all: to all places, on all occasions, without hesitation, reluctance or fear. The joy of the Gospel is for all people: no one can be excluded. That is what the angel proclaimed to the shepherds in Bethlehem: 'Be not afraid'" (EG, 23).

- "The primary reason for evangelizing is the love of Jesus which we have received, the experience of salvation which urges us to ever greater love of him. What kind of love would not feel the need to speak of the beloved, to point him out, to make him known? If we do not feel an intense desire to share this love, we need to pray insistently that he will once more touch our hearts" (EG, 264).

- "The Church's mission derives not only from the Lord's mandate but also from the profound demands of God's life within us" (RMI, 11).

that Christians have found in Christ. We proclaim that belief with the Lord's Prayer in every liturgy, as we remember the "blessed hope" (v. 13) we share as we await the coming of our Savior, our Lord Jesus Christ. This perspective on Christ's presence invites us to let that hope be the guiding beacon of our entire life.

LUKE 2:1–14 This selection from Luke's account of the Gospel portrays three distinct scenes. In the first we hear of Mary and Joseph, who undertook a journey of approximately ninety miles in the last days of Mary's pregnancy. That journey was necessary because the people of occupied Israel had to register for the purpose of taxation. The opening scene depicts a time of oppression for God's people.

In the second scene, Luke uses very few words to announce the birth of the Messiah. He simply tells us that Mary's time was completed and she gave birth to her son. There is no great drama, no miracles, just a simple birth. To emphasize the ordinariness of it all, Luke mentions that the baby was wrapped in swaddling clothes—a sign as spectacular as someone today saying that the baby was diapered. Finally, as if the birth were not unostentatious enough, Luke adds a crucial detail and the rationale for it. The child was laid in a manger because there was no room for him among his own people. In those few lines, Luke orients us to the entire Gospel he is about to recount. God's son comes among us unobtrusively, in adverse conditions, and not even the members of God's own people make room for him.

The third scene underlines the simplicity of God's involvement in human history. The first to hear of the birth of the child are poor shepherds—either hired hands or those who had not the means to hire others to work the night shift for them. They were often stigmatized as dishonest and for being unable to fulfill the strict requirements of the law. It was to them that the announcement came, with the assurance that they had nothing to fear from this great event that God was working among them.

ISAIAH 62:11–12 As we celebrate Christmas we take every one of our First Readings from the Book of the prophet Isaiah. In the Vigil, Isaiah told us that God would become Israel's husband. At the night Mass, we heard that the Savior would bring light and peace. In the last liturgy of the day we will see the coming of the one who brings glad tidings of God's comfort. In this short reading, the end of the section from which we took the reading for the Vigil, we hear that it is now God who proclaims the coming of that savior. This describes the simple and profound result of that coming: God's salvation will be known to the ends of the earth. In addition, the people will be made holy by the presence of God in their midst.

PSALM 97:1, 6, 11–12 This short selection from Psalm 97 highlights the theological message of the entire Psalter: God reigns! The heavens proclaim it, and all people, each in their own particular circumstances, will see God's glory. While we tend to underline the diversity of heaven and earth and all the distinct peoples, the underlying message is the same for all: the light dawns for the just. The upright will find it a cause for rejoicing.

TITUS 3:4–7 Like the passage from Isaiah, Paul's letter to Titus affirms the extraordinary results of the Savior's presence among us. With an interesting interplay between God's initiative and human response, Paul reminds us that all grace originates solely in God's gracious mercy. Nevertheless, each and every person must respond for that mercy to have its effect in their lives. Thus, Paul reminds us that Baptism is the source of our rebirth, the sign of our desire for the grace of conversion and the outpouring of the Holy Spirit in our lives.

LUKE 2:15–20 This selection continues the narrative of the Gospel for the Mass during the Night. We have here a depiction of the first evangelists and Mary, the contemplative theologian.

Throughout Scripture we hear of shepherds, both good and wicked. The figure of the shepherd often described a king's responsibility to protect the people. Psalm 23 thanks God for being our shepherd. Jesus describes himself as the

CONNECTIONS TO CHURCH TEACHING AND TRADITION

- "Through the Incarnation God gave human life the dimension that he intended man to have from his first beginning" (RH, 1).

- "The faithful still strive to conquer sin and grow in holiness. And so they turn their eyes to Mary who shines out to the whole community. . . . Devoutly meditating on her and contemplating her in the light of the Word made man, the church reverently penetrates more deeply into the great mystery of the Incarnation and becomes more and more like its spouse" (LG, 65).

- "And all the aspects of His mystery—the Incarnation itself . . . the cross and the resurrection, the permanence of His presence in the midst of His own—were components of His evangelizing activity" (EN, 6).

Good Shepherd. Nevertheless, as noted in the commentary on the Mass during the Night, shepherds did not always enjoy a sterling reputation among their contemporaries. Theirs was a lonely profession without days off. That meant that they could not fulfill the law of the Sabbath and other ritual requirements. In addition, shepherds often cared for the sheep of others and were frequently suspected of being less than honest when it came to accounting for the number of sheep born to those for whom they worked versus the additions to their own flocks. It should not surprise us that shepherds, simple people of questionable reputation, were the first to hear of the birth of the Savior.

Why did Luke bother to tell us about the shepherds? First of all, it was their response to the angelic message. They took to heart the angel's invitation to be unafraid, responding, "Let us go" (v. 15), and left their flocks "to see this thing that has taken place." One can hardly listen to that without hearing echoes of the first disciples, be it in John's account of the Gospel where the first invitation Jesus issued was "come and see" (see John 1:39; John 1:46; John 4:29; and John 11:34) or the accounts of those who left everything to follow Jesus. Of course, the newborn child was not one they might reasonably follow. Nevertheless, they did proclaim their faith in the message they had received—to the amazement of "all who heard it" (v. 18).

The second person Luke focuses on here is Mary. We know her from previous chapters as the self-offering young woman who, like the shepherds, believed the message of an angel. We have also seen her rejoicing with her kinswoman Elizabeth in their awareness of God's wondrous action in their lives and, by extension, in the whole of human history. While with Elizabeth, Mary sang the song that we use as a daily prayer celebrating God's care of the lowly. Now, we see Mary simply taking it all in, pondering these things in her heart.

These Scripture passages invite us to join Mary and the shepherds rejoicing in the signs of God in our midst. Like Mary, we need to ponder it all in our heart. Like the shepherds, we must be ready to move beyond our own little fields to see and then to proclaim what God is doing in our midst.

- "Christianity has its starting-point in the Incarnation of the Word. Here, it is not simply a case of man seeking God, but of God who comes in Person to speak to man of himself and to show him the path by which he may be reached" (TMA, 6).

The Nativity of the Lord (Christmas), Mass during the Day
We Too Are God's Own Children

ISAIAH 52:7–10 This song of joy announces God's salvation, calling a defeated and devastated people to wake up, dust themselves off, and prepare for a different future (52:2). We might well ask who it is who announces this, what it is that they see, and how we might respond.

The announcers are called watchmen, an allusion to those who stand guard, but also to the prophets who contemplate the situation and perceive God's finger in it all. The prophet Isaiah foresees God's triumph, the restoration of a ravaged people. He proclaims the renewal of Jerusalem, which implies a renewal of their freedom to worship as the Chosen People. What response does he call for? To open their eyes to what is happening, to stop limiting themselves to their own, often depressed, perspective; and to decipher God's presence in contemporary events. That is indeed reason for breaking into joyful song.

Ultimately, the people are challenged to perceive, and thus base their thinking, prayer, and behavior on the fact that God truly reigns on earth. That is asking a great deal, but the reading gives options for growth toward the goal. They can begin by listening to the proclamation, noticing the feet of those who bring Good News, even if they do not comprehend it all. They may learn to see as the prophets, getting an ever-clearer view of how God is saving them. Finally, they may come to the moment when they realize that all the earth sees God in action through the life of a holy people. No matter what their degree of understanding, it calls for songs of joy and gratitude. Moreover, their very prayer of thanks will deepen their understanding of the glad tidings.

PSALM 98:1, 2–3, 3–4, 5–6 (3C) Some scholars say that this one psalm could summarize the entire Psalter. We could hardly find a better psalm for Christmas, as it commands us to sing our joy at God's saving action. As we sing and pray, let us ask for the grace to see ever more clearly the signs of our Savior's reign in our own time and place.

CONNECTIONS TO CHURCH TEACHING AND TRADITION

- "The joy of the Gospel fills the hearts and lives of all who encounter Jesus. Those who accept his offer of salvation are set free from sin, sorrow, inner emptiness and loneliness" (EG, 1).

- "Preaching constitutes the Church's first and fundamental way of serving the coming of the kingdom in individuals and in human society. Eschatological salvation begins even now in newness of life in Christ: 'To all who believed in him, who believed in his name, he gave power to become children of God' (John 1:12)" (RMI, 20).

HEBREWS 1:1–6 The first four verses of Hebrews are actually one complex and theologically dense sentence contrasting the present and the past, the prophets and the Son, and proposing a timeline that moves from preexistence through the Incarnation to exaltation, all the while using alliteration that we miss in translation. For all its literary artistry, the message is key.

The reading focuses our attention first on God, who has reached out to humanity since the dawn of creation. Then we are told that God's ultimate word to us comes through the Son. It goes on to point out how the Son is unique; that he is "the very imprint" (v. 3b) of God's being.

With its proclamation of Christ's total union with God, this is an exceptionally apt reading for Christmas. What we should not miss is that the Son is fully human. That implies that humanity is capable of full union with God.

JOHN 1:1–18 Although this Gospel account may not have the charm of Matthew's and Luke's Nativity accounts, we might remind ourselves that in the liturgy prior to the Second Vatican Council, this passage, popularly called "the last Gospel," was read at the end of every Eucharistic celebration—an indication of how important the Church considered it to be. It is replete with allusions and multiple layers of meaning. Given such richness and complexity, perhaps we can best approach this Gospel text by choosing one dimension of it for our Christmas reflection.

A part of the message that is often overlooked comes just after the mention of Christ's rejection by "his own" (v. 11). It says that to those who did accept him, he gave the power to become "children of God . . . born . . . of God" (vv. 12–13). That seemingly simple statement summarizes the very meaning of Christian life. As we celebrate the Nativity, let us keep in mind that it is not just a celebration of God taking flesh, but of God's invitation to us to share divine life, what our Eastern brothers and sisters call divinization. Believing in this offer may require even more faith than we need to believe in the Incarnation. But that is the message here. The real Christmas gift is the future God has planned for us—a life in which we share fully in the family life of the Father, Son, and Spirit. The only condition is our willingness to accept that gift.

THE HOLY FAMILY OF JESUS, MARY, AND JOSEPH
My Family, Holy Family

SIRACH 3:2–7, 12–14 The book of Sirach, written in Hebrew by a Jewish scribe between 200 and 175 BC, is also known as "Wisdom of the Son of Sirach" and by its Greek name, "Ecclesiasticus." The author addressed his contemporaries to help them live a life of religious faith and integrity. The book comprises many sayings on a variety of topics about the relationship of individuals, families, and communities to one another and God. It also treats religious and social customs of the time including friendship, education, poverty and wealth, the law, and worship.

This passage speaks about the honor and respect that children are to give to their parents and lays out clear actions that one can do. It can be thought of as a practical explanation of how to follow the fourth commandment: "Honor your father and your mother, that you may have a long life in the land which the Lord, your God, is giving you" (Exodus 20:12). Its instructions teach how children are to act with love toward their parents.

PSALM 128:1–2, 3, 4–5 (SEE 1) Psalm 128 begins with the beatitude "Blessed is everyone who fears the Lord, / who walks in his ways" (v. 1). While most of us are familiar with the beatitudes that Jesus taught in Matthew 5:1–12, the psalms sometimes contain a beatitude that indicates a blessing or sign of God's favor, especially for those who live the way of the covenant.

The description of an olive plant in Psalm 128 would have given the listeners or singers of this psalm a clear image of what this kind of blessing would look like. An olive tree was seen as a symbol of health and vitality. When a tree grows old, young shoots start to grow up around it. The man's wife would be fruitful, and his children would gather in abundance around his table. The psalm suggests that dependence on God and following the ways of the Lord is the way to blessing and abundance. In their reliance on God, individuals and Israel as a whole are both blessed (vv. 5–6).

CONNECTIONS TO CHURCH TEACHING AND TRADITION

- "Christ chose to be born and grow up in the bosom of the holy family of Joseph and Mary. The Church is nothing other than 'the family of God'" (CCC, 1655).

- "The church is God's *farm* or field (see 1 Corinthians 3:9). In this field the ancient olive tree grows whose holy root were the patriarchs and in which the reconciliation of Jews and Gentiles has been achieved and will continue to be achieved (see Romans 11:13–16). . . . The true vine is Christ who gives life and fruitfulness to the branches, that is, to us" (LG, 6).

- "God, who has a parent's care for all of us, desired that all men and women should form one family and deal with each other as brothers and sisters. . . . Love for God and of one's neighbor, then, is the first and greatest commandment" (GS, 24).

COLOSSIANS 3:12–21 OR 3:12–17 This passage from Colossians is part of a longer section that tells how a Christian is to live ethically in the world (Colossians 3:1—4:6). It begins with a list of virtues and continues with a code of how members of a household are to act toward one another. Paul wrote in a patriarchal society. In that society, protecting the authority and responsibility of the patriarch was important for order and societal integration. In maintaining right relationships, Paul's lasting contribution is his emphasis that Christian relationships are to be guided by what God has done for all through Jesus Christ. God's love has saved us, forgiven us our sins, and given us peace. We are to put on that same kind of love in our families and in our relationships with all God's people.

MATTHEW 2:13–15, 19–23 This is our final look at Joseph in the Sunday Scriptures of this liturgical year and in Matthew's account of the Gospel. A central figure in Matthew's early infancy stories, Joseph now fades from its pages. He leaves behind a powerful impression of faith and obedience to God. Twice we hear that immediately after the angel's command to rise and take the child and his mother, Joseph rises and obeys. He does not protest about how hard the travel will be, does not object to leaving just after having made a long journey, and does not put it off to take care of other things first. Joseph responds in obedience (vv. 13–14, 21–22).

In this early chapter, the evangelist Matthew wants his community to see Jesus as the new Moses. Jesus comes out of Egypt, as did Moses. Innocent children were killed by a corrupt ruler when Jesus was born, as they were when Moses was born. Although Matthew wants his listeners to know of the continuity between Moses and Jesus, he also wants to communicate the truth that Jesus will be greater. As the narrative unfolds in Matthew, it is Jesus of Nazareth, who came from a family of faithful Jews, who fulfills human longing for a Savior, and who freely gave up his spirit on the Cross. The centurion and the men with him in the midst of an earthquake would proclaim him as the Son of God (Matthew 27:54).

NUMBERS 6:22–27 Aaron's blessing probably goes back to the time of Moses (1250 BC). It is believed to be one of the oldest biblical poems. Its setting is most likely the Temple and the priestly blessings upon the people. The sacred name of God, always abbreviated YHWH and translated into English as *Lord,* is used three times. The threefold blessing invokes God to enfold the people, to allow intimacy and graciousness to dominate the relationship, and to look upon us with kindness and grant us peace.

Peace entails a sense of wholeness in which everyone has what is needed for fullness of life. Peace demands that justice abound in all our dealings. As we begin the New Year, it is fitting to ask God to bless us so that we might live lives of justice that lead to peace. Mary, God's blessed, is our model as we begin a New Year. Her devotion and dedication to God brought abundant blessings upon her and upon all who follow the Son she brought into the world.

PSALM 67:2–3, 5, 6, 8 (2A) This psalm of praise is a prayer of thanks to God for a bountiful harvest. Such concrete realities are obvious indicators of God's blessing upon the people and the land. The beginning verses are similar to the Aaronic blessing from today's reading from Numbers. God's blessing is not just for the people, but also serves as a way of making God's way and salvation known among all the nations. The care lavished on the people, along with the just and loving manner in which God guides and sustains them, causes other nations to be glad, to exult, and to praise the God of Israel.

God's blessings on the people have a far greater purpose and effect. By invoking God to bless us, we are seeking to secure God's blessings, not only for ourselves, but for all of creation as well. Through us, others will come to know and experience God's goodness, love, and mercy. As we celebrate a new year, we call upon God to bless us. Mary, who was blessed by God in a unique and singular way, is a sign of God's blessings for us all. Through God's blessings upon Mary, we come to know God's graciousness more clearly, and come to the realization that God blesses all people in the same rich, lavish way he blessed Mary.

CONNECTIONS TO CHURCH TEACHING AND TRADITION

- "Jesus was born in a humble stable, into a poor family.[1] Simple shepherds were the first witnesses to this event. In this poverty heaven's glory was made manifest.[2] The Church never tires of singing the glory of this night" (CCC, 525).

- "To become a child in relation to God is the condition for entering the kingdom.[3] For this, we must humble ourselves and become little. Even more: to become 'children of God' we must be 'born from above' or 'born of God'[4]" (CCC, 526).

1 Cf. Luke 2:6–7.
2 Cf. Luke 2:8–20.
3 Cf. Matthew 18:3–4.
4 John 3:7; 1:13; 1:12; cf. Matthew 23:12.

GALATIANS 4:4–7 Paul's "fullness of time" (v. 4) refers to the time God deemed appropriate to become one of us. God became fully one of us—"born of a woman" (v. 4), and a Jew—"born under the law" (v. 4), while still fully retaining divinity as God's Son. Jesus' mission was to ransom us from the law and to make us adopted sons and daughters of God. Paul does not repudiate the law, but sees it as a tutor for one not yet of age. With Christ and the gift of the Spirit given through him, the law can be set aside for we have come of age and have been brought into a mature and intimate relationship with God.

Proof of this new mature status is God's gift of the Spirit, sent into our hearts, empowering us to call God "Abba," our loving Father. We are no longer slaves subject to the law, but are God's adult sons and daughters. Through Baptism into Christ, we become intimate members of God's family and heirs to all of God's love and blessings. Mary was among the first to experience that intimate and deep relationship to God in and through the Person of her Son, the second Person of the Holy Trinity. For this special gift, we honor her today as we thank God for the same rich gift that we have all received in Christ.

LUKE 2:16–21 The shepherds, usually social outcasts, are the first to see and experience God in this lowly birth in a stable. They come to believe the divine presence in this ordinary child and are the first evangelizers. Like the nations in today's psalm, they come to see God's gracious blessings in the ordinary events of this birth, as they go forth "glorifying and praising God for all they had heard and seen" (v. 20). Their lives changed through this experience of God's blessings. We, too, are called to hear, see, and believe in God's great love for us, manifested in life's ordinary events.

Both the shepherds and Mary model what such seeing and hearing entails. The shepherds are invited to hear, come, see, believe, and praise God for such rich blessings. Mary keeps all these things in her heart, reflecting on them as they invite her to deeper understanding and belief. Like the shepherds, we are invited to hear, come, see, believe, and praise God. Like Mary, we are asked to ponder God's ways in our hearts, so that we may attune our lives to God's many blessings.

▪ "Mary is acclaimed by Elizabeth . . . as 'the mother of my Lord.'[5] In fact, the One whom she conceived as man . . . was none other than the Father's eternal Son, the second person of the Holy Trinity. Hence the Church confesses that Mary is truly 'Mother of God' (*Theotokos*)[6]" (CCC, 495).

---

5 Luke 1:43; John 2:1; 19:25; cf. Matthew 13:55; et al.

6 Council of Ephesus (431): DS 251.

THE EPIPHANY OF THE LORD
Light in Darkness

ISAIAH 60:1–6 This Epiphany reading was selected for its reference to camels coming to Jerusalem bringing the wealth of nations, gold, and frankincense. Along with Psalm 72, it provides the backdrop to the account in the Gospel of Matthew of the Magi following the star to the newborn king of the Jews. Isaiah's historical setting is the Babylonian exile, with the land ravaged and the people dispersed. Isaiah consoles Jerusalem and all its inhabitants with a vision of light in darkness. While it appears that despoiled and ravaged Jerusalem is in darkness, God has not abandoned her. God's glory and light shines upon Israel, rescuing her from darkness to new light, from slavery to freedom, as it did at the Exodus.

God's glory and light shine on Jerusalem with such splendor that all its exiled inhabitants, young and old, return to experience it. The wealth of nations shall be brought to Jerusalem, both to rebuild and to pay homage to the Lord. Jerusalem, so richly manifesting God's light, glory, and presence, is the beacon that guides all nations to the Lord. Today, we celebrate the revelation and manifestation of God's glory to all nations in the birth of Jesus, the Light of the World.

PSALM 72:1–2, 7–8, 10–11, 12–13 (SEE 11) The psalm describes the ideal qualities that people hope their newly crowned king might manifest. The psalmist prays that God might endow the new king with right judgment, just decisions, and concern for the afflicted and the poor. Such a king would be remembered always, and would become the model of kingship for all the nations. Such a rule would be desired by all. God's ways would be incarnated in the king, with all nations admiring and honoring such a king with riches, tribute, honor, homage, and service.

Such manifestation of God's wisdom and right judgment by the king would lead all nations to acknowledge and honor God. Such ways of acting would be desired by all and for all time. Epiphany celebrates the manifestation of just such a king in the person of the child Jesus, true God and true man. All nations, represented by the Magi from the East, come to honor and offer homage, praying that his kingship would last forever.

CONNECTIONS TO CHURCH TEACHING AND TRADITION

- "Christ is the light of nations and consequently this holy synod, gathered together in the holy Spirit, ardently desires to bring to all humanity that light of Christ . . . by proclaiming his Gospel to every creature.[1] . . . The Church, in Christ, is a sacrament—a sign and instrument, that is, of communion with God and of the unity of entire human race" (LG, 1).

- "Christians are called to be the light of the world. Thus, the Church shows forth the kingship of Christ over all creation and in particular over human societies[2]" (CCC, 2105).

1 Cf. Mark 16:15.
2 Cf. AA 13; Leo XIII, *Immortale Dei* 3, 17; Pius XI, *Quas primas* 8, 20.

EPHESIANS 3:2–3A, 5–6 The author of Ephesians notes that through God's revelation, a mission—stewardship—was given for the benefit of all. God's mystery, the hidden plan of God from the beginning, was revealed by the Spirit to the author, as well as to the "holy apostles and prophets" (v. 5). The essence of that mystery is that the Gentiles are coheirs, members, and copartners "in the promise of Christ Jesus through the Gospel" (v. 6).

In Jesus, and through the power of the Spirit, God's mystery was revealed to the Jews. Correspondingly, a new way of thinking and acting was demanded of all Jews. No longer were they God's only Chosen People. Rather, God's plan from the beginning was that all would share in God's intimacy and blessings that they now enjoyed. The essence of Jesus' Good News is that Jews and Gentiles share equally in God's intimacy, blessings, and promises. Jesus' presence illuminates our minds and hearts; the Spirit's power enables us to be that same light to all the world.

MATTHEW 2:1–12 The Magi narrative, unique to the Gospel according to Matthew, developed out of several biblical and extrabiblical references intended to communicate beliefs concerning the identity and mission of Jesus. These post-Resurrection beliefs were projected into the early life of Jesus. The Magi represent the Gentiles who, guided by God's light, the star, come to Jerusalem to worship and honor the newborn king of the Jews. Herod and the Jewish leaders assert that the Messiah is to come from David's line and be born in David's town, Bethlehem. Herod, a Jewish king, represents those who are threatened by the new king and a new way of exercising kingship. Such people scheme to do away with Jesus and the values he manifests.

The Magi continue to follow God's light and are rewarded with an opportunity to recognize and honor the child Jesus as king with a completely different concept of kingship and ruling. Through this narrative, Matthew's wanted his to understand that Jesus came for all humanity. We who claim to be disciples of Jesus are called to bring that same insight, wisdom, and light to all the world. We are to manifest God's light to all, making certain that no one is excluded from membership in God's Kingdom. Epiphany celebrates Jesus' manifestation to the world, and our call to continue that mission in our lives.

- "The white garment symbolizes that the person baptized has 'put on Christ,'[3] has risen with Christ. The *candle*, lit from the Easter candle, signifies that Christ has enlightened the neophyte. In him the baptized are 'the light of the world'[4]" (CCC, 1243).

- "The magi's coming to Jerusalem . . . shows that they seek . . . in the messianic light of the star of David, the one who will be king of the nations[5]" (CCC, 528).

---

3 Galatians 3:27.

4 Matthew 5:14; cf. Philippians 2:15.

5 Cf. Matthew 2:2; Numbers 24:17–19; Revelation 22:16.

THE BAPTISM OF THE LORD
Walking in God's Way

ISAIAH 42:1–4, 6–7 Chapters 40 to 55 of the Book of Isaiah have been called the "Book of Consolation." God tells the people their time of exile is over and their deliverance is at hand. A new exodus will occur when the people return from Babylon through the wilderness to the Promised Land.

God wants more than deliverance for God's people; God wants to establish justice through the servant of the Lord. Chapter 42 contains the first of four "Servant Songs" in the Book of Isaiah (see 49:1–7; 50:4–11; 52:13—53:12). God's servant will be "a covenant to the people, a light to the nations" (42:6). This servant will be filled with the Spirit of God and will walk peacefully in God's ways. He will open the eyes of the blind and bring freedom to "those who sit in darkness" (v. 7). Although it is uncertain whom the prophet had in mind—Israel, a biblical personage, or the prophet himself— the Church sees Jesus as the fulfillment of the suffering servant of God.

PSALM 29:1–2, 3–4, 3, 9–10 (11B) This psalm may be an adaptation of an old Canaanite hymn, perhaps composed in honor of Baal, the pagan storm god. After an invitation to praise the Lord, the psalmist describes the majesty of God's revelation in a theophany, the manifestation of the divine in nature. The psalmist uses the imagery of a violent storm to show the might of God. As the storm arises over the Mediterranean Sea, God's voice is heard as thunder "over the waters" (v. 3a). God's mighty voice "breaks the cedars of Lebanon" (v. 5b) and makes the hills leap like "a young wild ox"(v. 6b). The storm passes east over the "wilderness of Kadesh" (v. 8b), which quakes at the voice of God. As the storm subsides, God is acclaimed as the Lord who "sits enthroned as king forever" (v. 10b) and blesses the people with peace.

ACTS 10:34–38 God sent Peter to the house of Cornelius, a Roman centurion, who asked to be received as a convert into the Christian faith. Although Peter was at first unwilling to associate with non-Jews, he had a vision that informed him "that God shows no partiality" (v. 34b). All who walk in God's way by living morally and ethically are acceptable to God.

CONNECTIONS TO CHURCH TEACHING AND TRADITION

- Through his baptism, Jesus is called to bring forth justice, fulfill the law, and become a covenant to the people (CCC, 580).

- Jesus' baptism by John marks the inauguration of his public life and mission (CCC, 444, 535–536, 608,701, 1224).

- Through Baptism, we enter into Jesus' Death and Resurrection and become disciples of Christ, continuing his ministry (CCC, 537, 1223).

Peter's kergymatic speech to Cornelius is the essence of the early Christian preaching about Jesus. Peter proclaims Jesus, who was sent by God with "the Holy Spirit and with power" (v. 38a). After his baptism, Jesus "went about doing good and healing" (v. 38b). Some opposed him and he was crucified on a cross. Death could not defeat Jesus, and God "raised him on the third day" (v. 40). After that, Jesus appeared to Peter and all "who were chosen by God as witnesses" (v. 41) to his Passion, Death, and Resurrection. As Peter spoke, the Spirit fell on Cornelius, who with his whole household, was baptized in Jesus' name.

MATTHEW 3:13–17 The baptism of Jesus is another epiphany, or manifestation, of the divine presence. The word *baptism* comes from a Greek word (*baptizo*) that means to be plunged or submerged in water. The Jews used baptism only for proselytes who came into Judaism from some other faith. Jews were members of the chosen people and assured of God's salvation; they could not conceive of the need for baptism for themselves. With John's call to repentance and the offer of forgiveness of sins, Jews realized their own need of God. Jesus was sinless and had no need to be baptized. He came to be baptized by John to "fulfill all righteousness" (Greek: *dikaiosune;* v. 15). But John was unwilling to baptize him. Jesus had no need of what John could give; it was John who needed what Jesus offered. By submitting to baptism, Jesus identified with those he came to save. He entered the waters of human sinfulness and sanctified them by his divine presence (2 Corinthians 5:21).

The voice heard from heaven, "This is my Son, the Beloved, with whom I am well pleased," is composed of two quotations. "You are my son; today I have begotten you" (Psalm 2:7) is a description of the Messiah, the mighty ruler to come. "Here is my servant, whom I uphold, my chosen, in whom my soul delights" (Isaiah 42:1) announces the suffering servant of God. In his baptism, Jesus was chosen to be king, but his throne would be the Cross. In Christian baptism, the elect plunge into the Passion, Death, and Resurrection of Christ (Romans 6:3–5), and become one with Christ's Body, the Christian community.

Lent

Lent begins on Ash Wednesday and concludes with the Mass of the Lord's Supper on Holy Thursday. In addition to being a penitential season, Lent is also known as the Period of Purification and Enlightenment for those catechumens (elect) preparing for Christian initiation. During this period, public rites such as the Rite of Sending for Election, the Rite of Election, the three Scrutinies, and the presentation of the Creed and the Lord's Prayer take place. The witness of the elect in these public rites reminds all of the faithful of the basis of their faith and their own need for God's mercy. The presence of the elect and the celebration of the rites fitting to this period help us understand the ancient and restored meaning of Lent as the season of immediate preparation for Christian initiation.

FIRST READINGS

During Lent, the Old Testament readings are about the history of salvation, a theme that coincides with the season of Lent. The progression of the readings from the First through Fifth Sundays presents the main aspect of salvation history from its beginning through the promise of the New Covenant fulfilled in Jesus Christ.

Beginning with the second creation story, the creation of Adam out of dust and from the breath of the Lord (the First Sunday of Lent) to the call of Abraham (Second Sunday of Lent) to the gift of water from the rock at Massah and Meribah (Third Sunday of Lent) to the anointing of David as Israel's king (Fourth Sunday of Lent) to the Lord promising to put his Spirit in the Israelites (Fifth Sunday of Lent), our faith becomes rooted in the wondrous life the Lord has given his people from the very beginning of time, despite their occasional lack of faith in him.

RESPONSORIAL PSALMS

From the First Sunday of Lent through the Fifth Sunday of Lent, the Responsorial Psalms repeatedly speak of the Lord's mercy. Whether it is a simple statement of the psalmist's and our confidence in the merciful nature of God (Psalm 130) or a personal prayer to the Lord asking him to shower his mercy upon us (Psalms 51 and 33), the idea of God's loving kindness is a primary theme of the Lenten psalms. The Lord's forgiveness and care for his people is so deep and constant that on the Fourth Sunday of Lent, the Responsorial Psalm is the beloved Psalm 23, in which the psalmist confesses that because the Lord is his shepherd, he is in want of nothing. On Palm Sunday, the Responsorial Psalm in each of the three years is Psalm 22, with the accompanying plea of one in need heard in the refrain "My God, my God, why have you abandoned me?"

SECOND READINGS

Unlike those of Ordinary Time, the Second Readings of Lent do correspond with both the First Reading and the Gospel. To the extent to which it is possible, the Second Readings also provide a connection between these two readings. During Year A, the Second Readings on the First, Third, and Fifth Sundays of Lent come from Paul's Letter to the Romans, his great treatise on justification by faith and the peace that comes from this grace. On the Second Sunday of Lent, we hear a selection from the pastoral letter 2 Timothy, which reinforces the truth that suffering for the sake of the Gospel comes with being a disciple of Christ. On the Fourth Sunday of Lent, the Second Reading is a passage from the letter to the Ephesians, a letter considered by Scripture scholars to be deutero-Pauline. This means it contains themes common to Paul, but was written by someone other than Paul and who was learned in Paul's teachings. On Palm Sunday, the Second Reading is the same in each year of the three-year cycle. It presents Christ's humanity and divinity in the form of a beautiful hymn. This hymn climaxes in the exaltation of Christ and the call to every tongue to confess him as Lord because of his obedience to the point of death on a cross.

GOSPEL READINGS

The Gospel readings of Lent provide some of the richest words with which people of all ages can pray, study, and grow spiritually as individuals and in relation to the Christian community. Year A of the Lectionary cycle of readings, in particular, gives us the great narratives of conversion on the Third, Fourth, and Fifth Sundays of Lent. These are the stories from John's account of the Gospel of the woman at the well, the man born blind, and the raising of Lazarus. The Gospel readings for the first two Sundays of Lent are always from one of the synoptic accounts. The temptation account sets us on the road to Easter, as we ponder those areas in our lives in which we give in to temptation and are in need of the saving grace of the One who did not. Hearing the account of Jesus' Transfiguration calls us to pause and remain in awe at his glory, just as the disciples who went up the mountain did.

First Sunday of Lent
Create in Me a Clean Heart

GENESIS 2:7–9; 3:1–7 In Genesis 2, God first creates the man out of the earth. After watching the creature, for the first time in the Bible, God says, "It is not good" (2:18). What was not good was that the human was alone. In the beginning, the man into whose nostrils God blew the breath of life could just as well be called "earth creature," for until the creation of Eve he was unique and alone. Although he could name everything around him including the animals (a sign of domination), the man's loneliness did not go away. Finally, God created a companion who could converse with him and call him by name. Now both of them knew what it meant to be human.

Immediately after, we hear the account of sin's entry into the world via temptation by the serpent. What the prince of lies told them was that they would be like gods if they ate of the forbidden fruit. They had forgotten that they were made in the image of God and, via their relationship with God and one another, they already were like gods. They who had been made in the image of God thought they could make themselves gods and, in their disobedience, they obeyed one who was not the true God.

PSALM 51:3–4, 5–6, 12–13, 17 (SEE 3A) Psalm 51 is the most well-known penitential psalm. Like Psalm 103, which appears a number of times in the lectionary, it is called a psalm of David, and it fits his experience. The psalm recognizes that every sin, no matter who the victim, is also a sin against God, destroying the divine order and plan for creation. The key to this prayer is that it recognizes God as the center and ruler of the universe, the only one who can forgive and restore. And so we look to God, begging for mercy and renewal.

ROMANS 5:12–19 OR 5:12, 17–19 Paul's Letter to the Romans is the only extant Pauline letter that was not written to a community that Paul knew well. Thus, in the beginning of the letter he introduces himself and the themes and topics he will treat, which include the early Church's basic teaching.

CONNECTIONS TO CHURCH TEACHING AND TRADITION

- "[Reason] becomes human only . . . if it looks beyond itself. Otherwise, man's situation, in view of the imbalance between his material capacity and the lack of judgment in his heart, becomes a threat for him and for creation" (SS, 23).

- "There are still others whose hopes are set on a genuine and total emancipation of humankind through human effort alone and look forward to some future earthly paradise where all the desires of their hearts will be fulfilled" (GS, 10).

- "But the world's Creator has stamped man's inmost being with an order revealed to man by his conscience. . . . Men 'show the work of the law written in their hearts. Their conscience bears witness to them.'[1] And how could it be otherwise? All created being reflects the infinite wisdom of God. It reflects it all the more clearly, the higher it stands in the scale of perfection[2]" (PT, 5).

---

1 Romans 2:15.
2 Cf. Psalm 18:8–11.

In today's liturgy we proclaim what he says in regard to the mysteries of sin and salvation. Paul contrasts Adam, counted as the first sinner, with Christ, the one who brought acquittal to all sinners who would accept him. Paul does not blame all sin on Adam, but rather recognizes Adam as the originator of sin and therefore of death. The point is not so much to teach about original sin and Adam, but rather to focus on Christ, who brings an abundance of grace, justification, and the promise that faithful disciples will reign with Christ.

MATTHEW 4:1–11 The account of Jesus' temptation in the desert occurs in all three synoptic accounts of the Gospel. The temptations that the devil puts before Jesus reprise the history of Israel. The first, creating bread for himself, recalls the trek through the wilderness, and is a temptation to use his power for himself. As if they were in a rabbinical debate, Jesus responds to the tempter with a Scripture quotation, citing Deuteronomy 8:3.

When the devil took him to the parapet of the temple and challenged him to jump, both the devil and Jesus quoted Scripture. The devil was asking Jesus to see if God really would care for him, and Jesus' response was to refuse to test God as the Israelites did in the desert (Deuteronomy 6:16).

Finally, the devil shows Jesus all the kingdoms of the world and offers them to Jesus if only he will worship him. This is the temptation that most closely resembles the Genesis account, because the devil is promising something that is not his to give. Not only that, but he is promising the kingdoms of the world, not the kingdom of God. Jesus' reply summarizes his vocation and his call to disciples: "The Lord, your God, shall you worship / and him alone shall you serve" (v. 10). For the rest of the Gospel, Jesus will be living that vocation and trying to get it across to his disciples. His message is that, with the grace of God, all disciples can make God the center of their worship and live in a way that gives witness to God's grace.

Listen to Him

GENESIS 12:1–4A Abraham is the chief figure in the First Reading for the Second Sunday of Lent of all three years in the lectionary (A, B, C). In this year's reading, we meet Abram as the model of faith, hope, and obedience. He listened to God and believed that the impossible could happen. Accepting the incredible plan of God, he left everything behind. We can paraphrase Paul and say that by faith, Abram was transfigured. His life became something he never could have imagined, but he believed in the power of God more than in his own fortunes.

PSALM 33:4–5, 18–19, 20, 22 (22) Following the account of the call of Abram and his faith-filled response, our psalm sings what might well have been in Abram's mind, even if the psalm itself was written in a future epoch. The refrain intimates that we stand with Abram as we place our trust in God. The body of the psalm proclaims our belief in the trustworthiness of the Lord, and recognizes the fact that the kindness of the Lord fills all of creation. The final strophe, which is also the end of the psalm itself, reminds us that the Lord, our help and our shield, is our only source of hope; therefore, our best act of faith is to wait for the Lord with a listening heart.

2 TIMOTHY 1:8B–10 Throughout Paul's Second Letter to Timothy we encounter a very human Paul writing to his protégé, Timothy, as one would write to a beloved son. He uses his own experience to counsel Timothy about how to be a good minister of the Gospel. That, of course, will entail suffering, but the strength to bear it comes from God who, as Paul has said in other places, has called us from the beginning of time. That theme is reminiscent of Psalm 139 and Jeremiah 1:5, and it provides a follow-up to the story of Abraham's call. In the context of the other readings, Paul invites us to consider our own call to a holy life and how the grace and appearance of Christ Jesus enlightens and changes—transfigures—our life.

MATTHEW 17:1–9 The account of the Transfiguration follows Jesus' first prediction of his Passion and his explanation that discipleship entails taking up one's own cross. In some ways, the real subjects of the Transfiguration are the

CONNECTIONS TO CHURCH TEACHING AND TRADITION

- "When we have spread on earth the fruits of our nature and our enterprise—human dignity, sisterly and brotherly communion, and freedom—according to the command of the Lord and in his Spirit, we will find them once again, cleansed this time from the stain of sin, illuminated and transfigured, when Christ presents to his Father an eternal and universal kingdom 'of truth and life, a kingdom of holiness and grace, a kingdom of justice, love and peace'[1]" (GS, 39).

- "Disciples must be formed in a spirituality of missionary action . . . based on docility to the impulse of the Spirit, to its life giving power which mobilizes and transfigures all dimensions of existence" (*Aparecida*, 284).

---
1 Preface for the Feast of Christ the King.

three disciples. The narrative speaks more about them than about Jesus, and only names Moses and Elijah as his conversation partners. We are not told of Jesus' own experience, but rather what the three saw and heard. We are not told whether or not this experience strengthened Jesus, but it was clearly meant to be a revelation to the disciples.

The description of the transfigured Jesus is almost like a resurrection appearance. It happens after six days, as did God's revelation to Moses in Exodus 24:13–16. It happens on a mountain, a prototypical place for divine revelations. Jesus is described as having a face that shone like the sun while his clothes became "white as light" (v. 2), recalling John the Evangelist's description of Jesus as the Light of the World. The two Old Testament figures that appear with Jesus, Moses and Elijah, are two of the most important figures in Israel's history and represent the Law and the prophets. Jesus is solidly in line with his Jewish heritage.

Here, as at the time of his baptism, a voice comes from the heavens and now proclaims "This is my beloved Son, with whom I am well pleased; listen to him" (v. 5). The voice certainly unnerved the disciples, causing them to fall over in fear. In one of the classic Orthodox icons of the Transfiguration, the disciples' reaction is portrayed vividly: the three seem to be hiding in plain sight. Like a child who closes her eyes and thinks she has erased the object of her fear, they have fallen down and cannot bear to behold the vision before them. In addition, we see other disciples in the distance, seemingly in caves from which they can see, hear, and understand even less than Peter, James, and John. The truth is that what Jesus and God are revealing about Jesus' nature as the second Person of the Holy Trinity, is beyond their ability to comprehend. As time goes on, through the Passion and Resurrection, they will gradually come to understand more.

At the end, the gentle Jesus touches the three and tells them not to be afraid. He also tells them that they are not to report the vision to anyone. Obviously, they have not yet understood it. The central point is that in order to understand, they must listen to him.

■ "Proclaiming the death of the Lord . . . entails that all who take part in the Eucharist be committed to changing their lives . . . It is his fruit of a transfigured existence and commitment to transforming the world in accordance with the Gospel which splendidly illustrates the eschatological tension inherent in the celebration of the Eucharist" (EE, 20).

THIRD SUNDAY OF LENT
Christ the Living Water

EXODUS 17:3–7 As a squeaky wheel gets its grease, so a cranky people get their water. Moses and God react differently to the thirsty people strewing complaints across the desert. Moses is exasperated, but God comes up with a practical solution. This passage tells the classic story of Moses striking a rock with his staff, and God opening the rock with a burst of water. The elders of Israel witnessed the event, lending credibility to an otherwise implausible story. God invited the people into this journey, wanted them to complete it, and offered them every aid. This episode serves as a prelude to the Gospel of the day, which in turn foreshadows the mystery of Baptism.

PSALM 95:1–2, 6–7, 8–9 (8) This psalm recalls the same event told in the First Reading. Here, though, God's response is not as bemused as it seems to be in Exodus. Instead of casually cooperating with the people's request, God issues a different command to a later generation: "'Harden not your hearts . . . / as in the day of Massah in the desert, / Where your fathers . . . / tested me though they had seen my works' " (vv. 8, 9). Basically, the psalm is asking a later generation of beleaguered people to have a better attitude than their forebears had.

ROMANS 5:1–2, 5–8 Just as God poured forth water for the people in the desert, so God pours love into the hearts of Christians through the gift of the Holy Spirit. St. Paul's challenging letter to the Romans has some of its meatiest material in chapter 5. He explores what came to be known as the theological virtues: Christians are justified by faith, which gives them hope, because they have received the love of God. By comparing this gift of the Spirit to something "poured out" (v. 5), Paul uses a metaphor that the Lectionary puts to eloquent purpose. It links this passage with the love of God in the First Reading and the Gospel's promise of the Spirit.

CONNECTIONS TO CHURCH TEACHING AND TRADITION

- Christ creates the gift of faith in those who seek him (RM, Preface for the Third Sunday of Lent).

- The Lord Jesus is the fountain for whom catechumens thirst; through the Son, the Father has offered salvation to all sinners (RCIA, 154).

- The human virtues are rooted in the theological virtues of faith, hope, and charity (CCC, 1812).

- "The woman of Samaria is a symbol of the Church not yet made righteous but about to be made righteous" (LH, II:212, from a treatise on John by St. Augustine, bishop).

JOHN 4:5–42 OR 4:5–15, 19B–26, 39A, 40–42 A woman who comes to perform an ordinary task finds herself in an extraordinary conversation. The story is one of the most vivid in the Gospel according to John.

In the time of Christ, Jews and Samaritans did not get along, partly because many generations earlier, upon their release from the Babylonian captivity, the Jews rebuilt the Temple without inviting the Samaritans to help. So, when Jesus, a Jew, asks a woman, a Samaritan, for a drink, he was already testing boundaries. That their conversation climaxed in a discussion on places of true worship showed their willingness to step right into the heart of a centuries-old conflict, played out in the ordinary lives of two people needing water on a hot, sunny day. Jesus wants something more than water. He wants the woman's faith. He probes and parries, demonstrating his prophetic knowledge of her life and his willingness to satisfy the deepest thirst in her heart. He offers her living water. He is that water, the one who can so slake those who receive him that they will never be thirsty, lifeless, and aimless again. He wants her to drink him in.

The woman herself shifts the discussion to faith, as she identifies the unrewarded thirst of the ancients: the coming of the Messiah, the one called Christ. Already she is wondering, could this be the one? At a well of water, echoing words Moses heard at a bush of fire, Jesus says to her, "I am he." Now, the woman acts like an apostle. She invites others to believe in Jesus, and they do, not just because of her testimony, but because they come to know Christ.

This entire story has long been associated with the Third Sunday of Lent. There is strong circumstantial evidence that it was proclaimed with the scrutiny rites in the early Church, in order to prepare catechumens for Baptism. This story, then, provides a paradigm in which those seeking the waters of Baptism today can find hope in the woman's story. Lent is observed not just by catechumens but also by the faithful. Those who mark the disciplines of Lent in order to renew their commitment to Christ will come to the end of their spiritual journey when they renew their baptismal promises at the Easter Vigil. Then they will be sprinkled with the blessed water of Baptism, living water that enables them to tell the world that Jesus is the Christ.

Christ the True Light

1 SAMUEL 16:1B, 6–7, 10–13A God chooses David as the king of Israel, and Samuel anoints him. This reading serves two purposes in today's liturgy. When lifted out of its context here, it can be placed in sequence with the other First Readings of the season; it then becomes one in a series of markers in the history of Israel. One workable method of preaching and catechizing during Lent focuses just on the First Readings of the six weeks, which together show how God was preparing for the salvation of the human race step by step throughout the generations of Israel. One of those milestones is the anointing of David.

The other reason this reading fits today's liturgy is its relationship to the Gospel account of the man born blind. Basically a story of how people who have physical sight may lack spiritual sight, this First Reading carries a similar message. Those who were looking for a likely candidate to be king overlooked the best of them all.

Note how dramatically the writer of 1 Samuel keeps the reader in suspense. The name of the future king is not revealed until the very last lines. A skilled reader of this passage will pause before announcing the name, as if to say, "And the winner is [*pause for excruciating suspense*] . . . David!"

PSALM 23:1–3A, 3B–4, 5, 6 (1) Unquestionably the most popular psalm in the Bible, Psalm 23 appears today because of its idyllic picture of the shepherd with his peaceful sheep. It looks back to the First Reading with reassuring confidence that David will shepherd God's people as no one has before. The psalmist at Mass can imagine David singing these words—he who is the shepherd acknowledging that the Lord is his shepherd. Then will come alive this phrase: "You anoint my head with oil" (v. 5).

This psalm has little to do with the theme of the Gospel, but matches up nicely with the story about the anointing of Israel's first king.

EPHESIANS 5:8–14 Addressing a Gentile community in words not complimentary about its past, Paul says, "You were once darkness, but now you are light in the Lord" (v. 8). Paul affirms the beautiful brightness that shines from the hearts of these believers and encourages them to shine their light upon others. The closing verses probably come

CONNECTIONS TO CHURCH TEACHING AND TRADITION

- "'This bath is called *enlightenment*, because those who receive this [catechetical] instruction are enlightened in their understanding.'[1]" (CCC, 1216).

- "By the mystery of the Incarnation, / [Christ] has led the human race that walked in darkness / into the radiance of the faith"(RM, Preface for the Fourth Sunday of Lent).

- "'I am the light of the world.' . . . That light shines on us now, for we have had our eyes anointed with the eye-salve of faith" (LH, II:276, from a treatise on John by St. Augustine, bishop).

- "Lord Jesus, you are the true light that enlightens the world" (RCIA, 167).

---

1 St. Justin, Apol. 1, 61, 12: PG 6, 421.

from an early Christian hymn, summoning those who sleep—and those who have died—to greet Christ who gives them light.

Obviously, this passage is chosen for today's liturgy because of its strong link to the theme of the Gospel. Whereas the Gospel will tell of a man born blind, Paul refers to a people born blind, but who now see with the eyes of faith.

JOHN 9:1–41 OR 9:1, 6–9, 13–17, 34–38 Jesus gives sight to a man born blind. But that is not even half the story. The miracle is dispatched rather quickly in the early verses of this chapter, and the rest of today's proclamation explores the effect this miracle has on the family, acquaintances, and the very person of the man born blind.

John does not conceal his main point. He contrasts physical blindness with spiritual blindness. This miracle story lies behind the opening verse of the popular hymn "Amazing Grace": "I once was lost, but now am found, / was blind, but now I see."

Like last week's Gospel, this one has a long history associated with the catechumenate. As catechumens elected for the Easter sacraments make their final preparations for Baptism, they experience scrutiny rites intended to drive out whatever keeps them from Christ and to strengthen their resolve to follow him. As did the woman at the well, so does the man born blind. Surprisingly, the man never asked Jesus for this miracle. His gift of faith came after, not before, his healing. Yet, it comes in a powerful statement: "I do believe, Lord," he says.

This story still strengthens those preparing for Baptism, even as it reminds those already baptized that following Christ means removing blindness. At this stage of Lent, the faithful should be more aware of their weaknesses, their dependencies, their addictions, and their sin. They may not have asked for the healing that Lent offers, but here it is, ready to open their eyes, that they might believe.

■ "The word 'Christ' comes from the Greek translation of the Hebrew *Messiah*, which means 'anointed.' . . . In effect, in Israel those consecrated to God for a mission that he gave were anointed in his name. This was the case for kings, for priests, and, in rare instances, for prophets"[2] (CCC, 436).

2 Cf. Exodus 29:7; Leviticus 8:12; 1 Samuel 9:16; 10:1; 16:1, 12–13; 1 Kings 1:39; 19:16.

FIFTH SUNDAY OF LENT
Christ the Resurrection and the Life

EZEKIEL 37:12–14 Through the prophet Ezekiel, God announces to captive Israel that freedom will come, as surely and miraculously as the dead shall rise from their graves. This short passage concludes a famous prophecy in which Ezekiel sees dry bones in a field coming to life as a mighty army, stirred by spirit—and not just any spirit—by God's Spirit. This powerful conclusion places a mighty prophecy before a dispirited people. God's comparison would have stunned even the prophet: captive Israel's future resembles the liberty of the dead from their graves. On this particular Sunday, this passage lifts a veil from the miracle that caps Jesus' career in John's account of the Gospel: the raising of Lazarus from the dead.

PSALM 130:1–2, 3–4, 5–6, 7–8 (7) The psalm today carries a refrain about God's mercy that prophetically pairs it with the "fullness of redemption" (v. 7). God's mercy is not just a compassionate feeling of pain, but one that intervenes to offer complete salvation. The faint drumbeat of the coming Easter victory can already be heard. More importantly, this psalm opens with the famous line, "Out of the depths I cry to you, O Lord."

Well known by its Latin title, *De profundis,* this prayer for mercy stresses the depths from which the psalmist cries out. In the light of the other readings today, Psalm 130 brings to the ears of the faithful the chilling voice of the dead, calling out from the depths of the grave for forgiveness, confident that God will redeem. This psalm has a classic position in the Catholic funeral rites for the same reason. Although the original psalmist was alive but feeling lonely, the psalm can be heard as the voice of the souls of the faithful departed, expressing their confident plea for forgiveness and life.

ROMANS 8:8–11 The Spirit of Christ gives life to those who are dead. Paul applies this statement in two ways, both to the living and to the dead. Those who are "in the flesh" live in sin, but those in whom the Spirit of God dwells are "in the spirit" (8:9). So throughout a Christian's days, the Spirit bestows righteousness. It does not end with death. Through the Spirit, God, who raised Jesus from the dead, gives life to bodies claimed by death.

CONNECTIONS TO CHURCH TEACHING AND TRADITION

- "The Christian Creed . . . culminates in the proclamation of the resurrection of the dead on the last day and in life everlasting" (CCC, 988).

- "I order you, O sleeper, to awake. I did not create you to be held a prisoner in hell. Rise from the dead, for I am the life of the dead. Rise up, work of my hands, you who were created in my image. Rise, let us leave this place, for you are in me and I am in you; together we form only one person and we cannot be separated" (LH, II:497, an ancient homily on Holy Saturday).

- "For as true man he wept for Lazarus his friend / and as eternal God, raised him from the tomb" (RM, Preface for Fifth Sunday of Lent).

- "Lord Jesus, / by raising Lazarus from the dead / you showed that you came that we might have life / and have it more abundantly" (RCIA, 175).

Throughout this central passage of the letter to the Romans, Paul is building his case about the triumph of spirit over flesh, life over sin and death. Because of the thematic content of the other readings today, this passage helps the Christian understand how the powers of Christ over death apply very personally to the lives of believers.

JOHN 11:1–45 OR 11:3–7, 17, 20–27, 33B–45 Jesus raises his friend Lazarus from the dead. John's dramatic account of this episode has Jesus appear indifferent to the sickness, but he is more interested in life than death, in preaching than in illness. When he tells the disciples that Lazarus has died, he adds, "I am glad for you that I was not there" (v. 15). Illness and death are merely the substance upon which Jesus builds the greatest prophetic stance of his career. This is the last of the great signs Jesus works in John's account of the Gospel. After showing his power over death here in chapter 11, the story of his Passion gets underway in chapter 12.

The conversation with Martha carries the most important teaching. Jesus tells her, "I am the resurrection and the life." The Resurrection is not just something that happened to him; he is the Resurrection, the one in whom all souls find hope.

This Gospel is the climax of three Johannine passages that build through the latter part of Lent. They were probably first associated with scrutinies in the early Church. The post–Vatican II lectionary recovered them, to be used even in Years B and C whenever there are elect present with whom to celebrate scrutinies. The images increase in drama: first water, the source of life; then light, the sign of faith; and now life, the fulfillment of the promise of birth. The elect can be brought to a deeper appreciation of the sacraments to which they are called, even as they leave behind whatever keeps them from Christ.

These readings also draw the faithful more deeply into the expectations of the Christian life. More aware of their sin, they seek God's forgiveness. Many will celebrate the Sacrament of Reconciliation before Easter. With today's reading they encounter the ultimate mysteries of life. God who summoned them through their birth now shows power over death. Those who repent die to their past, that they may rise as new people on Easter Day.

Palm Sunday of the Passion of the Lord
Jesus the Son of David

MATTHEW 21:1–11 Although we commonly speak of this day as Palm Sunday, its full title mentions the Passion of the Lord as well. Two Gospel passages are proclaimed on this day: one about the palms, the other about the Passion.

The first is proclaimed after the blessing of branches and before the entrance procession. In Matthew's account, the people recognize Jesus as the Son of David who comes in the name of the Lord. The word Hosanna means something like "save us." It comes from the same Hebrew root as Jesus' own name, Yeshua, which means "savior."

The evangelist seems to have misunderstood Zechariah 9:9, where the prophet uses two different ways to express a humble king astride an animal. Matthew thought he meant two different animals, so he has Jesus straddling them both.

ISAIAH 50:4–7 This is the third of Isaiah's four oracles of the servant of God. It poignantly foreshadows the suffering of Jesus as he approaches Calvary, giving his back to those who beat him, not shielding his face from buffets and spitting, yet confident that the Lord God will be his help.

This passage was newly added to the Palm Sunday Mass after the Second Vatican Council. There were very few Old Testament readings on Sundays prior to the Council. This passage broadens the Christian's appreciation of the role of the Son of God in the eternal plan of salvation.

PSALM 22:8–9, 17–18, 19–20, 23–24 (2A) Perhaps the line in the Passion that most wrenches believers is Jesus' impassioned cry "My God, my God, why have you abandoned me?" He is quoting Psalm 22, which the Church sings for the responsorial today. The liturgy, however, does not rest on the quotation of that single agonizing line. It excerpts three stanzas of suffering: scoffing enemies, pierced hands and feet, and garments divided by a roll of the dice. It concludes with a powerful fourth stanza presupposing a faith that stabilizes amid terror: all the descendants of Israel should revere God.

CONNECTIONS TO CHURCH TEACHING AND TRADITION

- Christ died for all without exception (CCC, 605).

- "It is love 'to the end'[1] that confers on Christ's sacrifice its value as redemption and reparation, as atonement and satisfaction" (CCC, 616).

- "In his humility Christ entered the dark regions of our fallen world and he is glad that he became so humble for our sake, glad that he came and lived among us and shared in our nature in order to raise us up again to himself" (LH, II:419, from a sermon by St. Andrew of Crete, bishop).

- "As Christ the Lord was about to celebrate with the disciples the paschal supper in which he instituted the Sacrifice of his Body and Blood, he commanded that a large, furnished upper room be prepared.[2] Indeed, the Church has always judged that this command also applied to herself . . . for the Celebration of the Most Holy Eucharist" (GIRM, 1).

---

1 John 13:1.
2 Luke 22:12.

PHILIPPIANS 2:6–11 For as long as there have been lectionaries, possibly at least since the fifth century, this passage has always been associated with Palm Sunday. It perfectly captures the mission of the Son of God, who takes on human form, humbling himself to death on a cross, and then is exalted as Lord above all creation. The Palm Sunday Gospel will tell of the Death of Christ, but this passage reveals already the mystery that will be proclaimed more grandly next week.

MATTHEW 26:14—27:66 OR 27:11–54 "Jesus cried out again in a loud voice, and gave up his spirit" (27:50). These are the words that galvanize the faithful today. Matthew's account of the Passion is a long, dramatic meditation on the final hours in the life of Jesus of Nazareth, but it all comes down to this line. If he had not died, there would be no meaning to his Resurrection. Because of his Death, believers who suffer from ailments, injury, and abandonment all know that they have an intercessor who understands.

Although all four Gospel accounts devote their largest section to the Passion and Death of Jesus, Matthew's account is the traditional one to be proclaimed on Palm Sunday. Prior to the publication of the lectionary revised after the Second Vatican Council, Catholics heard it at Mass every year. Matthew includes episodes with which every faithful Christian is familiar: Judas betrays Jesus for thirty pieces of silver, Jesus has a last supper with his disciples, Peter hears the prophecy that he will deny Jesus three times, Jesus prays in agony that the cup may pass from him, a violent mob descends on Jesus at his arrest, Caiaphas interviews Jesus, Judas hangs himself, Pilate questions Jesus, Barabbas is set free, soldiers mock and scourge Jesus, Jesus is crucified with two criminals and he dies on the Cross, the sanctuary veil is torn as the earth quakes, a centurion proclaims the divinity of Jesus, and Joseph of Arimathea reverently lays the body of Jesus to rest.

Even those who know this story well enter into its power every year. The proclamation of the Passion is more than a simple recitation of events. It is the Word of God thundering through the gathered assembly, making them present to the supreme sacrifice that even now saves.

The Sacred Paschal Triduum

Overview of the Sacred Paschal Triduum

We begin the Triduum celebration with the Holy Thursday Eucharist. The Scripture accounts of the Last Supper address the heart of our faith. We believe the Eucharist is the Body and Blood of Christ and that Jesus told us this and commanded us to eat and drink in remembrance of him. We are also called to engage in service to our neighbor, following Jesus' example of washing the disciples' feet.

On Good Friday, we journey with the Lord, the innocent servant of God, who has taken our sins upon himself as he walks the path to Calvary. At the end, Jesus says, "It is finished." It doesn't mean "It is over." It means "It is accomplished" or "It is perfected." He has completed the task he was given. He hands over his spirit.

That most sacred night when we gather at the Easter Vigil to rejoice in the Good News of Christ's Resurrection is the high point of the Triduum. All of Lent has led to this pivotal night of the entire liturgical year; even Advent and Christmas Time prepared us for this night. Everything we celebrate for the next fifty days until Pentecost results from our belief that Christ is risen from the dead. The Mass of Easter Day, which is included in this section because the Triduum lasts until Easter Sunday night, echoes and reechoes the Alleluias and baptismal promises of the Vigil.

FIRST READINGS

On Holy Thursday, the First Reading from Exodus is the remembrance of the Passover meal preceding the Exodus; on Good Friday, the First Reading is from another one of the servant songs in Isaiah. At the Easter Vigil, there are seven Old Testament readings. Their proclamation makes the saving works of God throughout history present and real to us.

RESPONSORIAL PSALMS

The psalms of Triduum are suitable to each of the three days. On Holy Thursday, the refrain used with Psalm 110, which comes from the New Testament's first letter of Paul to the Corinthians, speaks of the blessing cup as participation in the Blood of Christ. Good Friday's Responsorial Psalm each year is Psalm 22, and its refrain contains the words of the Gospel according to Luke spoken by Jesus as he hangs on the Cross: "Father, into your hands I commend my spirit" (Luke 23:46). The seven Responsorial Psalms of the Easter Vigil, which correspond to the seven Old Testament readings, abound with themes of the glorious nature of the earth and the Lord himself, the Lord's faithfulness to his people, the salvation the Lord offers, and the joyful nourishment that comes from following the Lord and his Word. Psalm 118, which serves as a responsorial psalm and the Gospel Acclamation at the Vigil, is also the Responsorial Psalm for the Mass of Easter Day.

SECOND READINGS

On Holy Thursday, the Second Reading from Paul's first letter to the Corinthians gives the oldest written account of the Eucharist and reminds us of what we celebrate each time we gather together to pray the Eucharistic liturgy. On Good Friday, the Second Reading is from Hebrews. This letter speaks of the high priesthood of Jesus Christ. In particular, Good Friday's passage emphasizes the sacrifice of the High Priest's own life as an offering for sin.

GOSPEL READINGS

During the three days of the Sacred Paschal Triduum the Gospel readings present Jesus' example in his washing of the feet of his disciples on Holy Thursday; John's account of the Passion, which emphasizes Jesus as Isaiah's servant of the Lord and the one High Priest; and Matthew's account of the women at the empty tomb and their announcement of the Resurrection to Jesus' disciples.

Jesus Gives a Model

EXODUS 12:1–8, 11–14 In this reading, God commands Moses and Aaron to institute the feast that would be known as Passover. At the time, the community of Israel suffered bondage in Egypt. This passage comes in the midst of the description of the ten plagues through which the Pharaoh became convinced to free the people of Israel from their captivity.

Passover came to mean the meal and the date fixed on the Jewish calendar. For the first observance, a family slaughtered a lamb or a goat, eating the meat, but sprinkling the blood on the two doorposts of each home. The blood became a sign for the angel responsible for the tenth plague to "pass over" the homes and spare the life of the firstborn. Ever since this event, the Jewish community has celebrated Passover each year.

PSALM 116:12–13, 15–16BC, 17–18 (SEE 1 CORINTHIANS 10:16) Several verses from a psalm of thanksgiving supply the Responsorial Psalm. The overall purpose of Psalm 116 is to give thanks to God, but the Lectionary designates these verses because they especially fit the themes of Holy Thursday. The psalmist gives thanks by taking up "the cup of salvation" (v. 13). The psalm proclaims, "Precious in the eyes of the Lord / is the death of his faithful ones" (v. 15). These verses foreshadow the Eucharistic cup that Jesus shared at the Last Supper, as well as his own Death looming on Good Friday.

The refrain is taken from the same epistle that gives us the Second Reading; it is not a verse from the psalm. As Christians experiencing anew the last days of Jesus, rooted in the meal traditions of our ancestors, we sing, "Our blessing-cup is a communion with the Blood of Christ." Normally, the Responsorial Psalm echoes a theme from the First Reading or the Gospel. This is a rare instance when it pertains to the Second Reading, which has not yet been proclaimed.

1 CORINTHIANS 11:23–26 St. Paul tells how Jesus instituted the Eucharist. With minor variations, this account also appears in the Gospel accounts of Matthew, Mark, and Luke. Scholars tell us, however, that Paul wrote these epistles before the evangelists wrote their Gospel narratives.

CONNECTIONS TO CHURCH TEACHING AND TRADITION

- "At the last supper, on the night he was betrayed, our Savior instituted the Eucharistic sacrifice of his body and blood" (SC, 47).

- "Moreover, the wondrous mystery of the Lord's real presence under the Eucharistic species . . . is proclaimed in the celebration of the Mass" (GIRM, 3).

- "In order to make society more human, more worthy of the human person, love in social life—political, economic and cultural—must be given renewed value, becoming the constant and highest norm for all activity" (CSDC, 582).

- The principle of the universal destination of goods also applies naturally to water, considered in the Sacred Scriptures as a symbol of purification (cf. Psalm 51:4; John 13:8) and of life (cf. John 3:5; Galatians 3:27)" (CSDC, 484).

- "In all of his life Jesus presents himself as *our model*. He is 'the perfect man,' who invites us to become his disciples and follow him" (CCC, 520).

This, therefore, is the oldest account of what happened at the Last Supper, the version that lies closest to the years of Jesus' life.

At this point in his letter, Paul is probably responding to some specific questions from the Corinthians. Apparently, they had asked about the proper way to celebrate the Eucharist. Paul hands on to them what others had told him. Paul says that the supper took place on the night before Jesus was betrayed, that Jesus took bread, gave thanks, said "This is my body that is for you," and commanded his followers to "do this in remembrance of me" (v. 24). Jesus repeated this command upon taking up the cup, which he called "the new covenant in my blood" (v. 25). Paul says we proclaim the "death of the Lord until he comes" whenever we "eat this bread and drink the cup" (v. 26).

These words address the heart of Catholic faith. We believe that our Eucharist is the Body and Blood of Christ, that Jesus told us this, and that he commanded us to eat and drink in remembrance of him. This passage is the key that unlocks the meaning of Holy Thursday.

JOHN 13:1–15 Jesus gives his followers a model of discipleship when he washes their feet. In John's account of the Gospel, at the Last Supper, the reader expects to find the institution of the Eucharist that appears in the synoptic accounts of the Gospel; it is not there. Instead, John gives a mystical interpretation of the Eucharist in the washing of the feet. Just as Paul's letter unlocks the meaning of Holy Thursday, John's narrative of the Gospel unlocks its implications. As Jesus stoops to wash feet, Simon Peter resists until Jesus warns him, "Unless I wash you, you will have no inheritance with me" (v. 8). His statement probably alludes to baptism, which became an initiation rite for all the followers of Jesus. Jesus pointedly advises the disciples, "If I, therefore, the master and teacher, have washed your feet, you ought to wash one another's feet" (v. 14). Whenever we engage in selfless, humble service of our neighbor, we follow the model that Jesus gave.

Jesus Dies for Us

ISAIAH 52:13—53:12 The Lectionary subtitles this passage the "Fourth oracle of the Servant of the Lord"; it is also called the Fourth Song of the Suffering Servant. Near the end of the Book of the prophet Isaiah, we meet a figure called God's servant, who represents God but suffers greatly for the sins of others. The figure may have been a historical person at the time of Isaiah or a representation of the people of Israel. Christians read these four passages with the specific view that they prophesy Jesus, the servant of the Father, who suffered for our salvation.

The passage opens with a startling description of this servant. He was "spurned and avoided by people, / a man of suffering, accustomed to infirmity" (53:3). In the most moving verses, read with a lump in our throats, we realize that the servant's suffering should have been ours: "Yet it was our infirmities that he bore, / our sufferings that he endured . . . / We had all gone astray like sheep . . . / but the Lord laid upon him / the guilt of us all" (53:4, 6). On Good Friday, these verses come to fulfillment in the crucified Jesus.

PSALM 31:2, 6, 12–13, 15–16, 17, 25 (LUKE 23:46) Psalm 31 appeals to God for rescue. The psalmist is desperate, "an object of reproach, / a laughingstock to my neighbors, and a dread to my friends" (Psalm 31:12). But the psalm does not dwell in despair. It trusts that God will redeem the one in distress. This singer is so convinced of salvation that the psalm concludes with an exhortation to the hearer: "Take courage and be stouthearted, / all you who hope in the Lord" (v. 25). The refrain for the psalm comes from the Gospel according to Luke. It was spoken by Jesus on the Cross. Jesus, who must have known its words by heart, quotes Psalm 31 when he makes his appeal for rescue: "Father, into your hands I commend my spirit" (Luke 23:46).

HEBREWS 4:14–16; 5:7–9 The sufferings of Jesus enabled him to sympathize with our weakness, making him a powerful mediator of mercy and grace. The Letter to the Hebrews explains the role of Jesus as the greatest of all high priests. This passage describes the events of Jesus' Passion. "In the days when Christ was in the flesh, he offered prayers and supplications with loud cries and tears to the one who

CONNECTIONS TO CHURCH TEACHING AND TRADITION

- "This sacrifice of Christ is unique; it completes and surpasses all other sacrifices.[1] First, it is a gift from God the Father himself, for the Father handed his Son over to sinners in order to reconcile us with himself. At the same time it is the offering of the Son of God made man, who in freedom and love offered his life to his Father through the Holy Spirit in reparation for our disobedience[2]" (CCC, 614).

- "The crucified Jesus has overcome divisions, re-establishing peace and reconciliation, precisely through the cross, 'thereby bringing the hostility to an end' (Ephesians 2:16) and bringing the salvation of the Resurrection to mankind" (CSDC, 493).

- "Christ's stay in the tomb constitutes the real link between his passible state before Easter and his glorious and risen state today" (CCC, 625).

---

1 Cf. Hebrews 10:10.
2 Cf. Jn 10:17–18; 15:13; Heb 9:14; 1 Jn 4:10.

was able to save him from death" (5:7). These words resemble the Gospel accounts of Jesus' agony in the garden of Gethsemane, but the passage does not linger on Jesus' suffering, as "he was heard" (5:7). The Father could save Jesus from death, and so did, through his Resurrection.

JOHN 18:1—19:42 This passage in the Gospel according to John is one of the most sublime testimonies to the glory of God. The narrative moves through several scenes, but it constantly teaches the meaning of Jesus' life, Death, and Resurrection. We hear it each year on Good Friday.

Early on, John presents "Jesus, knowing everything that was going to happen to him" (18:4). Jesus is no innocent bystander. He is the omniscient God in control of the events that follow. Three times in the opening confrontation he says, "I AM," boldly claiming the name that God revealed to Moses in the burning bush. His enemies end up proclaiming the truth about Jesus in spite of themselves. Caiaphas had told the Jews "It was better that one man should die rather than the people" (18:14), fulfilling Isaiah's fourth oracle. Pilate, unable to get a straight answer from Jesus about his identity, asks, "What is truth?" (John 18:38). But it is Pilate who has an inscription made for the Cross that calls Jesus, in three languages, the *King of the Jews*. The soldiers plait a crown from thorns and wrap Jesus' beaten body in purple cloth, intending to mock, but handing over the signs of his kingship.

The enemies of Jesus unintentionally speak the truth, but his friend Peter intentionally denies him three times. From the Cross, Jesus takes matters into his own hands, entrusting his mother and the disciple whom he loved to each other. From these faithful disciples the Church will be born.

Before he dies, Jesus says, "It is finished" (19:30). That does not mean "It's over." It means "It is accomplished" or "It is perfected." He has completed the task he was given. He hands himself over to God. John has Jesus dying on the Cross on preparation day, the day before Passover, so that we will see in the slaughtering of the Passover lambs a concurrent symbol of the one who gave his life that others might live.

Jesus Is Risen from the Dead

GENESIS 1:1—2:2 OR 1:1, 26–31A God created the heavens and the earth. The entire Bible opens with an account of how and why all things came to be. The heavens and the earth exist by the will of God. At the time these verses were written, science had not advanced beyond a rudimentary understanding of biology and zoology. The Catholic Church does not expect members to believe in the literal words of this story. Genesis, however, defends a vital belief that we recite at the beginning of our weekly profession of faith: God is the Creator of heaven and earth.

The Easter Vigil is the pivotal night of the entire liturgical year. Lent has led up to this night, and even Advent and Christmas have been preparing for this night. Everything we celebrate for the next fifty days results from our belief that Jesus is risen from the dead. Christ's Resurrection from the dead makes our own resurrection possible. As faithful followers, we believe that God created us, and that God will recreate us at the end of time. Our destiny is prefigured in the Baptisms we celebrate in Catholic churches throughout the world on this night. To reaffirm the foundation of our belief in a new creation, the Easter Vigil offers us the story of the first creation. Since God created everything out of nothing, it is not so hard to believe that God can re-create everything out of something.

PSALM 104:1–2, 5–6, 10, 12, 13–14, 24, 35 (30) God created all things and wondrously renews what he has made. Psalm 104 is a psalm of praise to God for the wonders of creation. It imagines the earth fixed upon a foundation, covered with the waters of the oceans, surmounted by waters enclosed in the sky, high above the tops of the mountains. Water, birds, cattle, and grain all supply the needs of humanity, the crown of God's creation.

It would be enough if this psalm praised God for the wonders of nature, but it does something more. It praises God for the way nature is renewed each year and from one generation to the next. The verse we use for the refrain calls upon God to send the Spirit to renew the face of the earth. This quality of creation, its inherent ability to renew, makes this psalm a perfect choice for the Easter Vigil. On this night, we praise God for the Resurrection of Christ, for the

CONNECTIONS TO CHURCH TEACHING AND TRADITION

- "Creation is the foundation of 'all God's saving plans,' the 'beginning of the history of salvation'[1] that culminates in Christ" (CCC, 280).

- "Thus the revelation of creation is inseparable from the revelation and forging of the covenant of the one God with his People. . . . The truth of creation is also expressed with growing vigor in the message of the prophets, the prayer of the psalms and the liturgy, and in the wisdom sayings of the Chosen People[2]" (CCC, 288).

- "A correct understanding of the environment prevents the utilitarian reduction of nature to a mere object to be manipulated and exploited" (CSDC, 463).

---

1 GCD, 51.

2 Cf. Isiah 44:24; Psalm 104; Proverbs 8:22–31.

new life bestowed upon the newly baptized, and for the promise of eternal life revealed throughout God's Word.

PSALM 33:4–5, 6–7, 12–13, 20–22 (5B) As an alternative to Psalm 104, Psalm 33, another psalm of creation, may follow the First Reading. It, too, praises God for the wonders of nature. This psalm envisions that the waters of the ocean are contained as in a flask, confined as though in cellars in the deep. Notably, Psalm 33 includes morality among God's creations. God's word is "upright," all God's works are "trustworthy," God loves "justice and right," and the earth is full of God's "kindness." Here is echoed the belief from the First Reading that what God made is "good." We praise God not just for the things that are, but for the goodness of things that are.

Christians interpret one of the verses of this psalm as a prophecy for our belief in the Holy Trinity. "By the word of the Lord the heavens were made; by the breath of his mouth all their host." In one verse we find references to the Lord, the word, and the breath, images of the Triune God, preexisting all that is.

GENESIS 22:1–18 OR 22:1–2, 9A, 10–13, 15–18 God puts Abraham to the test by asking him to sacrifice his son Isaac. This is one of the most difficult passages in the entire Bible, and it is hard to hear it without feeling uneasy about the God who would make this request, Abraham who would fulfill it, and Isaac who would be the innocent victim. There is a happy ending, but not before the story wrenches our hearts. Adding to the grim nature of God's request is that Abraham had no son until he was over one hundred years old. God had promised that Abraham's progeny would be as numberless as the sands on the shore of the sea, but at that point the patriarch was not even the father of one. Now, at advanced ages, Abraham and Sarah had become first-time parents, and this was the son God wanted him to sacrifice.

The story is retold at the Easter Vigil because it foreshadows the life of Jesus. He was an only child, as was Isaac. He was innocent, yet walked up a hill carrying on his shoulders the wood of his sacrifice. But there, the similarities end. Isaac was saved from death; Jesus saved through death.

- "Christian hope takes up and fulfills the hope of the chosen people which has its origin and model in the *hope of Abraham*, who was blessed abundantly by the promises of God fulfilled in Isaac, and who was purified by the test of the sacrifice[3]" (CCC, 1819).

- "But because of the union which the person of the Son retained with his body, his was not a mortal corpse like others. . . . [This statement] can be said of Christ: . . . 'For you will not abandon my soul to Hades, nor let your Holy One see corruption'[4]" (CCC, 627).

- "As proclaimed in the prayers for the blessing of the water, baptism is a cleansing water of rebirth[5] that makes us God's children born from on high" (CI, 5).

- "God's love is 'everlasting'[6]: 'For the mountains may depart and the hills be removed, but my steadfast love shall not depart from you'" (CCC, 220).

(continued)

---

3 Cf. Genesis 17:4–8; 22:1–18.
4 Acts 2:26–27; cf. Psalm 16:9–10.
5 See Titus 3:5.
6 *Isaiah 54:8.*

PSALM 16:5, 8, 9–10, 11 (1) God will reveal the path of life. Those in the most difficult circumstances yearn for the confident trust of Psalm 16. When things go wrong, we turn to God for assistance. Sometimes we demand help; often we hope against hope for it. But Psalm 16 airs an aroma of confidence: "with [the Lord] at my right hand, I shall not be disturbed." This psalm flows naturally from the story of Abraham and Isaac. Abraham, too, possessed the charism of confidence. He believed that even in the most difficult circumstances God would be faithful to the covenant. Psalm 16 fits the Easter Vigil because of its references to death and life. This psalm appears each week in Thursday Night Prayer. Before going to bed, Christians pray these words, confident that wakefulness will follow sleep, and life will follow death.

EXODUS 14:15—15:1 God frees Israel from slavery through the waters of the Red Sea. This paradigmatic reading from the Old Testament must be proclaimed in every celebration of the Easter Vigil. The liturgy encourages the use of all the Old Testament readings at the Vigil, but permits a smaller number for exceptional circumstances. This reading is never omitted because it roots our understanding of Baptism and resurrection.

In the story, Egypt has enslaved the Israelites, and God has appointed Moses to lead them from the clutch of the Pharaoh into freedom. Their only route traverses the Red Sea, which parts for their passage, but flows back to swallow up Pharaoh's pursuing forces. On the other side of the waters, Israel is poised to enter the Promised Land.

The Exsultet and the blessing of baptismal water, which are both proclaimed in the Vigil, point out the significance of this passage, and hence of this night. God freed Israel from its foes through water, and God will free the catechumens from the clutches of Satan and sin through the waters of Baptism. Set free from Pharaoh, Israel entered the Promised Land. Set free from sin, the neophytes enter the life of grace as members of the Body of Christ. At the center of all this imagery is Jesus Christ, who was set free from death to life through the mercy of the Father.

(continued from 59)

- "When she delves into her own mystery, the Church, the People of God in the New Covenant, discovers her link with the Jewish People,[7] 'the first to hear the Word of God'" (CCC, 839).

- "Jesus, the Son of God, also himself suffered the death that is part of the human condition. Yet, despite his anguish as he faced death, he accepted it in an act of complete and free submission to his Father's will.[8] The obedience of Jesus has transformed the curse of death into a blessing[9]" (CCC, 1009).

- "By its very nature water cannot be treated as just another commodity among many, and it must be used rationally and in solidarity with others" (CSDC, 485).

7 Cf. NA 4.
8 Cf. Mark 14:33–34; Hebrews 5:7–8.
9 Cf. Romans 5:19–21.

EXODUS 15:1–2, 3–4, 5–6, 17–18 (1B) The people of Israel sing praise to God for granting them freedom. The response that follows this reading from Exodus also comes from Exodus. It is the very song that Israel sings upon reaching the dry shores beyond the Red Sea. It retells the events of this Passover night: the loss of Pharaoh's chariots in the Red Sea and the redemption of God's Chosen People when God "planted them on the mountain" (v. 17). Throughout the song, the people give praise to God. It is the Lord who has covered himself in glory. Yes, they have experienced freedom from slavery, but they do not rejoice in their own accomplishment. They praise God.

ISAIAH 54:5–14 God reestablishes the covenant with Israel. The Maker of Israel becomes the Spouse of Israel. This passage from the prophecy of Isaiah meets Israel at a very different moment in history. Many years have passed since the dramatic rescue of the Chosen People from the hand of Pharaoh. The people have dwelled in the Promised Land and have enjoyed too much prosperity. They have been lured away by other beliefs.

But God did not relinquish the covenant. Isaiah uses a startling image: "The Lord calls you back, / like a wife forsaken and grieved in spirit" (v. 6). God says through Isaiah, "For a brief moment I abandoned you, / but with great tenderness I will take you back" (v. 7). God compares this event to the days of Noah, when God swore never again to cover the earth with the waters of wrath. God is not angry with the Chosen People. God takes them home.

God still takes pity on us in our sin. Even those who have not yet been baptized are God's children. God is yearning to receive them with great tenderness as they enter the waters of Baptism. Catholics who have spent this Lenten season in repentance can hear these consoling words and take heart that their penance has been noticed, their prayers have been heard, and God is anxious to renew with them the everlasting covenant of mercy.

- "All evangelizing activity is understood as promoting communion with Jesus Christ. Starting with the 'initial' conversion of a person to the Lord, moved by the Holy Spirit through the primary proclamation of the Gospel, catechesis seeks to solidify and mature this first adherence" (GDC, 80).

- "He who makes the profession of faith takes on responsibilities that not infrequently provoke persecution" (GDC, 83).

- "Baptism is therefore, above all, the sacrament of that faith by which, enlightened by the grace of the Holy Spirit, we respond to the Gospel of Christ" (RCIA, CI, General Introduction, 3).

- "Baptism, the cleansing with water by the power of the living word, washes away every stain of sin, original and personal, makes us sharers in God's own life (see 2 Peter 1:4) and his adopted children" (RCIA, CI, General Introduction, 5).

(continued)

PSALM 30:2, 4, 5–6, 11–12, 13 (2A) In thanksgiving, we sing praise to God. We thank God not for just any unexpected gift, but for release from a serious threat. The writer of Psalm 30 experienced death threats from enemies. Death seemed near, but somehow God rescued the singer "from among those going down into the pit" (v. 4). At the time, it seemed as though there were no way out, but in retrospect, it seems as though God's anger lasted "but a moment" and his good will lasts "a lifetime" (v. 6). This psalm takes up the main theme of the Easter Vigil: the triumphant Passion of our Lord Jesus Christ. He could have sung this psalm himself: "O Lord, you brought me up from the netherworld . . . / At nightfall, weeping enters in, / but with the dawn, rejoicing" (vv. 4, 6). All the participants in the Easter Vigil can sing this along with Christ. Those to be baptized are to be lifted from their former way of life to membership in the Body of Christ. Those who have already been baptized have expressed sorrow for their sins and experienced the joy of God's mercy. With Christ, we are all brought up from the netherworld on this night that shines more brightly than the dawn.

ISAIAH 55:1–11 God invites us to life-giving water, renews the covenant, and shows the power of his Word. Isaiah offers a second prophecy for our reflection. It extends again to a people who had drifted from the covenant, but who discover that God's mercies are without end. The prophecy opens with an invitation to drink water, a symbol that will occupy center stage at the Easter Vigil in the next part of the ceremony. We cannot live without water, and our relationship with God slakes our spiritual thirst. The Lord is near, and Isaiah urges us to call upon him, forsaking the ways of sin. The Risen Christ is very near to all who seek him. Catechumens have left the desert of life without Christ, and the faithful have abandoned their sins through the penance of Lent. The waters of the covenant will renew us. Strengthening the image of water, God speaks through Isaiah about the effectiveness of rain and snow. They come down from the heavens and do not return there "till they have watered the earth, making it fertile and fruitful" (Isaiah 55:10). God's Word does that in our lives. It comes to us like living water, and it produces the effect for which it was sent.

(continued from 61)

- "It is desirable that the liturgy of Lent and Paschal time should be restored in such a way that it will serve to prepare the hearts of the catechumens for the celebration of the Paschal Mystery, at whose solemn ceremonies they are reborn to Christ in baptism" (AG, 14).

- "For this reason the Church, especially during Advent and Lent and above all at the Easter Vigil, re-reads and re-lives the great events of salvation history in the 'today' of her liturgy. But this also demands that catechesis help the faithful to open themselves to this spiritual understanding of the economy of salvation as the Church's liturgy reveals it and enables us to live it" (CCC, 1095).

ISAIAH 12:2–3, 4, 5–6 (3) With joy, we draw water at the fountain of salvation. We sing praise to God. Isaiah supplies not just the two previous readings, but also the responsorial for the second one. Like the passage from Exodus that follows the Third Reading, this canticle resembles the structure and content of a psalm, but it exists in another book of the Bible. The Lectionary offers us this passage to follow the previous reading because of the similarity in the way it applies the image of water, and because it comes from the same biblical book.

The canticle rings forth with praise of God. The singer proclaims, "I am confident and unafraid" (v. 2). God is the source of salvation, just as a fountain is the source of life-giving water. On this Easter night, preparing for the celebration of Baptism, we are reminded of all that God promises, and how confidently we stand in faith.

BARUCH 3:9–15, 32—4:4 To know wisdom is to know God. Changing the tone of the evening, the prophet Baruch chides Israel for forsaking the fountain of wisdom. He ascribes the troubles of Israel to the people's infidelity to the covenant. The solution? "Learn where prudence is, /where strength, where understanding" (v. 14). To know wisdom is to know God. Just as creation unveils the wisdom of God, so to know the wisdom of God is to draw near to our Maker. On this wondrous night, we grasp the wisdom of God's plan. The plan existed from the beginning of creation, but it was revealed to human beings slowly, through history. At the time of Baruch's prophecy, people still did not fully comprehend that Jesus would reveal the resurrection. Yet even without complete knowledge, people were able to perceive the wisdom of God in imperfect ways.

Hearing this reading, and standing on the other historical shore from the Passion of Christ, we praise God for the gift of revelation made plain to us. Those who are approaching the waters of Baptism have come to the same insight. They put their faith in the Resurrection of Christ, and they participate in his life because of the interior wisdom they have received.

- "To accomplish so great a work Christ is always present in his church, especially in liturgical celebrations. . . . He is present in his word since it is he himself who speaks when the holy scriptures are read in church" (SC, 7).

- "The Resurrection of Jesus is the crowning truth of our faith in Christ, a faith believed and lived as the central truth by the first Christian community; handed on as fundamental by Tradition; established by the documents of the New Testament; and preached as an essential part of the Paschal mystery" (CCC, 638).

PSALM 19:8, 9, 10, 11 (JOHN 6:68C) Psalm 19 has two parts, and these verses come from the section that revels in the beauty of God's Word. It resembles the longest psalm in the Bible, 119, which meditates line by line on the Word of God through a variety of synonyms and attributes. These verses of Psalm 19 praise the "law," "decree," "precepts," "command," and "ordinances" of the Lord, which rejoice the heart and enlighten the eye. This psalm builds upon the theme of wisdom from the previous reading. We come to know God through meditation on his decrees. God revealed these to us in the covenant, so they detail the wisdom that exudes from the very being of God. For Christians, Jesus Christ is the perfect expression of God's wisdom. He is God's wisdom. He is the Word made flesh. For this reason, the Lectionary gives us a refrain taken from the Gospel according to John, not from the psalm itself. The verse is spoken by Peter after Jesus has given the discourse on the bread of life. The teaching revealed the very reason Jesus came, to offer us eternal life through the eating of his Body and drinking of his Blood. Many of those who heard him speak these words, however, turned away. Jesus looked fearfully at his closest followers and asked if they, too, were going to leave him now. Peter said no. "Lord, you have the words of everlasting life" (John 6:68c). That statement of faith becomes the refrain we sing to a psalm that praises the wisdom of God. It also foreshadows the initiation of those who will share Holy Communion for the first time at this Mass.

EZEKIEL 36:16–17A, 18–28 The prophet Ezekiel addresses a people who had experienced exile from their homeland because of their infidelity, but who also had learned that God had not abandoned them. As a sign of renewing the eternal covenant, God offered the people cleansing and renewal through the gift of a new spirit. Israel's sin was not covered up, but it was forgiven, and the people grew stronger in faith.

On a night when the waters of Baptism symbolize new life, this passage prophesies all that Christianity has to offer. Those who have failed to love God as they should are cleansed from all sin. Some are baptized and others will renew their baptismal covenant through promises and holy water. All will experience the gift of the new spirit that God places in the heart of believers. God never goes back on the covenant; it is eternal. Even though we sometimes fail to keep the covenant, God always gives us the opportunity to renew it.

PSALM 42:3, 5; 43:3, 4 (42:2) Our souls thirst for God like a deer that longs for running streams. The Lectionary offers three possible responses to the seventh reading. The first, from Psalm 42, is sung whenever Baptism will be celebrated at the Vigil.

The psalm asks God for the gift of God's light and fidelity, so that those who receive it may approach the dwelling place of God, and specifically the altar of God. These verses eloquently prophesy the journey of the catechumens, who thirst for the waters of Baptism, and attain it through the light and fidelity that God extends to new believers through the covenant. Having been refreshed by the waters of Baptism, the neophytes come to the altar of God, where they participate in Holy Communion, the intimate union that makes them fully the Body of Christ, a dwelling place for God most high.

ISAIAH 12:2–3, 4BCD, 5–6 (3) In this song of praise, we thank God for all that he has accomplished. This is exactly the response that follows the Fifth Reading of the Easter Vigil. It is offered again as one of the alternatives following the Seventh Reading. In practice, it could logically be sung here whenever the seven readings are abbreviated and the Fifth Reading has been eliminated.

The English-language Lectionary recommends it as one of the options if Baptism is not celebrated during the Vigil. This may seem puzzling because the image of water is so strong at the beginning of these verses. In fact, the liturgical books are not consistent on this point. The *Ordo Lectionum Missae,* actually recommends this psalm, not the previous one, when Baptism is to be celebrated.

PSALM 51:12–13, 14–15, 18–19 (12A) We ask God to create within us a clean heart. Tradition calls seven of the 150 psalms penitential. This one is perhaps the greatest of them. It expresses the remorse we feel after sinning, and our cries for forgiveness. These particular verses, coming at the end of the psalm, focus on renewal. Although we have sung this text often during Lent, we may complete its sentiments at the Vigil, when we put our sinful ways behind us and seek a clean heart. These verses work well after the passage from Ezekiel, which employs a similar image—a new heart. In reestablishing the covenant with us, God remakes us. We reenter the covenant not as the same people, but as those who have known sin, repented of it, received forgiveness, and resolved not to sin again. This psalm is recommended for an Easter Vigil that does not include Baptism. It more nearly suits the faithful Christians coming for renewal after observing a rigorous Lent.

ROMANS 6:3–11 Christ has been raised from the dead. Through Baptism, we enter the mystery of his Death and Resurrection. After hearing and singing up to fourteen passages from the Old Testament (seven readings and seven psalms or canticles sung responsorially), the New Testament makes its bright appearance. We hear Paul say, "We know that Christ, raised from the dead, dies no more; death no longer has power over him" (v. 9). This is the first scriptural proclamation from tonight that Jesus is risen. Paul compares the Resurrection of Christ and Baptism. This passage underscores our liturgical practice of celebrating Baptism at the Easter Vigil. It also affirms our preference for baptizing infants on any Sunday, our weekly observance of the Resurrection.

PSALM 118:1–2, 16–17, 22–23 This psalm gives many reasons for thanksgiving. It opens with the simple assertion that the Lord is good, and that "his mercy endures forever" (v. 1). It then announces the power and deeds of God's right hand. Two of the verses prophesy the meaning of this Easter night. You can imagine Jesus singing this psalm: "I shall not die, but live, / and declare the works of the Lord" (Psalm 118:17). Christians can affirm, "The stone which the builders rejected / has become the cornerstone" (v. 22). His enemies thought they had put Jesus to death, but he has become the cornerstone of life.

The refrain for this psalm is a triple Alleluia. It doubles as the Gospel acclamation. No words can fully express the joy of this night, so we resort to a Hebrew acclamation that needs no translation: Alleluia! Throughout Lent, we have abstained from singing that word. We have introduced the Gospel with a different acclamation of praise. But now, the word returns. Our "fasting" from the Alleluia is over. We rejoice that Christ is risen.

MATTHEW 28:1–10 Jesus has been raised from the dead. After many readings, we finally come to the account in the Gospel according to Matthew that announces the meaning of this night. At dawn, Mary Magdalene and the other Mary go to the tomb, where they see an angel of the Lord who tells them not to be afraid. "I know that you are seeking Jesus the crucified. He is not here, for he has been raised just as he said" (Matthew 28:5–6). That is truly the Gospel: the Good News of this night.

The encounter with the angel takes place just as the day after the Sabbath is dawning. For this reason, we celebrate the entire Easter Vigil at the same time. It begins after dark, and it finishes before light. The angel wears white clothing, the uniform of heavenly beings throughout the New Testament. The angel sends the women on. "Go quickly and tell his disciples," the angel says (Matthew 28:7). Easter is not just about hearing good news, it is about telling good news.

Throughout this glorious Vigil, the faithful encounter Christ in many ways: in the fire, in Baptism, and most importantly in the Eucharist. But they also meet Christ in the proclamation of the Word. He is present as we hear the Good News. Tonight the response the people make to the Gospel reading has special power: "Praise to you, Lord Jesus Christ." They do not address those words to the priest. They address those words to the Risen Christ, who is present as his Gospel is proclaimed.

ACTS 10:34A, 37–43 Jesus' earthly ministry was limited mostly to Jews (see Matthew 15:24). At Jesus' Ascension, he commanded his followers to be his witnesses "to the ends of the earth" (Acts 1:8). In obedience to Christ's mandate, the Gospel moved beyond Israel's borders. Peter's offer of baptism to Cornelius, an uncircumcised Roman centurion, was a pivotal incident. Underlying the event were key questions: Did Christians have to obey Jewish dietary laws and practices? Could non-Jews become Christians without being circumcised? God prepared Peter to break through his narrow understanding of the law by giving him a vision of "unclean" animals that the Jews were forbidden to eat. God tells Peter, "What God has made clean, you must not call profane" (10:15). For the first time in Acts, Peter proclaims the kerygma to a non-Jew. As at the first Pentecost, the Spirit pours forth on all those listening.

PSALM 118:1–2, 16–17, 22–23 (24) Psalm 118 is the Great Hallel (Hebrew for "praise"), the last of the Hallel Psalms (Psalms 113–118), which recount God's deliverance of the Hebrew slaves from Egypt. Psalm 118 was sung at all major festivals. During the Feast of Tabernacles, it was a processional hymn on entering the Temple. The crowds that greeted Jesus as he entered Jerusalem sang, "Blessed is the one who comes in the name of the LORD" (v. 26, see Matthew 21:9). Jesus quoted Psalm 118: "The stone that the builders rejected has become the chief cornerstone" (v. 22) to describe his own rejection but ultimate victory. The Hallel Psalms were also sung during the Passover meal. Jesus and his disciples sang Psalm 118 before he went out to the garden of Gethsemane to face death.

COLOSSIANS 3:1–4 The early Christians regarded Baptism as a dying and a rising again. As the person was immersed in the waters, it was as if he or she were buried in death. As they emerged from the waters, it was like being resurrected to a new life. Therefore, Christians must rise from Baptism as different persons. Their thoughts must be set on the things of God and no longer concerned with the passing things of earth. This was not another worldliness in which Christians withdraw from the activities of this world; ethical principles follow that make it clear what was expected of newborn Christians (vv. 5–25). They would now view

CONNECTIONS TO CHURCH TEACHING AND TRADITION

- Jesus is revealed as Savior of the world in his life, Death, and Resurrection (NCO, 90) and fulfills both the promises of the Old Testament and his promises (CCC, 652).

- Easter is the feast of feasts, the focal point of the church year (CCC, 1169–1171).

- Christ is alive in a new way after the resurrection (CCC, 554–556, 645–647, 999–1000).

everything in light of eternity and no longer live as if this world was all that mattered.

SEQUENCE: *VICTIMAE PASCHALI LAUDES* The Easter Sequence, *Victimae paschali laudes,* is a song of praise to the Paschal Victim that also reflects the Gospel account of Mary's encounter with the Risen Lord.

JOHN 20:1–9 Two stories of the Resurrection were widely circulated in John's time. One story centered on the empty tomb; the other involved appearances of the Risen Lord. One of these stories involved Mary from Magdala, a fishing village on the Sea of Galilee. There is no basis for identifying her with the repentant sinner of Luke's Gospel (Luke 7:36–50). Mary was a faithful follower of Jesus and, along with Jesus' mother and other women, was a witness to his crucifixion and burial (John 19:25). In John's Gospel, she was the first to discover the empty tomb. She believed Jesus' body had been stolen, and she ran to report the news to Peter and John. Jewish law held that two men were required as witnesses; therefore, Mary could not serve as a witness. The two apostles rushed to the tomb. John arrives first, but out of respect for the elder apostle, waits for Peter to enter the tomb. They observe the burial clothes lying folded neatly, which refuted any claim that Jesus' body was stolen. Peter is slow to understand the meaning of the empty tomb, but John "saw and believed" (20:8). Even though they did not yet understand the Scripture that Jesus must rise from the dead, John served as the example for all "those who have not seen and yet have come to believe" (v. 29).

MATTHEW 28:1–10 Matthew's Gospel shows Mary Magdalene and "the other Mary" arriving at the tomb at a critical moment. An earthquake and an angel announce to the women, and to Matthew's audience, "He is not here, for he has been raised, as he said" (v. 6). The women are invited to see the emptiness of the tomb for themselves and then to "go quickly and tell his disciples" (v. 7). Like Mary in John's Gospel, the Marys in Matthew's account meet Jesus on their way, and he sends them forth as his messengers. Both the women and the disciples whom they tell are instructed to move beyond their immediate experience to the work Jesus still has for them to do in Galilee.

Easter Time

Overview of Easter Time

Like Christmas, Easter has its own season that lasts long beyond the day itself. The focus of all we do as a parish community and as individuals during Easter Time is meant to be filled with the joy and glory of the Resurrection: from the sacramental celebrations of Baptism, Confirmation, and first Holy Communion, "Alleluia" should resound from the rafters of the church and in the depths of our souls. Easter Time is also the period of mystagogy for the neophytes, those newly initiated into the Church. During this time, they are instructed more deeply in the mysteries of the Church, particularly the sacraments.

Easter Time includes the solemnities of the Ascension and Pentecost. The first is the celebration of the Risen Lord's return to the Father. The second is the celebration of the coming of the Holy Spirit and birth of the Church. Traditionally, the celebration of the Ascension is forty days after Easter, but in many dioceses bishops have transferred the celebration to the following Sunday, so that it replaces the Seventh Sunday of Easter. Pentecost, the Greek word for *fifty*, originally began as a celebration in thanksgiving for the "firstfruits," when winter grains and spring vegetables were harvested, enjoyed, and offered to God. For Christians, Jesus is the "firstfruits" of those who have died (1 Corinthians 15:23). His Resurrection heralds our own at the end of time. For now, we live as Christians in the world, empowered by his Spirit of peace and forgiveness. While Pentecost concludes Easter Time, the gift of the Holy Spirit compels us to resound with Easter joys for days to come.

FIRST READINGS

During Easter Time, you will notice a shift in the First Readings. At this time of the liturgical year, they are from the New Testament book the Acts of the Apostles. The passages describe the life and growth of the early church and evidence how the church witnessed to faith in the Resurrection. On the Solemnity of the Ascension of the Lord, the First Reading is always the account of the Ascension from Acts, which concludes with the question to the disciples about why they are still staring at the sky. This is a question that leads them to embrace the Spirit given to them at Pentecost and leads us today to discern how the Spirit leads us to live out our Christian mission. On Pentecost, the First Reading is one proclaimed in the Church for centuries. The account from the Acts of the Apostles narrates the dramatic coming of the Holy Spirit upon those gathered in the house and how everyone, regardless of his or her homeland, is able to hear everyone else speaking of God's mighty acts.

RESPONSORIAL PSALMS

As Lent and Holy Week give way to Easter Time, the tone of the Responsorial Psalm changes. The joy of the Resurrection first celebrated at the Easter Vigil can be heard from Easter Sunday through Pentecost. Note that each Sunday of Easter Time, including Pentecost, includes the option for the refrain of the Responsorial Psalm to be "Alleluia." Choosing this option makes the celebration of the Resurrection palpable and obvious to the assembly.

The Responsorial Psalms as a whole during Easter Time communicate a sense of thanksgiving for the works of the Lord, joy for the Lord's Day, hope for seeing the goodness of the Lord, and confidence that the Lord himself will show his followers the path to life. Interspersed with the joyful psalms is a repetition of Psalm 23 on the Fourth Sunday of Easter, also referred to as Good Shepherd Sunday, and a prayer for the Lord's mercy on the Fifth Sunday of Easter. On the Solemnity of the Ascension, Psalm 47 fittingly speaks of God mounting his throne and those around him shouting with joy. As the liturgical assemblies of today sing this psalm, they, too, shout for joy as they remember and celebrate Christ the Lord ascending to his throne at the right hand of the Father. The concluding Responsorial Psalm of Easter Time, sung on Pentecost, calls upon the Lord to send out his Spirit and renew the face of the earth. Our contemporary singing of this psalm gives voice to our belief that the Spirit the Lord sends will be present, always and everywhere, renewing the earth and her peoples.

SECOND READINGS

Most of the Second Readings of Easter Time come from the pastoral letter 1 Peter. Written as an instruction to the newly baptized, its appropriateness to Easter Time is obvious. The Second Readings from 1 Peter are meant to carry forth the spirit of joyful faith and hope that is fundamental to Easter Time.

Only on the solemnities of the Ascension and Pentecost do the Second Readings come from another New Testament work. On the Solemnity of the Ascension, the passage from Ephesians includes petitions for the Church as it spreads after Christ's Ascension. On Pentecost, the reading from 1 Corinthians leads those gathered as the Church today to reflect on the many diverse gifts that exist among them, and the unity that exists because of their common Baptism in Christ.

GOSPEL READINGS

In the proclamation of the Gospel readings throughout Easter Time, we experience both joy and trepidation at the event of the Resurrection. As Easter Time progresses, our sense of joy continues while our awe and fear subside as we come to know the Risen Lord in the peace he brings, in the conversation on the way to Emmaus, in the meal he shares with two of his disciples, in the catch of a large number of fish, and in his call to Peter to tend his sheep. We learn from the readings from the Gospel according to John, interspersed with those from the Gospel according to Luke, that this Risen Lord is the gate and the way, the truth, and the life. The excerpts from the Lord's discourse and prayer at the end of the Last Supper from John on the Fifth, Sixth, and Seventh Sundays of Easter show how deeply the Lord cares for those who follow him and will remain after him. He is the one who promises another Advocate on the Solemnity of Pentecost, when the Gospel tells of Jesus breathing the Holy Spirit upon the disciples.

Second Sunday of Easter / Divine Mercy Sunday
Christ Our Strength and Courage

ACTS 2:42–47 This passage is one of four idealized descriptions of the early Christian communities that are present in Acts. Although they are idealized descriptions, they do highlight the ethical implications of what Jesus' mission and ministry demand. The communities "devoted themselves to the teaching of the apostles and to the communal life, to the breaking of bread and to the prayers" (v. 42). The teaching of the Apostles connected the communities with the eyewitness that Jesus instructed and guided. Communal life was integral to Jesus' ministry, a life of care and concern for the other, rooted in our common bond as members of God's family. Sharing of possessions was voluntary, not mandatory, and Christians were called to be mindful of the concern for those in need. The breaking of bread was a common designation for the Eucharistic meal that was held in homes, in which Jesus' presence and memory was kept alive. The prayers said in the Temple linked Jesus' Jewish roots with those of his followers. This was and still is a bold way to proclaim our new life in Christ. It attracted many new members then, and it should characterize Jesus' disciples to this day. In the Spirit, we make bold to live as Jesus modeled.

PSALM 118:2–4, 13–15, 22–24 (1) Psalm 118, also used on Easter Sunday, returns with a different refrain and a slightly different focus. We are invited to give thanks to the Lord, whose goodness and love are everlasting. This thanksgiving psalm of praise calls upon the liturgical assembly (house of Israel), the priests and liturgical ministers (house of Aaron), and all those who fear the Lord to acknowledge and affirm God's faithful and enduring covenant love (mercy). The psalmist has personally experienced God's love and saving help in times of trouble. Acknowledging God's saving help, the psalmist affirms the Lord as "my strength and my courage" (v. 14) leading to "joyful shout of victory" (v. 15). The one rejected was rescued by God and made the cornerstone. God's love and care have accomplished this, eliciting great joy. In its liturgical context, the community affirms that the Lord continues to love and save us this very day. We truly rejoice and are made glad in our loving God, who gives strength and courage this day and always.

CONNECTIONS TO CHURCH TEACHING AND TRADITION

- "The virtue of fortitude enables one to conquer fear, even fear of death, and to face trials and persecutions. It disposes one even to renounce and sacrifice his life in defense of a just cause. 'The Lord is my strength and my song.'[1] 'In the world you have tribulation; but be of good cheer, I have overcome the world'[2]" (CCC, 1808).

- "Jesus, 'the Author of life,' by dying destroyed 'him who has the power of death, that is, the devil, and [delivered] all those who through fear of death were subject to lifelong bondage.'[3] Henceforth the risen Christ holds 'the keys of Death and Hades,' so that 'at the name of Jesus every knee should bow, in heaven and on earth and under the earth'[4]" (CCC, 635).

---

1 Psalm 118:14.
2 John 16:33.
3 Hebrews 2:14–15; cf. Acts 3:15.
4 Revelation 1:18; Phil 2:10.

1 PETER 1:3–9 This passage begins with the "new birth to a living hope" (v. 3) that is ours in the Risen Christ. In Christ, we have salvation and an inheritance that lasts forever, kept for us in heaven till "the final time" (v. 5) when all will be revealed. Until then, the community's faith struggle with persecution and rejection is viewed as a time of testing and purification, ultimately producing a more genuine and purified faith to the glory of God. Even though the community has not seen the Lord, they love him and believe in him. This stance eventually leads to great joy and lasting hope as the community strives to attain the goal of their faith: ultimate union with God.

Easter Time celebrates this new birth in the Risen Christ with those baptized at the Easter Vigil, as well as with all the baptized. The Risen Christ is our strength and courage, enabling us to face any and all challenges to faith as we await ultimate union with God. Through our baptismal commitment, the Holy Spirit, the third Person of the Trinity, emboldens us to act in the Lord's name no matter the cost, living in love and enduring hope until the Lord returns.

JOHN 20:19–31 This passage, proclaimed every Second Sunday of Easter, recounts two Easter appearances to the disciples. In both cases, the Risen Christ appears on the first day of the week. Fear and locked doors are dispelled by the Risen Christ, who stands in their midst and wishes them peace. Showing them his hands and his side, he assures them that it is he. Jesus commissions them just as the Father commissioned him, by breathing new life into them and emboldening them with the Holy Spirit. Their ministry is to be characterized by reconciliation and forgiveness.

Thomas is not present and refuses to believe until he sees and touches Jesus. This occasions Jesus' second appearance. Wishing them peace, the Risen Lord calls forth Thomas to touch, see, and believe. Thomas responds with the strongest affirmation of Jesus' identity in the entire Gospel: "My Lord and my God" (v. 28). Thomas believes because he has seen. Jesus blesses all those who have not seen and yet believe. We who have not seen and yet believe are made bold by the Risen Christ, through his gift of peace and the Spirit, to go out to the world and proclaim the Father's love, leading to forgiveness and reconciliation.

- "Spiritual progress tends toward even more intimate union with Christ. . . . God calls us all to this intimate union with him" (CCC, 2014).

- "Christ is Lord of the cosmos and of history. In him, human history and indeed all creation are 'set forth' and transcendently fulfilled[5]" (CCC, 668).

5 Ephesians 1:10; cf. Ephesians 4:10; 1 Corinthians 15:24, 27–28.

ACTS 2:14, 22–33 Here is another summary of the early Christian Gospel, courtesy of Luke. Peter's first speech, given on the day of Pentecost, like the speech we read last week, is tailored to fit both Peter's audience (Jews from all over the empire who had made pilgrimages to Jerusalem for the festival) and Luke's readers (gentile Christians and Christian sympathizers). The summary resembles the summary we saw on Easter Day: God was at work in the ministry of Jesus. According to God's plan as laid out in Scripture, Jesus was handed over for execution and was raised on the third day, also according to God's plan. Now Jesus is at the right hand of the Father. The Apostles, Peter says, are witnesses to these things through the power of the Spirit they have just been given. To emphasize his point, Peter quotes Psalm 16, citing King David as another witness.

Peter's words point out two very different responses to Jesus. The religious leaders saw the mighty deeds of Jesus but did not recognize him. They believed Jesus to be a threat, and they conspired with the Romans to have him killed. The Apostles, on the other hand, not only saw Jesus but also recognized him. They even ate and drank with him following his Resurrection. Their response is faithful witness, full of the Holy Spirit. How will we respond to Jesus? What will our witness be?

PSALM 16:1–2, 5, 7–8, 9–10, 11 (11A) Tradition has attributed this psalm to King David, and Luke follows that tradition in our Gospel today. However, it is more likely that a Levite or other temple functionary wrote it. Either way, the psalm powerfully expresses trust in God's care. The psalmist does not request deliverance from what is clearly a life-threatening situation. Instead, he asks for God's protection. Using images that call to mind God's gift of the Promised Land, the psalmist proclaims trust in God. He recalls God's goodness to him and his own faithfulness to God and his Law. The psalmist is so confident of God's protection that he says God will never let him see corruption.

CONNECTIONS TO CHURCH TEACHING AND TRADITION

- Jesus' appearances after his Resurrection most clearly reveal the Trinity, the fundamental mystery, and our destiny (CCC, 65–66, 638–655).

- Jesus' Resurrection is both a historical and a transcendent event, a work of the Trinity offering salvation to all (CCC, 639, 648, 655).

- Church charitable organizations are responsible for reinforcing members so that through their words, silence, and example they may be witnesses to Christ (DCE, 31).

1 PETER 1:17–21 The author of 1 Peter again addresses his congregation of "exiles." This time, he is more explicit about their alienation. Believers are strangers to this world, he says. Having been redeemed (that is, brought out of slavery), they no longer belong to the world. Having been purified by the Blood of Christ, they no longer fit. Instead, their hope and faith are in God, who raised Jesus from the dead and glorified him.

In Christ, God has delivered us from the past. Christ's Death and Resurrection have forever freed us from the ways of life that once took us away from God. How shall we respond to this grace? We are to be a holy people. For 1 Peter, that means living our lives in reverence for God. It means remembering the high price Christ paid for our deliverance. It also means obeying the truth; and the truth, the author says, is love.

LUKE 24:13–35 The story of the road to Emmaus illustrates how hard Jesus works to make us aware. No wonder he calls the disciples "slow of heart." They had read the Scriptures, which said the Messiah would suffer and then be vindicated. They had heard Jesus say he would return on the third day. They had heard the witness of the women. The Risen Christ was right there with them, explaining the Scriptures, yet they did not recognize him. Perhaps their grief kept them from seeing Jesus. Perhaps their fear blinded them. Or perhaps they did not recognize Jesus because they were looking for someone else, someone who would "restore Israel." But the minute Jesus broke bread, their eyes were opened. They saw their Risen Savior.

God has given us many opportunities to recognize the Risen Christ too. Like those disciples on the road to Emmaus, we also have the witness of Scripture to help us see. We have Jesus' own words to help us recognize him. Most of all, we have the Eucharist, where through the presence of the assembly, the proclamation and preaching of the word, and the breaking of the bread, the Risen Christ meets us. Grief and disappointment, fear and false expectations may blur our vision at times, but even then we can always be sure that Jesus is with us.

ACTS 2:14A, 36–41 Luke has Peter close his Pentecost speech on a climactic note. Overcome, the crowd demands to know, what shall we do? This gives Luke the opportunity to introduce some of his favorite themes. "Repent, and be baptized," Peter says. "Be baptized for the forgiveness of your sins, and you will receive the Holy Spirit" (v. 38). This promise is for everyone, even future generations. Luke tells us that more than three thousand people were added to the Church that day. They devoted themselves to the Apostles' teaching, to fellowship together, and to the breaking of bread.

Although Luke does not use the shepherd image, we see hints of Jesus as the Good Shepherd. Jesus is obedient to God, faithful as a shepherd, and God has made him Messiah of all nations. Jesus not only keeps his "flock" of believers safe, but he also rescues us from sin. He not only feeds his believers, but he also nurtures us with the gift of the Holy Spirit.

PSALM 23:1–3A, 3B–4, 5, 6 (1) This psalm seems so calm and gentle that it is easy to imagine the psalmist sitting undisturbed in reverent meditation. But if we read between the lines, a different image emerges. The psalmist is running from enemies. He may even have taken refuge in the temple, where he may indeed have eaten in front of his adversaries and they legally could not touch him.

It is no surprise, then, that the psalmist dreams of God as a perfect shepherd. The shepherd had to be strong to defend the flock and powerful enough to provide them with nourishment. With God as his shepherd, the psalmist says, he has everything he needs. He fears no evil, for God leads him to places where he can get food and water in peace. His cup overflows.

Today we celebrate Jesus as the embodiment of the psalmist's hope. We celebrate God's protecting, guiding, and nurturing power. Even when we experience distress or danger, we can still celebrate Jesus, who shepherds us and leads us in "right paths."

CONNECTIONS TO CHURCH TEACHING AND TRADITION

- Jesus is the way, the truth, and the life (NDC, 1).

- Jesus is the Good Shepherd (LG, 5, 6; CCC, 754, 764, 2158).

1 PETER 2:20B–25 At first, the author's advice seems to invite us to become doormats. He specifically speaks to Christians who are slaves (as many were), saying, "Suffer patiently." He reminds them that Christ did not fight back even when his enemies were killing him. Instead, Jesus endured gracefully, trusting that God would vindicate him in the end. But the author of 1 Peter is not talking about just any suffering; he is talking about unjust suffering, the kind that comes because we have done what is right in the face of evil. When we face that kind of suffering, the best thing to do is be patient and, like Jesus, not return insults but trust God.

In this reading, the Good Shepherd turns out to be a vulnerable lamb who endures all patiently so that evil and violence might be shown for what they really are—sins against God. Through this, 1 Peter assures us, we have been healed. We once strayed like lost sheep, but now we are safe in the care of the "shepherd and guardian of our souls."

JOHN 10:1–10 John 10:1–18 is probably the closest thing we find to a parable in John's Gospel. John's "parable," however, is really an extended metaphor. Indeed, John weaves several metaphors together. His purpose here is to contrast Jesus with others who claim religious authority. The Pharisees are the most obvious target, but John hints at others too, most notably bandits (anti-Roman revolutionaries who were quite popular in Galilee and often hailed as messiahs). John may even have had in mind certain Church leaders in his own time. These, he says bluntly, are thieves and predators.

While false leaders are only out for their own interests, Jesus looks out for the interests of those who believe in him. Like a good shepherd, he knows each of his flock by name. And like the door of the sheepfold (where sheep were kept safe overnight), Jesus guards his flock and protects them from predators. This reading reminds us that Jesus is not some distant ruler but a nearby shepherd who cares for us deeply enough to give his life for us.

Jesus Is the Way, the Truth, and the Life

ACTS 6:1–7 This Sunday's reading from the Acts of the Apostles twice tells us that the number of disciples continued to increase. That increase created the need to appoint new ministers, or deacons. Luke says the Greek-speaking Christians complained that their poor were not being treated as well as those who spoke Aramaic. In response, the Twelve convened a formal assembly and announced that because their first responsibility was to preach, others should serve at the table of the Lord. Among those who were appointed were Stephen, who would become the first martyr, and a Greek-speaking man named Nicholas, who would have been a convert to Judaism before he joined the young Christian community. The task of the seven newly named ministers was to preside at the table and to assure that all the poor received what they needed.

PSALM 33:1–2, 4–5, 18–19 (22) This hymn is addressed to the faithful, reminding them of the many reasons they have to praise God. Their God is absolutely trustworthy; the signs of God's kindness are everywhere to be seen. Most of all, God never stops watching over them and caring for them.

1 PETER 2:4–9 Peter addresses this letter to people he describes as sojourners: Gentile Christians who already know persecution. Peter encourages them to keep turning to the Lord, and even more than that, to imitate him. Although they are Gentiles, Peter's message is so full of Hebrew images that he seems to be passing the vocation of Israel on to the Christian community. Peter's four descriptions of the diverse community insist on one central reality: they are called not as individuals but as a people. They are a priesthood, a people of God whose vocation is to spread the Word of God. Like their Master, they will be rejected, but built on him they will also be a spiritual house, a dwelling place of God forever.

JOHN 14:1–12 In this selection from Jesus' last discourse, two disciples ask questions to which they should already know the answers. As a matter of fact, the two questions are simply variations on the same theme. Thomas asks about "the way" (v. 5), and then Philip says, "Master, show us the

CONNECTIONS TO CHURCH TEACHING AND TRADITION

- "Faith . . . means abiding with [Jesus] in the Father who, in him, so loves us that he abides with us" (CCC, 2614).

- "[I]n every nation, anyone who fears God and does what is right has been acceptable to him (see Acts 10:35). He has, however, willed to make women and men holy . . . to make them into a people who might acknowledge and serve him in holiness" (LG, 9).

- "The first and last point of reference of this catechesis will always be Jesus Christ himself, who is 'the way, and the truth, and the life'[1]" (CCC, 1698).

- "[Christ] tells us who man truly is. . . . He shows us the way, and this way is the truth. He himself is both the way and the truth, and therefore he is also the life which all of us are seeking. He also shows us the way beyond death; only someone able to do this is a true teacher of life" (SS, 6).

---

1 John 14:6.

Father" (John 14:8). Both requests indicate that the disciples do not understand that Jesus is the Way. They do not grasp the fact that to see him is to see the Father.

In typical fashion, John uses uncomprehending characters to allow Jesus to explain something far deeper than they imagined. In the first section of the reading, Jesus explains his departure and the fact that he will return for his own. Then, he reminds them that they know the way to the life he is promising. Thomas disagrees, seemingly asking for a road map for Jesus' upcoming journey. To that, Jesus responds: "I am the way and the truth and the life."

The image of "the way" has a rich scriptural history. The word occurs over 150 times in the psalms, beginning with Psalm 1, which says, "happy those who do not . . . go the way of sinners" (v. 1) and "the Lord watches over the way of the just, / but the way of the wicked leads to ruin" (v. 6). Jesus' way is the way of the just, a way of life that the disciples are to imitate.

While imitation characterizes the ordinary relationship between a disciple and a teacher, Jesus' statement has additional implications. In John 8:31–32, Jesus invited his disciples to remain in his word so that they would know the truth that would set them free. As he stood before Pilate, Jesus said, "Everyone who belongs to the truth listens to my voice" (18:37). The truth of which Jesus speaks comes from taking him in, listening, and being freed by him.

The prologue to John (1:1–14), describes Jesus as the source of life. In chapter 6, Jesus says "I am the bread of life" (John 6:35), and later on he identifies himself as "the resurrection and the life" (John 11:25). The life he offers is nourishment for the present and an everlasting future.

Jesus' statement "I am the way and the truth and the life" (John 14:6) is a summary of who he is for his disciples: the ones who heard the words and all those who would come after. Jesus is the "way" not simply as an example, but much more because he dwells in the disciples as source of life and truth. Later, in 15:1–10, he will describe that indwelling as akin to a vine and its branches. To accept Jesus as our way, truth, and life means to open ourselves to his dwelling in us. It is a communion that could hardly be more intimate.

SIXTH SUNDAY OF EASTER
God's Presence

ACTS 8:5–8, 14–17 Luke recounts the way the Gospel, which had been confined to the area around Jerusalem, now spreads to Samaria. At first, Philip's trip to Samaria sounds very much like one of Paul's missionary journeys. However, Philip did not take this journey voluntarily. As we find in the verses preceding this reading, persecution, led by the yet unconverted Saul (Paul), caused all the believers in Jerusalem to be evicted. Most scattered to Judea, but some, like Philip, ended up in Samaria.

Much to everyone's surprise, the persecution did not interfere with the ministry of the Church at all. In fact, the eviction from Jerusalem was a catalyst that propelled the Gospel outward to even more people. Philip may have fled Jerusalem in danger, but he was clearly not defeated. Through the power of the Spirit, he was able to convince multitudes of Samaritans to believe in Jesus. People who might never have heard the Gospel at all were saved in part because of the hostility faced by believers in Jerusalem.

PSALM 66:1–3, 4–5, 6–7, 16, 20 (1) This psalm is rather unique. The psalmist vacillates between community praise and individual praise, between addressing God and addressing the gathered community, between Exodus images and images from the Exile.

The psalmist's message, though, is crystal clear: no matter what has happened in the life of the people, God has never abandoned or left them. The psalmist praises God, for when Pharaoh's army was about to drive the Israelites into the sea, the waters of the sea parted for them. When God tested the people in the wilderness, God still helped them arrive safely in the Promised Land. Even when the people sinned, even when the psalmist himself sinned, God was always there, ready to forgive.

CONNECTIONS TO CHURCH TEACHING AND TRADITION

- The Holy Spirit unfolds the divine plan of salvation within the Church, animates the Church, and directs her mission (NDC, 28).
- The Holy Spirit makes the Paschal Mystery present in the human mind (NDC, 28).
- The Holy Spirit animates creation (CCC, 703).
- The Holy Spirit continues God's work in the world (NDC, 92) by awakening faith (CCC, 684), by enabling communion with Christ (CCC, 683), by granting gifts to all (LG, 12; CCC, 2003), by making possible spiritual freedom (CCC, 1742), by allowing and enabling prayer and holiness (CCC, 741, 744, 2652), by having written the Scriptures (CCC, 304), and by revealing God in myriad ways (CCC, 244, 687), primarily but not exclusively through the Church.

1 PETER 3:15–18 In this reading, the author of 1 Peter returns to the issue of proper responses to persecution. He has just told us that if we suffer for doing good, we will be blessed. Now he urges us not to fear those who harm us for doing what is right. Instead, he says, have reverence for Christ. Always be ready to witness to the hope that is in us. Instead of retaliating or lashing out in what may be justifiable anger, 1 Peter counsels us to respond with gentleness. Our behavior, the author says, should be so commendable that those attacking us will be ashamed. This is the model Christ showed us, to "bring you to God."

- In these ways and in others unique to the Church, the Spirit makes present the mystery of Christ (CCC, 737, 1380–1381).

JOHN 14:15–21 John continues Jesus' response to Philip's request. In last week's reading, Jesus pointed to the unity he shares with the Father and how the Father will be glorified when the disciples also share in that unity. Now Jesus becomes even more direct. He says that if the disciples truly love him, they will keep his commandments, the most important of which he has just given them: "Love one another even as I have loved you" (15:12).

Jesus picks up their unspoken reservations: "How can you expect us mere mortals to love like you do?" Jesus does not expect them to do it by themselves. He will send them the Holy Spirit, through whom Jesus will continue to be with his disciples, guiding them and helping them keep the commandments he has given them.

Again, John weaves the early disciples' concerns about Jesus' departure with his own congregation's sense of Jesus' absence. The promise here is for both groups and for all of us. Even if we have not seen Jesus in person, he neither leaves us desolate nor leaves us to fulfill his commandment to love on our own power. Through the Spirit, Jesus is with all of us more closely than he could ever be in person.

THE ASCENSION OF THE LORD
Taken into Heaven

ACTS 1:1–14 This is the only place in the entire New Testament that speaks of a forty-day period between the Resurrection and the Ascension. Even the Gospel according to Luke implies that the Ascension took place on Easter evening. This forty-day time of waiting, however, fits perfectly into Luke's purposes in Acts. It gives him a chance to rehabilitate the disciples, most of whom abandoned Jesus at his arrest. More importantly, this transitional period also gives Luke an opportunity to address a major concern in the Church, the delay in the return of Jesus. "Lord, are you at this time going to restore the kingdom to Israel?" The disciples might not have used these exact words, but clearly they were wondering what God is going to do next and when it will happen. Those were natural questions. Jesus, however, is not concerned with times or places. "Wait for the Spirit," he says. "There is still work to do before God's realm comes in full. The realm will come, but until then I need you to be my witnesses. To do that, you will need the Spirit to help you. So wait until you have been "clothed with power from on high" (Luke 24:49).

Luke's account of the Ascension gives us at least three clues about what is next for us. First and foremost, Jesus wants us to be conscious of the Holy Spirit, which is given at Baptism and Confirmation and is invoked at every Eucharist. Second, he wants us to be his witnesses in the world. And third, he wants to reassure us that he will indeed return when the time is right.

PSALM 47:2–3, 6–7, 8–9 (6) Ancient Israel often imagined God as a king sitting high on a heavenly throne, looking down on the rulers of the nations. Such images were particularly popular whenever a new king was enthroned. Indeed, Israel may even have held regular festivals celebrating the enthronement of God and his representative on earth, Israel's king. Psalm 47 was composed for just such an occasion. It celebrates God as the ruler of the nations. It calls on the people of the world to acknowledge God's rule and includes a processional liturgy to help them do so (vv. 5–7).

This psalm leaves us no doubt what is next—Christ's enthronement at the right hand of the Father. For much of Christian tradition, the Ascension is Christ's coronation, his ascension to the throne from which he will exercise

- We pause between our celebrations of the Ascension and Pentecost to contemplate our task. The Church's mission is twofold: we are called to continuous conversion, and we are called to bear the Gospel of salvation to all the world (NDC, 10; CCC, 767–769).

- Jesus and the Holy Spirit's mission is accomplished in us (CCC, 737, 778).

- We are to announce, bear witness to, make present, and spread the mystery of the Trinity (CCC, 748–975).

God's sovereignty over creation. Today we celebrate that rule, and with the psalmist, we sing praises to the Father and to Christ who is highly exalted.

EPHESIANS 1:17–23 "I pray that . . . you may know . . . the immeasurable greatness of his power. . . . God . . . seated him at his right hand in the heavenly places, . . . not only in this age but also in the age to come." No wonder the author of Ephesians prays for his readers that their hearts might be enlightened. "[God] has put all things under his feet and has made him the head over all things for the church." Those are staggering claims. They put Christ's Ascension not only on a spiritual plane but also on a cosmic one. Christ rules everything, the author says— everything on earth and in the heavens. What is next is for that rule to become fully manifest. Christ is even now at the right hand of God, our author tells us, but we still wait to see his rule recognized in the world. We also wait to fully enjoy the benefits of that rule, benefits that the author of Ephesians assures us are ours already.

MATTHEW 28:16–20 Matthew's account of the Ascension differs markedly from either of Luke's accounts. In Matthew, the Ascension takes place in Galilee, not in Jerusalem. In Matthew, the Ascension takes place shortly after the Resurrection, presumably not long after the disciples arrived in Galilee, according to Jesus' instructions (Matthew 28:7, Mark 16:7). Most remarkable, however, is Matthew's emphasis on the Ascension as the foundational moment for the birth of the Church. Indeed, Matthew is the only New Testament writer to even hint that Jesus consciously intended to found a Church and certainly the only one who recounts that Jesus expressly commanded his disciples to baptize. While Luke leaves the disciples staring into space and not sure what to expect next, Matthew has Jesus leave them with explicit instructions. Their next task is to "go therefore and make disciples" (a deliberate change on Matthew's part from Mark's "proclaim the good news"[16:15] and Luke's "you are witnesses" [24:48]). The disciples are to baptize all nations and teach them to obey "all that [Jesus has] commanded."

SEVENTH SUNDAY OF EASTER
They Devoted Themselves to Prayer

ACTS 1:12–14 After the Ascension on Mount Olivet, the disciples return to Jerusalem and gather in the upper room, the room in which tradition claims Jesus and his disciples celebrated the Last Supper. The upper room is a Sabbath day's journey from Olivet, roughly one kilometer or six tenths of a mile, the distance Jews were permitted to walk on the Sabbath. There, the disciples, minus Judas, gather with some of Jesus' female disciples and Mary. There is no fear or anxiety expressed concerning their state. Rather, all devoted themselves to prayer in preparation for God's promised gift of the Spirit. Luke sees prayer as an essential preparation for the important events that occur in both his account of the Gospel and in Acts of the Apostles. We, too, are invited to devote ourselves to prayer as a way of continually seeking God's presence and direction in our lives.

PSALM 27:1, 4, 7–8 (13) The psalm expresses strong confidence in God along with a desired longing to seek intimacy with the Lord at all times. The psalmist associates three images with the Lord: light, salvation, and refuge. All three express great confidence in the Lord as one having the power to aid the psalmist in life's distress. As a result of the psalmist's strong confidence in God's gracious presence and power exercised on the psalmist's behalf, the psalmist yearns to seek God's face and dwell with the Lord always. The intimacy, power, and presence of the Lord experienced in the temple is what the psalmist yearns for each and every day. Such yearning for the Lord emboldens the psalmist to call upon the Lord in times of distress, already confident that the Lord will hear and respond. This confidence in and yearning for the Lord should be the prayer stance of all believers.

1 PETER 4:13–16 Suffering again surfaces as an integral component in the life of believers. Fidelity to Jesus' values and lifestyle made his followers' behavior stand out, especially when contrasted with the values and practices of their neighbors. As a result, misunderstanding, rejection, opposition, and persecution surfaced, causing much suffering for Jesus' disciples. The author exhorts them to rejoice because, in their innocent suffering for Christ, they share in Christ's own innocent suffering. Just as God raised up and

CONNECTIONS TO CHURCH TEACHING AND TRADITION

- "While awaiting the Spirit, 'all these with one accord devoted themselves to prayer.'[1] The Spirit who teaches the Church and recalls for her everything that Jesus said[2] was also to form her in the life of prayer" (CCC, 2623).

- "In prayer the Holy Spirit unites us to the person of the only Son, in his glorified humanity, through which and in which our filial prayer unites us in the Church with the Mother of Jesus[3]" (CCC, 2673).

- "Jesus fulfilled the work of the Father completely. . . . Our high priest who prays for us is also the one who prays in us and the God who hears our prayer" (CCC, 2749).

- "In this prayer Jesus reveals and gives to us the 'knowledge,' inseparably one, of the Father and of the Son[4], which is the very mystery of the life of prayer" (CCC, 2751).

---

1 Acts 1:14.

2 Cf. John 14:26.

3 Cf. Acts 1:14.

4 Cf. John 17:3, 6–10, 25.

glorified Christ, so too will we, in the Spirit's power, be raised up and glorified. We are reminded, however, that it is suffering for Christ's sake that brings about ultimate glory in God, and not suffering due to immorality. "Whoever is made to suffer as a Christian, should not be ashamed but glorify God because of the name" (4:16). The name "Christian" might have been used by others as a slur or insult, but disciples should glorify God with it, even in the face of shame or disgrace. Prayer enables us to continually seek the Lord, to endure suffering, and to even rejoice in the face of suffering, assured of God's glory.

- "This is Christian prayer: to be wholly God's, because he is wholly ours" (CCC, 2617).

JOHN 17:1–11A Chapter 17 of the Gospel of John is an extended prayer of Jesus, culminating his farewell address to his disciples at the Last Supper. Jesus first prays that his mission on earth may be brought to a successful conclusion as his "hour" approaches—John's word for Jesus' Passion, Death, and Resurrection. Jesus' Crucifixion is his ultimate act of glorifying the Father, and by glorifying the Father, the Father will glorify Jesus in return. In the process, all those who have believed in Jesus will benefit from the eternal life that Jesus accomplished in this world.

Jesus' prayer now extends to his disciples, "those whom [God] gave [him] out of the world" (17:6). Everything that Jesus shared with them has its origin in the Father. They have understood all he shared with them and have come to accept it and to believe in Jesus as the one sent by the Father. His prayer is for them and not for the world, understood by John as those who refuse to believe. Since all that Jesus has comes from the Father, and he has glorified the Father by sharing it all with his disciples, both the Father and he are glorified in the disciples as well. By sharing with his disciples the Father's words, and in their understanding of them and their belief in him, both the Father and Jesus are glorified in them. Jesus asserts that he is praying for his disciples, the ones God gave him (17:6), because they will remain in the world to carry on his mission while he returns to the Father. Like Jesus, we too are to call upon the Lord in prayer, seeking to glorify the Lord in all our words and actions.

From Confusion to Belief

GENESIS 11:1–9 OR EXODUS 19:3–8A, 16–20B OR EZEKIEL 37:1–14 OR JOEL 3:1–5 The Lectionary gives a series of four options for the First Reading for the Vigil Mass of Pentecost. These comments will focus on the reading from the Book of Genesis. One point of interest is that this is the first time since the Easter Vigil that we are hearing a text from the Old Testament. The Church's liturgy during Easter focuses our attention on the unfolding story of the power of Christ's Resurrection. As we come to the end of the Easter season, we are taken back in the readings to primeval salvation history. In Hebrew rhetoric, an author repeats a word or phrase for the sake of emphasis. Though it is not as clear in the English translation of this passage from Genesis, the Hebrew word for language or speech recurs five times, and of those, the words "the same language" appear twice (11:1, 6). Language, which had been the fundamental means of communication and communion, has become a source of confusion and disunity. This reading stands in direct contrast to the experience of Pentecost as described in Acts, when the different languages of the people gathered in Jerusalem are all understood by the Spirit-filled Apostles (see 2:4–13).

PSALM 104:1–2, 24, 35, 27–28, 29, 30 (SEE 30) Psalm 104 is a hymn of Creation, recounting both the wondrous works of God and the wisdom with which God has ordered the world in harmony and goodness. The opening phrase, "Bless the Lord, O my soul!" (104:1), is a powerful expression of praise. The Hebrew word for soul, *nefesh*, refers to that part of the human person which sustains life and vitality, the life force within an individual. Here the psalmist is calling to his own inner being, that which gives and sustains his life, to lift up praise to God. The opening three stanzas of the responsorial psalm give the psalmist's reasons for giving voice to this praise.

The last stanza twice employs the word spirit, in Hebrew, *ruach*. This word can variously refer to one's breath, the wind, or the spirit. In the Hebrew imagination, both human breath and the wind were mysterious things. In Genesis 1:2, a mighty "wind" swept over the chaotic waters. In Genesis 2:7, the Lord God blew "breath" into a mass of earth and it became a living being, Adam. Likewise in this verse, when

CONNECTIONS TO CHURCH TEACHING AND TRADITION

- "The Holy Spirit was sent on the day of Pentecost in order that he might sanctify the Church continually and so that believers might have access to the Father through Christ in the one Spirit[1]" (LG, 4).

- "On the day of Pentecost when the seven weeks of Easter had come to an end, Christ's Passover is fulfilled in the outpouring of the Holy Spirit, manifested, given, and communicated. . . . Christ, the Lord, pours out the Spirit in abundance[2]" (CCC, 731).

- "The word of God is thus expressed in human words thanks to the working of the Holy Spirit. The missions of the Son and the Holy Spirit are inseparable and constitute a single economy of salvation. The same Spirit who acts in the incarnation of the Word in the womb of the Virgin Mary is the Spirit who guides Jesus throughout his mission and is promised to the disciples" (VD, 15).

---

1 Cf. Ephesians 2:18.
2 Cf. Acts 2:33–36.

God sends forth "spirit," things are created and the face of the earth is renewed. Such images from the Old Testament serve as a prelude to the act of new creation by which Jesus sends his Spirit upon Mary and the Twelve, as well as those in Jerusalem at the Pentecost.

ROMANS 8:22–27 St. Paul writes about the human condition: our fragility and weakness in the lifelong process of growth into Christ. Yet as Jesus promised, he has not left us orphans (John 14:18–26). He has given us the Holy Spirit as the pledge of his presence, as a helper in time of distress, and as a guide to live faithfully as his disciples. It is this same Holy Spirit that teaches us to pray, even when we feel our prayer to be inadequate. St. Paul speaks of the Spirit who "intercedes with inexpressible groanings" within us (8:26). St. Paul is here referring to that ache we experience in prayer when we cannot even find words to wrap around what we know we should pray for, yet the feeling stays within us, almost haunting us. That is the Spirit praying in us, leading us to intercession, to praise, to gratitude, and to whatever might draw us into that intimate communion with God that is true prayer. Such a gift is reason for great hope and comfort.

JOHN 7:37–39 This very short Gospel is packed with meaning appropriate to our celebration of Pentecost. "The last and greatest day of the feast" refers to the last day of the Festival of Tabernacles, or in Hebrew, Sukkoth. This feast commemorated the wandering of the Hebrew people in the desert on the way to the Promised Land. It also eventually came to be associated with the end-of-the-year gathering in of the harvest. It was marked by seven days of grateful rejoicing for God's abundant goodness to them. So when Jesus exclaims, "Let anyone who thirsts come to me and drink," he is asserting that he has something far greater than what is being celebrated on these festive days. A new harvest of grace is to be received by those who believe.

Jesus' words about "rivers of living water" (7:38) can be understood as a reference to Baptism, that initial sacrament which imparts the gift of the Holy Spirit. It is worthwhile to meditate on how the evangelist John has placed the bread of life discourse (John 6) immediately adjacent to this chapter on Baptism and the Holy Spirit.

PENTECOST SUNDAY
Re-created by the Spirit

ACTS 2:1–11 This reading from Acts is an account of Pentecost. In the Old Testament, Pentecost, the "feast of Weeks," recalled the giving of the Law on Mount Sinai, one of the pilgrim feasts when Jews would come to Jerusalem for the fiftieth day after Passover. The mention of "a noise like a strong driving wind" (2:2) draws our minds to the account of the giving of the Law in Exodus ("there were peals of thunder and lightning . . . and a very loud trumpet blast" [19:16]). Luke draws a clear line of connection between the Book of Exodus with the experience of Pentecost in the new Christian dispensation.

When the text mentions "they were all filled with the Holy Spirit" (2:4), another resemblance to an earlier section of Luke's account of the Gospel is evoked. At the baptism of Jesus, Luke tells us, "the Holy Spirit descended upon him" (Luke 3:22), and when he returns from the desert temptations, we are told, "Jesus returned to Galilee in the power of the Spirit" (Luke 4:14), where in his hometown Nazareth he reads from the scroll of Isaiah, "The Spirit of the Lord is upon me" (Luke 4:17–18). Acts 2:1–11 asserts that the same Holy Spirit that descended upon Jesus has now come upon his followers who are to be baptized.

PSALM 104:1, 24, 29–30, 31, 34 (SEE 30) This is the same Psalm used for the Vigil Mass of Pentecost. The only difference is the concluding stanza. Please refer to page 90 for its commentary.

1 CORINTHIANS 12:3B–7, 12–13 This passage explodes with a message of hope that must be understood on two levels: the historical church of St. Paul, and our own circumstances as Christians today. First, St. Paul saw the factions within the Corinthian community as a threat to their intended unity created by Christ's Resurrection. By their Baptism, the Christians of Corinth had become the Body of Christ, his visible image on earth. While that is a great challenge to living Jesus' new law of love, Christians are given the profound gift of the Spirit to lead, guide, strengthen, and inspire them. In this Sunday's passage from 1 Corinthians 12, Paul chides these people to live in accord with what they have been given: the Spirit. Second, this passage stands as a weighty reminder of both what we have

CONNECTIONS TO CHURCH TEACHING AND TRADITION

- "When the Father sends his Word, he always sends his Breath. In their joint mission, the Son and the Holy Spirit are distinct but inseparable. To be sure, it is the Christ who is seen, the visible image of the invisible God, but it is the Spirit who reveals him" (CCC, 689).

- "To evangelize is first of all to bear witness, in a simple and direct way, to God revealed by Jesus Christ, in the Holy Spirit, to bear witness that in his Son God has loved the world—that in his Incarnate Word he has given being to all things and has called [all people] to eternal life" (EN, 6).

- "The Church, however, which is so full of youthful vigor and is constantly renewed by the breath of the Holy Spirit, is willing, at all times, to recognize, welcome, and even assimilate anything that redounds to the honor of the human mind and heart, . . . which, from the beginning of time, had been destined by God's Providence to be the cradle of the Church" (PP, 19).

been given, and how we are to use this precious gift within us. Our Baptism, our incorporation into Christ, bestows on us the very gifts of the Spirit which Paul lists in Galatians: love, joy, peace, patience, kindness, generosity, gentleness, self-control (5:22–23). Through these gifts of the Spirit, the mission of Jesus continues to be established in our world today. Could we ever preach this message of St. Paul strongly enough? It is not merely our duty to act in this way; rather, our Baptism marks us in an organic way, showing us our deepest nature in Jesus Christ. We preach it persuasively when we live it!

SEQUENCE: *VENI, SANCTE SPIRITUS* This Sunday, the Church sings one of four sequences, ancient poetic songs preceding the Gospel Acclamation on solemn occasions. In the *Veni, Sancte Spiritus,* the Church prays for the Holy Spirit to come as the Father of the Poor, the Comforter, Divine Light, Sweet Rest, and Healer, asserting that in the absence of the Holy Spirit, we stand in utter need. When the Holy Spirit is present, we have the Lord's salvation.

JOHN 20:19–31 In contrast to St. Luke, the evangelist John describes the coming of the Holy Spirit to the Eleven happening on Easter Sunday evening, not fifty days later. The powerful depiction of the gift of the Spirit is portrayed in relation to forgiveness. After the words of commission ("As the Father has sent me, so I send you" [20:21]), Jesus breathes on them, passing onto them his Spirit. They now possess the Spirit, and what will they do with it? Exactly what the Risen Christ has first done to them: offering them "peace," wholeness by means of forgiveness, and then authorizing them to offer that same forgiveness to others. How wounded the Apostles must have been, having betrayed the One who had loved them so completely, even with all their weaknesses. Jesus, risen from the dead, comes among them and with that single word, "peace," he pushes aside their sinfulness and offers them what they need most, forgiveness. On that first Easter night, the Risen Christ comes to those who have betrayed him, offering them forgiveness, the fruit of his saving Passion and Death. The Spirit enables us to be instruments of Jesus' own forgiveness and reconciliation.

Ordinary Time

Ordinary Time does not have its own distinctive character. Rather, the Sundays of Ordinary Time focus on the entirety of the mystery of Christ and all its dimensions. This period is called Ordinary Time because its Sundays are counted, or numbered. This time is not ordinary in the usual sense of the word; rather it is time marked by ordinal numbers, such as the fifth or twenty-first Sunday. These Sundays provide us with an extraordinary opportunity to ponder and live out the truth of Christ's Paschal Mystery, the salvific events of his birth, life, Death, and Resurrection.

Ordinary Time includes two periods: the shorter period of Ordinary Time comprises the Sundays and weekdays after the Feast of the Baptism of the Lord through the Tuesday before Ash Wednesday. It may last as few as four weeks or as many as nine, depending on the date of Easter. While winter's days may seem to drag on during this time, at least in the Northern Hemisphere, the Church's liturgy fills us with a sense of celebration because of our call to be followers of the Savior.

The lengthier part of Ordinary Time begins after Evening Prayer on Pentecost Sunday. But even after Ordinary Time resumes, the joy of Pentecost continues in the first two Sunday celebrations of the Most Holy Trinity and Most Holy Body and Blood of Christ. The first celebrates the rootedness of creation, the Church, and all human relationships in the Trinity—the Father, Son, and Holy Spirit—one God in three Persons. The second recalls the historical basis of the Eucharist as the Lord shepherds the Israelites, his people, out of Egypt, feeding them with manna in the desert. As Christians, we celebrate that Christ is indeed the living bread come down from heaven to feed all those who believe in him. The Eucharist is our participation in Christ's very life, and through it, Christ nourishes us to live as his faithful disciples. The celebrations of the solemnities of the Most Holy Trinity and the Body and Blood of Christ recall two fundamental beliefs of our faith, and thus prove a fitting beginning to the resumption of Ordinary Time. The scriptural backgrounds for these two Sunday are in the final chapter of this book.

When the counted Sundays begin again after these two solemnities, we begin not where we left off before Ash Wednesday. Rather, we skip a few Sundays. Why? Easter is known as a "moveable feast"; that is, it does not occur on the same date each year. Its date depends on the time of the spring equinox. Once the date of Easter is set, the other Sundays of the liturgical year are fixed around it. Since the liturgical year must end after the Thirty-Fourth Sunday of Ordinary Time (which is the Solemnity of

Our Lord Jesus Christ, King of the Universe) we count backward from that last Sunday of the year. Sometimes this does not match up with our counting forward from the first Sunday in Ordinary Time after the Christmas season.

FIRST READINGS

Over the course of the counted Sundays of Ordinary Time we hear from a variety of Old Testament books. The readings do not follow the order of the books in the Old Testament, but are chosen to complement the Gospel readings. During this time, we will hear readings from the prophets Isaiah, Jeremiah, Ezekiel, and Zechariah. We will also hear selections from the Book of Wisdom, 1 Kings, Exodus, Sirach, Leviticus, and Proverbs.

The First Readings of Ordinary Time in Year A include many of the themes of major significance to our faith: humility, the fruitfulness and power of the Word, the freedom to repent from sin, God's mercy, the gifts of wisdom and the everlasting covenant, the awe-inspiring presence of the Lord, God's justice, and Davidic ancestry.

RESPONSORIAL PSALMS

The Responsorial Psalm for each Sunday is an integral part of the Liturgy of the Word. The lyrical nature of the psalms lends itself to song. Meant to help everyone in the assembly give voice to their acceptance of the Word of God proclaimed in the First Reading, the Responsorial Psalm is another reading from Scripture, almost always with a short, simple refrain from one of the psalms. Occasionally, the refrain for the Responsorial Psalm comes from a different book, as is the case on the Fifteenth Sunday in Ordinary Time.

SECOND READINGS

In the earlier portion of Ordinary Time, the Second Readings come from Paul's First Letter to the Corinthians. Beginning with an opening address and greeting to the Corinthians on the Second Sunday in Ordinary Time, the Second Readings urge the Corinthians, a people divided on questions of faith and morality as well as who should be part of a community of faith, to agree to be united with each other in the same mind, the mind of Christ. The strong in the community are to take care of the weak. The strong are to make sure their actions do not negatively influence the faith of the weak. All are to be brothers and sisters in Christ.

On the Ninth Sunday we begin a semicontinuous reading of Paul's Letter to the Romans, his major theological treatise on faith and justification. From the Twenty-Fifth Sunday in Ordinary Time on, we listen to Second Readings from Paul's Letter to the Philippians, in which he lovingly exhorts them to continue their growth in Christ and strive for a deeper unity with him and one another.

After the proclamation from Philippians, there are three Sundays—though not consecutive—when 1 Thessalonians is proclaimed. The First Letter to the Thessalonians is the oldest of Paul's letters. Like all of the authentic Pauline letters, it was composed before the four New Testament Gospel accounts. In the letter, Paul offers thanksgiving for the Thessalonian Christians' perseverance in faith, hope, and love, and exhorts them to show their dedication to the Gospel by following a moral code of conduct.

On the Solemnity of Our Lord Jesus Christ, King of the Universe, the Second Reading is from Paul's First Letter to the Corinthians. Focusing on the unity of the Christian community in the Body of Christ, Paul tried to get the Corinthians to understand that their relationships with one another should reflect their belief in the oneness of the resurrected Body of Christ.

GOSPEL READINGS

With the onset of Ordinary Time after Christmas we hear first from John's account of the Gospel on the Second Sunday in Ordinary Time. This Gospel reading helps us transition from Christmas Time to Ordinary Time every year because it continues to focus on the manifestation of Jesus' identity. In Year A, the focus is John's proclamation of Jesus as the Lamb of God. Then, beginning with the Third Sunday in Ordinary Time each year, there is a semicontinuous proclamation of the synoptic account of the Gospel assigned to the current liturgical year, Matthew in Year A. After Easter Time ends we hear two passages from the Gospel according to John for the two solemnities that occur as Ordinary Time resumes, then we again proclaim Matthew's account of the Gospel. The Gospel according to Matthew is the lengthiest of the three synoptic Gospels. He understands Jesus as Emmanuel, God-with-us, the one who comes to save. For Matthew, Jesus is the great and humble teacher who forms his disciples in the way of following him. Jesus is also the new Moses who fulfills the prophecies of the Old Testament.

Second Sunday in Ordinary Time
You Are My Servant

ISAIAH 49:3, 5–6 This passage from Isaiah speaks either to an individual servant or to all of Israel as a servant of the Lord. Regardless of the addressee, the first verse we hear from Isaiah sounds like a commission: the servant is called and sent. The following verses indicate an even greater trust: "I will make you a light to the nations, / that my salvation may reach to the ends of the earth" (v. 6). The servant is called to go among the Gentiles and offer God's welcome, grace, salvation, and justice. Whoever the servant is, the servant has a role in history to live and offer the reign of God to all. Jesus Christ accepted the mission to spread the Good News of salvation to all by obediently submitting to the Father's will. His life, Death, and Resurrection invite his followers to do the same.

PSALM 40:2, 4, 7–8, 8–9, 10 (8A, 9A) Psalm 40 almost seems to be two different psalms. The first verses (2–11), a part of the psalm for this Sunday, are a song of thanksgiving; the second set of verses (14–18) are a song of lament. It differs somewhat from the typical psalm form, in which lamentations are usually sung first. Perhaps the author is reminding the servant of the Lord about his dependence on God. The psalmist reminds the servant that God wants more than offerings—he wants an obedient heart. This theme is heard from several Old Testament prophets. The psalm verses speak of the actions of an obedient servant and the Lord's response to that servant. The Lord hears the servant's cry and gives him a new song. The Lord also gives ears open to obedience and sends the servant forth to proclaim and announce justice to the vast assembly. The psalm speaks plainly of God's actions and the servant's response.

1 CORINTHIANS 1:1–3 Paul's opening verses in his letter to the Corinthians seem to set the tone for a glowing affirmation of their community and witness, if only we did not know what followed in the letter. The Corinthians have splintered into various rival groups. Paul writes to correct and address mistakes among them, including moral disorders and divisions in the community, offerings to idols, and problems in the liturgical assemblies. He reminds them that the Spirit is the source of all gifts and admonishes them about envy or rivalry with the striking image of the

CONNECTIONS TO CHURCH TEACHING AND TRADITION

- "By his loving obedience to the Father, 'unto death, even death on a cross' (Philippians 2:8), Jesus fulfills the atoning mission (cf. Isaiah 53:10) of the suffering Servant" (CCC, 623).

- "The teaching and spreading of her social doctrine are part of the Church's evangelizing mission. And since it is a doctrine aimed at guiding people's behavior, it consequently gives rise to a 'commitment to justice,' according to each individual's role, vocation and circumstances" (SRS, 41).

- "The members of the Church are impelled to engage in this [missionary] activity because of the charity with which they love God and by which they desire to share with all people the spiritual goods of both this life and the life to come" (AG, 7).

body and its interconnected parts. Paul later makes it clear that love is the greatest gift of all in the often-quoted verses about love in chapter 13.

Paul begins this letter, saying, "I give thanks to my God always on your account for the grace of God bestowed on you in Christ Jesus" (1 Corinthians 1:4). Knowing that all of these admonitions and concerns are addressed in the following chapters makes it touching that Paul begins his letter with an offering of grace, peace, and thanksgiving to the community at Corinth.

JOHN 1:29–34 Last Sunday, we heard Matthew's account of Jesus' baptism by John (unless the feast of Baptism falls on a Monday). This Sunday's Gospel provides the Baptist's testimony from the Gospel according to John. Throughout this Gospel, John the Baptist is mentioned almost twenty times. We hear about the places he preached, his discussions with followers, his testimony about Jesus, and even Jesus' own words to his opponents about John: "He was a burning and shining lamp, and for a while you were content to rejoice in his light" (John 5:35). John the Baptist is a strong witness to Jesus.

In today's passage he says he comes to testify about the one to come after him. He speaks of Jesus as the light to come and says that he came to give witness so that others may believe (John 1:7). John clearly states in this passage that the Baptist saw the Spirit come down on Jesus. He is bold and clear in his testimony that this is the Son of God. He speaks and acts so that others may come to know and believe that the Son of God will take away the sins of the world, bringing God's salvation to all. John himself is obedient to his call to testify, but he points out unmistakably Jesus' willingness to be obedient in giving himself to the Father's will, sacrificing his life for all of humanity. Jesus is the living expression of this Sunday's psalm refrain: "Here I am, Lord, I come to do your will" (Psalm 40:8a–9a).

ISAIAH 8:23—9:3 This reading includes the well-known and inspiring line "The people who walked in darkness have seen a great light" (9:1). What was this darkness? The lands of Zebulun and Naphtali were the northernmost tribes of Israel and were geographically close to Assyria. They were the first captured and the last restored when the Assyrians invaded Israel.

The great light that Isaiah proclaims to the Hebrews is a hymn of thanksgiving (9:1–6) for their deliverance from their captors. However, Isaiah also expresses concern for the Hebrews who remain under Assyrian power.

PSALM 27:1, 4, 13–14 (1A) "The Lord is my light and my salvation." The theme of this psalm, which we sing only a part of today, is confidence and trust in the Lord (27:1–3). Light is a biblical image for life and happiness. "The Lord is my light and my salvation; / whom should I fear?" (v. 1). In verses 4–6, the psalmist expresses confidence in the Lord, wishing to dwell in God's house, away from enemies. The Temple shines as God's house and is the perfect refuge. With the psalmist, we pray that we may gaze on the loveliness of God, who is our light and salvation.

1 CORINTHIANS 1:10–13, 17 Paul's preaching of the kingdom was built on the common union of all believers. As members of Christ's Body, this union was nourished and centered in the Eucharist. Paul is very sensitive to the lack of this unity, and addresses it here. It was clear that the Corinthians did not all share the same vision but were, in fact, hostile to one another.

To help make his point, Paul asks: "Is Christ divided?" In this question, "Christ" means the community of believers (1 Corinthians 6:15, 12:12). He asks why the community is divided according to who baptized them. Was it Paul, Apollos, or Cephas? He reminds them they are baptized into Christ. Paul also teaches them that his vocation is not to baptize, but to preach. To preach is to release the power of the Gospel (2 Corinthians 4:7–12). Authentic preaching builds up the Body of Christ.

CONNECTIONS TO CHURCH TEACHING AND TRADITION

- "Even when preoccupied with temporal affairs, the laity can and must be involved in the precious work of evangelizing the world" (LG, 35).

- "The apostolate of the Church and of all of its members is primarily designed to manifest Christ's message by words and deeds and to communicate his grace to the world" (AA, 6).

- "Divine providence works also through the actions of creatures. To human beings God grants the ability to cooperate freely with his plans" (CCC, 323).

MATTHEW 4:12–23 OR 4:12–17 After John the Baptist was handed over, Jesus came to Capernaum by the sea, on the northwest shores of the Sea of Galilee in the tribal land of Zebulun and Naphtali. This was to indicate that the beginning of Jesus' public ministry in Galilee was in accord with the Scriptures, as we hear in the First Reading. Jesus began his public preaching saying, "Repent, for the kingdom of heaven is at hand" (v. 17). He begins his preaching with the words of the Baptist, but now with the difference that the kingdom is near and has begun to be present. This kingdom of heaven indicates that time when God's power and judgment are made fully manifest and acknowledged by all.

The Sea of Galilee was large, and was an important trade route and home to a major fishing industry. In Matthew's account of the beginning of Jesus' public ministry, Jesus introduces the key disciples of his inner circle. These first disciples, Simon and Andrew, were fishermen and brothers. They owned their nets and boats, but left behind their possessions and source of income when Jesus called them to follow him in a new mission to become "fishers of men." James and John, two other brothers, who worked with their father, Zebedee, were also called that day.

Their immediate response highlights Jesus' attractiveness and persuasiveness. They had no understanding of what this invitation would mean or how it would change their lives. Yet, each of them immediately dropped their nets, left their boats, and followed Jesus.

Jesus went all over Galilee teaching the Good News of the kingdom. He taught and preached this Good News to all: the rich and poor, the learned and unschooled, the sinner and pious. Furthermore, he acted as a healer and exorcist for their ills and sufferings. What did the disciples learn and question as they walked the dusty paths of Galilee? What did this "fishing for men" mean in their daily lives? How are we called to "fish for men" today?

ZEPHANIAH 2:3, 3:12–13 The prophet Zephaniah addressed Judah during the seventh century BC. Politically, the world shifted from a power base in Assyria to one in Mesopotamia. The northern kingdom of Israel had been destroyed in 721 BC; a similar fate faced the tiny nation of Judah. Judah, as a vassal of the Assyrians, participated in the worship of Assyria's gods.

Zephaniah believed that Judah, too, would suffer from the enemy's hand, but like Isaiah, he believed that God's hand would save Judah. The "day of the Lord's anger" refers perhaps to the threat of conquest on the political horizon. Faithfulness to God, expressed as obedience, justice, and humility (v. 3), is the means to salvation.

The reading for this week skips down to 3:12–13. These verses describe the aftermath of the day of the Lord. A few people will survive and these few will live according to the ways of God. Their life will be as peaceful as sheep which graze.

Zephaniah's words are both a consolation and a warning. Those who trust in God will survive, but for those who live unfaithfully, the future cannot be guaranteed.

PSALM 146:6–7, 8–9, 9–10 (MATTHEW 5:3) The Gospel for today provides the antiphon for the psalm response. Like the psalm, it celebrates God's care for the needy. Psalm 146 is a hymn of praise of God, the source of justice. Faithful and true, God protects all those who have no hope of protection. The psalm names what would be considered the least important of society: widows, orphans, strangers, the imprisoned. Israel knows that God gave food to the hungry in the desert, set the captive slaves free, and continues to care for the needy. The mercy and compassion of God is their motive for praise.

1 CORINTHIANS 1:26–31 Paul addresses the wisdom and foolishness of faith by reminding the Corinthians of their status. If the Corinthians think that their new faith makes them superior to others, Paul is quick to deflate their egos. He reminds them that before becoming believers they were among the lowly of their society. In fact, their lowliness was the very thing that enabled them to receive the gift of faith in Christ.

CONNECTIONS TO CHURCH TEACHING AND TRADITION

- The closest we can get to knowing God's wisdom is in following Jesus' obedient example, as taught in the Beatitudes (NDC, 25, 45; CCC, 1716–1729).

- God created everything as an expression of divine wisdom (CCC, 295, 302–305, 315).

Through the lowly, God's reign is established. God, not the wise, not the powerful, not the wellborn, is the greatest. God gives the Corinthians life through faith in Christ Jesus. He is the true source of wisdom and the way to a right relationship with God. If the Corinthians find it necessary to boast of anything, Paul asks them to boast about God, not about their own wisdom or status. God is the source of all life.

MATTHEW 5:1–12A Like a rabbi instructing his students, Jesus teaches the disciples and the crowds what the reign of God is like. The mountain setting (unlike the plain in Luke's Gospel) evokes another important mountain, Sinai, where the Law was given to Israel.

Who are the truly happy, the truly blessed? In the reign of God, they are those who have moved beyond themselves to recognize their need for God. Those who care enough to grieve will find themselves healed of their grief. The meek, who place others ahead of themselves, will dwell in God's land. Those whose passion for justice cannot be quenched will be satisfied. People who forgive readily and easily will find this action extended to them in God's reign. Those who can focus on God to the exclusion of all else will be rewarded with a vision of God. People who care for the community, who try to bring reconciliation and peace, will be honored by God. Those willing to die for what they believe are already within the reign of God. Finally, those who forego honor and the acclaim of others in order to proclaim Christ will find themselves honored and acclaimed.

True happiness is found easily but not without great cost. Disciples must be willing to put their lives on the line for others. They must move beyond a "Me first!" mentality to an altruistic spirit empowered by compassion, courage, and faith.

Taste and See

ISAIAH 58:7–10 Isaiah, writing to the returned exiles from Babylon, answers the question, what will restore God's favor to us? The people are disillusioned and unhappy in their devastated environment. In the verses just prior, the people complain that they have tried fasting as they did in the days of old and still they have no positive response from God (58:3).

Isaiah condemns their unjust business practices and querulous behavior (vv. 3–4). Perhaps in the depressing days following the return, the sight of the ruined land and cities robbed the returnees of their faith. They imagined they could control God's responses to them through religious observances. Instead, Isaiah gives them the challenge: care for your neighbors, attend to their needs, and you will find God quick to respond to you. The people have ignored the poor and homeless and turned against each other, speaking falsely about their neighbors. Isaiah does not look sympathetically on their plight. He forces the people to face their behavior as the source of their alienation from God. Caring for their neighbors both physically and socially is the way to God.

PSALM 112:4–5, 6–7, 8–9 (4A) The praise of the just person is the psalm response. The just are rooted in God and have nothing to fear from either life's circumstances or from evil itself. God is a steadfast companion to the person who treats the poor and weak with compassion. Like light, the just person is a source of hope and consolation to those who seek God (v. 4). Immortality of a sort is given to the just; the memory of kindness and generosity will live on.

1 CORINTHIANS 2:1–5 In an antithesis to the "wisdom" the Corinthians want to claim, Paul claims weakness. Paul does not want the Corinthians to think that they have acquired a new kind of wisdom in the same way that other philosophical systems of the day promoted wisdom.

Unlike other preachers and philosophers of the first century, Paul tells the community that he came as a weak human being with a message about weakness—a crucified Christ. That they were convinced by his message had nothing to do with the power of his person, but rather was a result of the power of the Spirit.

CONNECTIONS TO CHURCH TEACHING AND TRADITION

- "It is necessary, then, . . . to keep a watchful eye on this our world . . . whose . . . affairs pose problems and grave difficulties. . . . This is the field in which the faithful are called to fulfill their mission . . . to be the 'salt of the earth' and the 'light of the world' (cf. Matthew 5:13–14)" (CL, 3).

- "The church, the salt of the earth and the light of the world (see Matthew 5:13–14), is even more urgently called upon to save and renew every creature, so that all things might be restored in Christ, and so that in him men and women might form one family and one people of God" (AG, 1).

- "The disciples of Christ . . . hope to offer . . . an authentic Christian witness. . . . They seek to enhance the dignity of women and men . . . so people are helped to attain salvation by love of God and love of humanity; the mystery of Christ begins to shine out" (AG, 12).

MATTHEW 5:13–16 The faith of the Corinthians is not based on human wisdom, but on a far greater wisdom, the wisdom of God (v. 5). The danger of treating Christianity as another philosophical fad must have been great for the Corinthians.

Like the prophets who themselves were persecuted (5:12), the disciples have a responsibility to fulfill. Jesus uses two images, salt and light, to explain how his followers are to relate to the world.

Salt, an important preservative and seasoning, was a valuable commodity in the first century. It also had other meanings. In Numbers 18:19 salt was used in a covenant ceremony. Salt was also offered with sacrifices (Leviticus 2:13). The disciples, therefore, are important. They are what seasons and preserves life, they are signs of covenant and friendship between peoples, and they are signs of God's relationship with humanity.

The second part of verse 13 contains a warning: enthusiasm and commitment are required, and if that is lacking, they are as useless as salt that has lost its flavor. How salt loses its flavor has a variety of interpretations: salt used in Jewish rituals can become unclean; the impure salt from the Dead Sea can lose its taste; the salt used to fire the baking ovens can lose its ability to season food. The message is that the salt changes from useful to useless. The disciples, unless they preach the reign of God, are not really disciples. Like the people Isaiah addressed in the First Reading, those who do not bring God's message of mercy and love to others are worthless.

Light, another necessity of life, is the second image Jesus uses to explain to his followers their role in the world. Light is often associated with the saving acts of God (Isaiah 2:5, Psalm 44:4) and with the suffering servant of God (Isaiah 42:6, 49:6). God's intent is to bring salvation to all peoples through those who are faithful.

The good works done by Jesus' followers are not to be hidden away but to shine forth. God's salvation is made known through the actions of the disciples. The praise and glory their works will receive is part of the praise and glory of God. In other words, to act justly, to care for the weak and needy, is another form of praise. To "be salt" or to "be light" is to heal, to teach, to forgive, and to love.

Sixth Sunday in Ordinary Time
Fulfillment of the Law

SIRACH 15:15–20 The selection we proclaim from Sirach today is part of a larger discussion of human responsibility addressed to people who held God to blame for the conduct of the wicked. In a religious milieu in which God was seen as the ultimate author of every action, some people held God responsible for evil and suffering, thereby undercutting faith in God's goodness. Sirach responds to that with a resounding affirmation of personal responsibility, emphasizing that those who choose to do so can keep the commandments. He insists that each of us account for our own choices, reminding us that God's commandments offer the path of true life.

PSALM 119:1–2, 4–5, 17–18, 33–34 (1B) With 176 verses, Psalm 119 is by far the longest prayer in the Psalter. Focusing on God's law, it uses eight synonyms for the law which, when added together, equal 174 references to God's Law. In spite of its focus on the Law, the psalm is not legalistic. Rather, it is a loving meditation on the blessings offered to those who set their hearts on God's way, seeking, loving, and following the Law. The author and any who spend time praying this psalm immerse themselves in the wonders of God's Law.

1 CORINTHIANS 2:6–10 It is hard to know whether or not Paul is being tongue-in-cheek when he addresses himself to the "mature" Corinthians. Other parts of this letter indicate that he had little esteem for their spiritual development (3:1, 5:1–2, 6:1–6). Here, however, the word he uses singles out people who have reached their goal, whose lives are fulfilling their deepest meaning. That they are Christians would indicate they are living the truth of the mystery God has revealed. As he continues talking to the Corinthians about true wisdom, Paul puts together citations from Isaiah 64:3 and Jeremiah 3:16, fashioning a beautiful image of God's indescribable revelation. This is a mystery, something that God has been working out since the beginning of the world (see Ephesians 1:3–14).

CONNECTIONS TO CHURCH TEACHING AND TRADITION

- "The Law of the Gospel fulfills the commandments of the Law. . . . Far from abolishing or devaluing the moral prescriptions of the Old Law . . . it reveals their entire divine and human truth" (CCC, 1968).

- "The gift of the commandments and of the Law is part of the covenant God sealed with his own. . . . Man's moral life has all its meaning in and through the covenant" (CCC, 2060–2061).

- "The Church proclaims human rights. . . . There is a temptation to feel that our personal rights are fully maintained only when we are free from every restriction of divine law. But this is the way leading to the extinction of human dignity, not its preservation" (GS, 41).

- "The Church feels the duty to defend the human dignity which belongs to every person, and 'denounces discrimination, sexual abuse and male domination as actions contrary to God's plan'[1]" (EIA, 45).

---

1 *Propositio* 11.

According to Paul, God's mystery, like his wisdom, is unlike anything of this world, which is in the process of passing away. Although this passage does not mention the Law, as it speaks of the mystery of God it draws our attention to the wonders of God's plan for humanity.

MATTHEW 5:17–37 OR 5:20–22A, 27–28, 33–34A, 37 The part of the Gospel that we call the Sermon on the Mount is a collection of Jesus' teachings that Matthew wove together in one carefully constructed discourse. In this section, Jesus expresses profound respect for his Jewish tradition, which he both interprets and fulfills.

Although the sayings introduced with "you have heard" and "but I say" are often called antitheses, implying that Jesus is abrogating the Jewish law, that is not necessarily the case. In some instances, he takes a teaching and goes to its root meaning. He demonstrates that the sin of murder has its roots in anger and disrespect of another. Adultery, which was understood at that time as an offense against the husband whose property had been abused by another, has its roots in looking at someone as an object of self-gratification rather than as a person and image of God. Thus, it is better to lose an eye or hand than disdain another person.

That teaching leads directly to the prohibition of divorce. Under traditional law, only the man could initiate a divorce, and, according to some interpretations, he was free to do so for the slightest of provocations. Jesus, however, promotes the dignity of women, saying they cannot simply be handed off as property.

Regarding interpersonal relationships and religion, Jesus calls his disciples to seek reconciliation with anyone who is angry with them. Otherwise, their sacrifice is hollow. So, too, since their word should be their bond, there is no reason to swear an oath. People can control their own behavior, but are powerless over heaven, Jerusalem, or even something as trivial as their natural hair color.

Taken together, this Sunday's readings sound a call to deep integrity. Those who have been called by God have the freedom to choose obedience to God and the wonders of his kingdom. To choose anything less than the unfolding of God's mystery is to tie your fate to that which is already passing away.

Seventh Sunday in Ordinary Time
Imitate God's Holiness

LEVITICUS 19:1–2, 17–18 Today's passage from Leviticus summarizes the intent of all God's laws: "Be holy, for I, the Lord, your God, am holy" (v. 2). Our vocation is to imitate God. The passage ends with a synopsis of what that implies "You shall love your neighbor as yourself" (v. 18).

This reading invites an examination of the kind of God our behavior proclaims. Are we like the God we meet in Scripture, slow to anger and rich in compassion, or does our behavior give witness to a false god of success, beauty, or materialism? Are we more apt to proselytize for our sports team or political party than for the Gospel?

PSALM 103:1–2, 3–4, 8, 10, 12–13 (8A) The *New American Bible* includes the subscript that this is a psalm of David. Whether or not it is of Davidic origins, it fits his experience.

In the context of our First Reading, we sing this psalm remembering what God has done for us. The psalm also describes what our God is like. God pardons sin and heals us, redeems us from destruction and treats us with kindness and compassion. By forgiving us, God makes our transgressions the opposite of our self-definition: "as far as the east is from the west" (v. 12). This is the God who offers compassion and mercy to us and is the God whom we are called to imitate.

1 CORINTHIANS 3:16–23 In this selection we are reminded of our intimate relationship with God. We, each and all of us, are the temple in which the Holy Spirit dwells. As a community, we replace the Temple where the people used to seek God's presence. In this context, the destruction of that Temple implies doing harm to the community.

Verses 18–23 of this reading summarize all that Paul has so far said. It reprises his themes of true wisdom versus human wisdom, and of the importance of remembering that the Corinthians do not belong to their favorite teacher. Rather, all belongs to them through Christ who belongs to God, and who brings them and us along with him to the Father.

MATTHEW 5:38–48 The last line of this reading looks back to the message of the First Reading. "Be holy as I am holy" is another expression of "Be perfect, just as your heavenly

CONNECTIONS TO CHURCH TEACHING AND TRADITION

- "Jesus, the Good Shepherd, wishes to communicate his life to us and place himself at the service of life. . . . He likewise invites his disciples to reconciliation . . . love for enemies . . . and to opt for the poorest" (*Aparecida*, 353).

- "The Word became flesh *to be our model of holiness*" (CCC, 459).

- "Although the Church possesses a 'hierarchical' structure, nevertheless this structure is totally ordered to the holiness of Christ's members. And holiness is measured according to the 'great mystery' in which the Bride responds with the gift of love to the gift of the Bridegroom" (MD, 27).

Father" (v. 48). This section of the Gospel according to Matthew has been misinterpreted by many over the years, who think that it means that those who suffer great injustice should just acquiesce to it, without doing anything to try to change things. In Jesus' environment, this was more of a call to justice than a call to suffer in silence. To understand the passage well, we must remember that the people in Jesus' time lived in a class system. There was a great distinction between slaves and masters, the occupying army and the nationals, and the rich and poor.

When Jesus tells the people to turn the other cheek, note that he says to do this "when someone strikes you on your right cheek" (v. 39). A right-handed person can only strike the right cheek of another with the back of the hand, a gesture that a master would use with a slave. By turning the other cheek, the person is essentially challenging the attacker to hit him or her squarely, like an equal. This recalls the Civil Rights marchers' commitment to avoid retaliation, but to remain strong in demonstrating their own humanity in an attempt to challenge their oppressors' prejudices and sense of righteousness.

The tunic and cloak that Jesus mentions were the primary garments of his day. Typically, when a poor person had nothing left with which to pay a debt, his tunic and cloak would be offered as collateral. According to the law, the lender had to return the cloak in the evening, because it was also the debtor's blanket. Handing over both cloak and tunic would be a persuasive sign demonstrating that the economics of the day left the poor naked.

The mention of "going the extra mile" is also better understood with some context. In Jesus' time, it was legal for a Roman soldier to force a local person to carry the soldier's heavy pack for just one mile—any more, and he would be subject to punishment. One can imagine the confusion and embarrassment a Roman soldier would feel trying to wrest his pack away from the Jew who is offering to carry it further. In all of these cases, loving the enemy comes down to asserting one's own humanity and attempting to call forth the humanity of the other. It is creative nonviolence, the most genuine way to love one's enemy.

- "At all times and in every nation, anyone who fears God and does what is right has been acceptable to him.[1] He has, however, willed to make women and men holy and to save them, not as individuals without any bond between them, but rather to make them into a people who might acknowledge him and serve him in holiness" (LG, 9).

---

1 Cf. Acts 10:35.

EIGHTH SUNDAY IN ORDINARY TIME
God Will Never Forget Us

ISAIAH 49:14–15 This reading follows the second of the four Songs of the Servant of the Lord in Isaiah and a prophecy of liberation (see Isaiah 42:1–4, 49:1–6, 50:4–9, 52:12—53:13). The prophecy (see Isaiah 49:8–13) promises the people: "In a time of favor I answer you, / on the day of salvation I help you" (49:8). It is a promise that God's will and God's people will prevail, with a reminder that the timing belongs to God, not to human beings. This section ends with the invitation to sing out and rejoice because the Lord comforts his people. Our reading today follows that promise and good news.

In this reading we meet Zion lamenting God's absence. The people see themselves as forsaken. What follows is God's motherly response. God is more than any human mother. Even if the human mother should forget, God will not forget the chosen people. In verse 16, we hear God say, "Upon the palms of my hands I have written your name." When one became a slave, they were often scarred or branded so that everyone would know to whom they belonged. Thus, the message here is that God, their Lord, belongs to them as a slave belongs to a master.

This reading encourages us to broaden our image of God. Do we need to dwell more on the image of God Isaiah gives us today, the God who will never forget us and who sends the Son to serve, to seek, and to find the lost? How often do we pray to that God of motherly tenderness? How often do we realize that, as St. Paul says, "If God is for us, who can be against us?" (Romans 8:31).

PSALM 62:2–3, 6–7, 8–9 (6A) In this psalm, a proclamation of the love of God, we have moved away from the image of God as a mother. Now God is our rock and stronghold. Nevertheless, this rock does not project a hard image, but rather a protective one. We proclaim God as our hope, our salvation, and our refuge. At the end of our prayer we return to a more human, and perhaps motherly, image: God is the one to whom we can pour out our hearts.

CONNECTIONS TO CHURCH TEACHING AND TRADITION

- "After the patriarchs, God formed Israel as his people by freeing them from slavery in Egypt. He established with them the covenant . . . so that they would recognize him and serve him as the one living and true God, the provident Father and just judge, and so that they would look for the promised Savior[1]" (CCC, 62).

- "We have come to believe in God's love: in these words the Christian can express the fundamental decision of his life. Being Christian is not the result of an ethical choice or a lofty idea, but the encounter with . . . a person, which gives life a new horizon and a decisive direction" (DCE, 1).

1 Cf. DV 3.

1 CORINTHIANS 4:1–5 Paul begins this section of the letter describing what he thinks the Christian self-concept should be: Christians should present themselves as servants of Christ and stewards of the mysteries of God. From there, Paul goes on to say that no one can rightly judge him or them. In fact, Paul cannot even judge himself. God is the only one who knows the depth of the human heart, and therefore God is the only one who can judge. The very good news at the end of the reading is that God will give praise to everyone.

MATTHEW 6:24–34 In this selection from the Gospel according to Matthew we have two seemingly unrelated teachings connected by the word *therefore*. The first, talking about serving more than one master, seemingly refers to the condition of slaves: they cannot serve a master and the master's enemy. The last sentence sums that up: you cannot serve God and "mammon," or material gain. We must set our priorities. What is the first thing that we seek? Is it wealth? Is it reputation? Is it fine food and drink, or fancy cars and homes? Or do we honestly choose the building up of God's Kingdom as our primary task as servants of the living God?

Jesus deepens the teaching in the rest of the reading by showing the futility of trying to assure our own security. Pointing to the birds and the flowers, he reminds his audience that worrying cannot add a single moment to their lifespan. He teaches that a focus on seeking material well-being is pagan. We need but seek God's Kingdom, as Matthew 6:33 says, and the rest will come in its turn.

This, of course, is not a divine insurance policy. We know that God's own Son was crucified, but we also know that God raised him from the dead. So, trust in God does not take away our legitimate responsibility or save us from all adversity, but it does tell us that no matter what happens, God will go through it with us and never forget us.

• "It is a grave duty of conscience not to cooperate, not even formally, in practices which, although permitted by civil legislation, are contrary to the Law of God. Such cooperation in fact can never be justified, not by invoking respect for the freedom of others nor by appealing to the fact that it is foreseen and required by civil law. No one can escape the moral responsibility for actions taken, and all will be judged by God himself based on this responsibility²" (CSDC, 399).

---

2 Cf. Rom 2:6; 14:12.

Ninth Sunday in Ordinary Time
Justified by Faith

DEUTERONOMY 11:18, 26–28, 32 Deuteronomy 11 is the finale of a homily Moses preached to introduce the Law. It reminds the Israelites that the law is not a set of ordinances, but a way of life. Here, as in three other places in the Pentateuch, the people are told to take the law to heart, to bind it to their wrist, and to place it between their eyes. That command led some Jews to don phylacteries, small boxes holding scripture quotations that are tied to the forehead and left arm, when they prayed. Clothing themselves with the Word reminded them to hold God's Law in their hearts. Moses tells his people that knowing the Law of God gives them responsibility for their own futures. If they allow the law to enlighten their hearts, they will be blessed. If they turn from it, they will bring curses upon themselves.

PSALM 31:2–3, 3–4, 17, 25 (3B) While this psalm is a lament, the verses we pray stress absolute trust in God. As we did last week, we use various images as we call on God.

Verse 17 reminds us that there is more to our relationship with God than deliverance. When we pray "let your face shine upon your servant" (v. 17), we ask God to be present, to look on us lovingly. That gaze will impel us to put the last verse into practice. It will become our second nature to encourage everyone we meet to hope in the Lord.

ROMANS 3:21–25, 28 When Paul wrote to the Romans, he was writing to a community he hoped to visit and from whom he hoped to get help for his planned missionary journey to Spain. Because it was a community that he had not founded, he did not know the Roman Christians well. What they did know was that there were great debates about what he taught about the law. One of the things Paul tries to clarify in this letter is his position on the law and God's justification.

Justification is a legal and relational term. In a theological sense, people are not justified by what they do, but rather because God justifies them by bestowing grace on them and declaring them righteous. As a result, they have allowed his judgment to have an effect on them. The relationship of justification begins with God, but requires a wholehearted human response.

CONNECTIONS TO CHURCH TEACHING AND TRADITION

- "Justification is the *most excellent work of God's love* made manifest in Christ Jesus and granted by the Holy Spirit" (CCC, 1994).

- "The first work of the grace of the Holy Spirit is *conversion*, effecting justification. . . . 'Justification is not only the remission of sins, but also the sanctification and renewal of the interior man'[1]" (CCC, 1989).

- "God's passionate love for his people—for humanity—is at the same time a forgiving love. It is so great that it turns God against himself, his love against his justice . . . so great is God's love for man that by becoming man he follows him even into death, and so reconciles justice and love" (DCE, 10).

- "When St. Paul speaks of Jesus . . . he means that in Christ's humanity 'God was in Christ reconciling the world to himself'[2]" (CCC, 433).

---

1 Matthew 4:17; Council of Trent (1547): DS 1528.

2 Romans 3:25; 2 Corinthians 5:19.

Paul teaches that everyone, Jews and Gentiles alike, have been deprived of God's glory as a result of sin. While there is nothing they can do to restore their grace, he who created them is free to restore it. That is what God did in Jesus. For Paul, the only way human persons can attain right relationship with God is by accepting what God has done for them in Jesus. That is justification by faith. While no one can attain justification on his or her own, being justified by God will manifest itself in concrete expressions of love of God and neighbor.

MATTHEW 7:21–27 At the end of the Sermon on the Mount, Jesus, like Moses before him, warns his listeners to take his words to heart. He presents a question of faith and works with an interesting twist. Jesus says that there will be many who call him by the right title and who prophesy, exorcise, and work miracles in his name whom he will not recognize in the end. Because this is the last section of the Sermon, when Jesus speaks of listening and acting on his words, he is referring to everything he had taught, beginning with the Beatitudes. He is warning his would-be followers that there is more to discipleship than dogmatically correct vocabulary and showy performances. In every age, there have been people who claimed to prophesy, to speak in the name of God, without being poor in spirit. There are many who struggle to rid society of its demons, to reform social or political life, but who have no concept of loving their enemies. So, too, people can perform mighty deeds, miracles of science or medicine, for their own self-aggrandizement, caring little or not at all for the people who need their services.

Jesus' message here is very close to Paul's teaching in Romans 3: one attains righteousness through faith in what God has done in Jesus. In Matthew, Jesus says that entry into the Kingdom will be granted to those whose lives are dedicated to God and doing his will. The strong foundation on which disciples begin is nothing more or less than love of God and gratitude for God's gifts. Building on that rock, their works will give true witness to the one they call Lord.

Tenth Sunday in Ordinary Time
Table of Outcasts

HOSEA 6:3–6 Hosea is a master of irony and understatement. He begins chapter 6 with what sounds like a corporate call to worship God. "God is for us," the people cry. "God will save us." But God is not pleased. The people want to offer service only with their lips, to observe the rituals, and then do whatever they want the rest of the week. They want God's help and protection, yet still spend money on military weaponry and political alliances, "just in case."

Hosea asks, when will they learn that it is not religious observance that God wants as much as obedience and faithfulness to God's ways? Hosea is clear. Our worship life and our daily lives are inexorably intertwined. Worship that does not influence our daily actions is not really worship at all, but empty forms. Daily lives that are not infused with the presence of God are hollow.

PSALM 50:1, 8, 12–13, 14–15 (23B) The psalmist echoes the sentiments of Hosea, even using some of Hosea's biting irony. In the psalm's opening verse, God summons the people before the divine judgment seat. The charge? A lack of sincerity in worship. Not only have the people been simply going through the motions of worship, but they have also imagined that doing so will protect them from God's displeasure. Again we find our worship and daily lives connected. God does not need our worship, but we need to worship. Indeed, our daily lives depend on it. It gives us perspective. It keeps us in touch with what is really important in life.

ROMANS 4:18–25 Paul concludes his discussion of justification by faith through grace. It is not an easy concept to grasp, so he uses an illustration. The patriarch Abraham, Paul says, was not a friend of God because he lived a saintly life. Abraham was justified in the sight of God because he showed faith. It was this faith alone, by the grace of God, that made it possible for Abraham to be "reckoned to him as righteousness."

Paul mentions two components to this faith: complete trust in God and heartfelt thanksgiving. When we think of Abraham, our attention is often so drawn to his trust in God that we tend to overlook the devotion to God that Paul also mentions. For Abraham, faith was not just being

CONNECTIONS TO CHURCH TEACHING AND TRADITION

- God offers mercy and forgiveness to all and calls all to repentance (CCC, 210–211).

- Through Jesus' example, we see the importance of love of neighbor and compassion for all, showing mercy toward sinners, and associating without regard to social convention (CCC, 589).

- Liturgy is the experience of ritual and Scripture proclaimed and the experience of Christ's action in the lives of the people (NDC, 33).

willing to follow God in his daily life, it also meant taking time to praise and worship the God he followed. According to Paul, it all flowed together.

Paul's point, however, is not simply to extol Abraham and his faith. Paul has even better news. Because of Christ, the faith that made Abraham righteous in God's sight is available to anyone. That is why Christ came, Paul says. That is why Christ died and was raised: to make possible for all of us the kind of trusting, thankful faith that so distinguished Abraham, not only when we feel especially close to God in worship but also in our daily lives.

MATTHEW 9:9–13 Matthew offers us two vignettes from Jesus' ministry in Galilee. Jesus sees a tax collector (whom Matthew does not name) and invites the man to follow him. Like James and John, the tax collector shows no hesitation; he follows Jesus immediately. Next, we find Jesus at dinner, perhaps in Matthew's own home. The friends he has invited are not the kind of people good religious folk like the Pharisees choose to associate with. Jesus eats with them anyway. After all, is not this what Hosea said God wants?

Jesus has come to show mercy, not judgment. He has come to those who need him most. He has even come to the Pharisees, but because they do not realize their own need, they do not recognize that his open invitation includes them.

The inclusive way of Jesus is not an easy one. It not only goes against human nature, but it can also open us up to criticism. Learning to be like Jesus takes practice, and one place we practice this is in worship. Worship gives us an opportunity to interact with many people with whom we might not otherwise interact. It also gives us a chance to practice the open hospitality demonstrated by Jesus. How is everyone welcome in worship? What about people who use wheelchairs? Have hearing problems? Cannot read? Have been in prison and are trying to get their lives back together? By being inclusive in the worshiping assemblies of God's people, we, like Jesus, show in one time and place what God intends for all times and places.

A Holy Nation

EXODUS 19:2–6A God calls Moses and the Israelites to Mount Sinai, the mountain where God was first revealed to Moses in the burning bush (3:1, there called "Horeb"). On the mountain, Moses was reminded that God brought them out of slavery in Egypt. On Sinai, God entered a covenant with the people, a special relationship by which they became God's people. God previously made covenants with the human race through Noah (Genesis 9:9) and to Abraham and his descendants (Genesis 15:18).

In the covenant with Abraham, God unilaterally promised him posterity and the possession of the land. On Sinai, God goes further by making demands of the people. If the people obey God's voice and keep the covenant, they would be God's "treasured possession" (Exodus 19:5b). When Moses summons the people and tells them the words God pronounced, Israel replies, "Everything that the LORD has spoken we will do" (v. 8a; the details of the covenant and the Ten Commandments are enumerated in chapter 20). The people are told to prepare themselves for God's revelation. A dense cloud, thunder and lightning, smoke, fire, and an earthquake (a theophany, or divine manifestation in nature) herald God's presence. These awesome forces emphasized the sacredness of the moment. God's people were not only chosen, but they were also formed by God to be "a priestly kingdom and a holy nation" (v. 6a).

PSALM 100:1–2, 3, 5 (3C) Psalm 100 is among the shortest in the Psalter. The people probably sang it while they made solemn entrance through the gates of the Jerusalem Temple and into the courts to offer up sacrifice to God. The people are invited to serve God "with gladness" (v. 2a) and rejoice in God's presence. The psalmist reminds the people that they are not only God's creatures, but they are also God's Chosen People, the flock that God shepherds. The worshipers are exhorted to come before God with thanksgiving and praise for God's goodness and care. God's love is eternal; God's faithfulness is without end.

ROMANS 5:6–11 Paul writes to the Roman Christian community, explaining that Jesus Christ dying for the human race was proof of God's love. Paul says it would be hard enough to convince someone to die for a just person or for

CONNECTIONS TO CHURCH TEACHING AND TRADITION

- The Church has a mission, and we must do our best to fulfill it: we must work for the salvation of all (AG, 1, 2, 5, 7–9, 15; GS, 40–43; CCC, 849–856).

- A most important aspect of our mission is the reconciliation of the world with God and healing rifts among people (LG, 8, 11, 22, 40; CCC, 1427–1449).

- Everyone is called to enter the kingdom of heaven, even the poor and the lowly (CCC, 543–544), so Jesus enlisted the help of others for his ministry (CCC, 858).

some great principle. It might be possible for individuals to have such great love for their friends that they would lay down their lives for them. But Jesus Christ died for humanity when they were still sinners and in a state of alienation from God. Through Jesus, the status of sinners was changed, and they were put into a right relationship with God. This change of status is called justification, the saving process by which people are made right with God through Christ's Death on the Cross. The saving process goes on through sanctification; that is, God's grace whereby sinful men and women are made God's holy people. Jesus did not come to change God's wrathful attitude toward the human race; he came to show what was always there, that through God's love, people have received reconciliation and salvation.

MATTHEW 9:36—10:8 When Jesus healed a possessed mute (9:32–33), the last miracle in a series of them in Matthew's Gospel (chapters 8–9), the people were in awe at this unprecedented event. Everywhere Jesus went, in the towns, villages, and synagogues, the good news of the kingdom was ushered in through Jesus' words and works. Many responded to these miracles with faith, but some refused to believe in him. The religious leaders, who should have welcomed the appearance of God's reign, rejected Jesus' works, claiming they came from the evil one. Jesus was moved with compassion because the people were like "sheep without a shepherd" (9:36). The Greek word Matthew uses for "compassion," *splagchnizomai*, is formed from the word that means "the bowels." It describes the depths of human feeling. The people longed for God, and the religious leaders had nothing to offer them. Jesus asks his disciples to pray that the "Lord of the harvest" (v. 38) would send out more laborers to care for God's people. The divine shepherd and harvest master needed human cooperation. Jesus chose twelve ordinary men to be his apostles. The word *apostle* literally means one who is "sent out" (10:5). Those Jesus called to share his authority and mission had no wealth, no special education, no social standing. Yet Jesus sent them forth to announce God's reign to the "lost sheep of the house of Israel" (v. 6). The miracles that accompanied their proclamation were signs of God's presence in them. The gift that they received was to be shared freely with others.

Twelfth Sunday in Ordinary Time
Do Not Be Afraid

JEREMIAH 20:10–13 Jeremiah, one of the four major prophets in the Old Testament, was chosen by God when he was very young, and he served faithfully for five decades. When Jeremiah received his call, Judah was under Assyrian domination; the people had fallen into the worship of pagan gods; the Temple was in disrepair; the Law of Moses was disregarded. Jeremiah's prophetic call came in the year 626 BC, on the eve of the religious reform of King Josiah. Unfortunately, Josiah died in a military campaign in 609 BC, and the reforms were never fully realized. During the last half of Jeremiah's career, the Assyrian empire collapsed and Babylon became the supreme power, which eventually led to the destruction of Jerusalem and the Exile of God's people in 587 BC. Chapter 20 of Jeremiah contains his confessions, his inner struggle with his vocation, and his complaints for the persecution that he suffered on behalf of God. Despite his lamentation, he ends with praise: "Sing to the LORD; praise the LORD! For he has delivered the life of the needy from the hands of evildoers" (v. 13).

PSALM 69:8–10, 14, 17, 33–35 (14C) Psalm 69 is a lament. The psalmist was faithful to God, and ardent zeal for the Temple of God had consumed him. Nevertheless, the psalmist suffered shame and dishonor. He became a "stranger" to his own "kindred," and an alien to his "mother's children" (v. 8). The scorn of those who insulted God fell on him. Brokenhearted and in despair, he "looked for pity, but there was none; and for comforters, but I found none" (v. 20). Although the psalmist expresses intense misery, he ends on a note of hope, a declaration of praise and confidence in God's ability to save: "The LORD hears the needy, and does not despise his own that are in bonds" (v. 33).

ROMANS 5:12–15 The Easter Proclamation (Exsultet) proclaims Adam's sin as a "happy fault" that led to the redemption of the human race in Jesus Christ, which far outweighed what was lost in the fall. Paul explained that through Adam's sin, all people were alienated from God. Yet, by the righteousness of Jesus Christ, all were restored to a right relationship with God. For just as in Adam all die, so also all shall live in Christ. To understand Paul's thought, it is necessary to recognize the Jewish self-understanding of

CONNECTIONS TO CHURCH TEACHING AND TRADITION

- God alone rescues us (CCC, 169).
- The prophets heard God's call to repentance and faithfulness. They prepared for the intervention of God in human history (CCC, 2584).
- The Church is the instrument of God's works, an assistant in God's work of salvation (CCC, 737, 778).
- The Church's deepest vocation is to live as communion. The Church is a community (LG, 51; CCC, 959), even a family.

the time. The Jewish people did not think of themselves as individuals, but as part of a family, a clan, or a nation. Because of human solidarity, all people actually sinned in Adam. Adam's sin was not one person's sin but the sin of all. Thus, through one person, Adam, death entered the world. Likewise, through one person, Jesus Christ, all have a share in his resurrection of the dead. Paul emphasized that this gift of eternal life is a free gift that sinful humanity did not deserve. Through God's mercy, the free gift of righteousness was given "in the grace of the one man, Jesus Christ" (v. 15).

MATTHEW 10:26–33 Jesus came as the full revelation of God to the world, but many were obstinate and refused to believe the truth of his words. Despite the darkness of unbelief, light came through the proclamation of Jesus' faithful apostles. Jesus warned them, however, that just as they shared his mission of proclaiming God's reign, they would also share in his Passion. Students were not above their teachers, and slaves could not outrank their masters (v. 24). Jesus' disciples would be despised by their fellow Jews and rejected by members of their own families. When they were brought to trial for their faith, they should not be concerned about how they would defend them selves. The Holy Spirit would inspire them to be faithful witnesses (v. 19). Fear of persecution and death should not deter them from boldly speaking the message they received. They should not fear those who could kill them; a greater peril would be to lose their immortal souls. The one they should fear is the evil one who could lead them to eternal destruction.

Jesus encouraged his followers by reminding them of their worth before God. If God cared for the tiny sparrows that were sold in the Temple for sacrifice, how much more valued were God's children? Despite the coming darkness and opposition, the Twelve must be fearless in proclaiming the light and truth of the Gospel. If they are faithful in their task, Jesus would defend them on the Day of Judgment.

THIRTEENTH SUNDAY IN ORDINARY TIME
Give without Expectation

2 KINGS 4:8–11, 14–16A The books of 1 and 2 Kings span the four-hundred-year history of Israel, from the royal dynasty of David's son Solomon to the division of the united kingdom and the destruction of the Temple in 587 BC. It chronicles the reigns of incompetent and ruthless kings whose policies led to the Exile, and the religious reforms of good kings, Hezekiah and Josiah. The author's purpose was not so much to write a history as to explain why things happened as they did. The author wanted to instill faith in those who saw the last king in David's line defeated and deported to Babylon. The books of Kings report the prophetic careers of Elijah and his disciple, Elisha, who continued the work of the great prophet by proclaiming God's faithfulness to the covenant. Elisha's encounter with the Shunammite is the story of a prominent woman who was interested in promoting the work of God, as shown in the hospitality she provided for the prophet without expecting anything in return. In due time, the woman was rewarded for her service. She conceived and bore a son as Elisha promised.

PSALM 89:2–3, 16–17, 18–19 (2A) Psalm 89 begins with a proclamation of God's "steadfast love" and "faithfulness" (v. 1). In the covenant made with David, God promises, "I will establish your descendants forever, and build your throne for all generations" (89:4; see also 2 Samuel 7:16). In Psalm 89:38, the mood changes radically. God's people were in anguish, their country was in ruin, and the king was removed from the throne and deported to Babylon. Had God renounced the covenant with David and forgotten the promise made to him? The psalmist proclaims that God did not abandon the people. God would fulfill the promises made to them and restore them to their land. In Jesus Christ, the "firstborn" son (v. 27), the descendant of David would rule forever.

ROMANS 6:3–4, 8–11 In his letter to Roman Christians, Paul carried on an argument against an imaginary opponent. He wanted to help them know that God forgave sins, but he also wanted them to know something more important. In Baptism, all sins are remitted because God cannot punish sins committed before a person is born. Paul went

CONNECTIONS TO CHURCH TEACHING AND TRADITION

- Christian charity should be genuine, and hospitality should be practiced (CCC, 1971). God rewards those who are patient in need and constant in prayer.

- Through Baptism, we enter the life, Death, and Resurrection of Jesus (CCC, 1213).

- Jesus calls us to conversion through Baptism. Through God's mercy and love, we continue the process of conversion (CCC, 1427–1428).

on to explain what happens in baptism. The person is "dead to sin and alive to God in Christ Jesus" (v. 11). In the early Church, Christian converts often came from pagan roots. They had to make a decision that meant leaving their former lives behind and beginning life all over again. When they were immersed in the baptismal font, the water closed over them, and it was like being buried. When they emerged from the water, it was like rising from the grave. They were not only united with Christ's Death, but also his Resurrection. The Church expresses this new life in Christ as sanctifying grace. Through Baptism, Christians are joined to Christ, and the life of God is infused in them, a gift that they must continue to live by faith.

MATTHEW 10:37–42 As opposition to Jesus' message grew, he exhorted his disciples to have courage under persecution. Jesus knew that not everyone would accept the Gospel his followers proclaimed. Even members of their families might be their adversaries. In Jesus' time, one of the beliefs concerning the "day of the LORD," when God would break into history through the coming of the Messiah, was that a division would occur among families. Jesus preached a message of total renunciation. His disciples must be willing to sacrifice everything for the sake of the Kingdom. Nothing or no one must deter them from their dedication to Christ and his mission. To encounter Jesus demands a choice: to accept him or to reject him. Those who deny Jesus to save their earthly lives risk losing eternal salvation. Those who choose this difficult path can be sure that they will share Jesus' destiny of persecution and suffering. Those who wish to follow in Jesus' footsteps must be willing to put the Gospel before all else, even their own lives. Whoever refuses to "take up the cross" and follow him was "not worthy" of being his disciples (v. 38). Like the prophets of old, they must be prepared to suffer for speaking God's Word. Jesus' disciples were Christian "prophets" who spoke God's saving message of the New Covenant. Whoever offered them hospitality received Jesus himself and God who sent him. They will be rewarded for their kindness to God's messengers.

FOURTEENTH SUNDAY IN ORDINARY TIME
Jesus Reveals the Mysteries of God's Kingdom

ZECHARIAH 9:9–10 Zechariah encourages Jerusalem to rejoice as he pronounces the coming of a future king who will be humble in appearance and demeanor. Instead of parading on a war horse, the king will ride an ass to demonstrate his humble reliance on God as the source of the king's victory and rule. In establishing his peaceful kingdom, the king will banish all instruments of war—namely the chariot, the war horse, and the bow. Relying on God's power and help, the king will proclaim peace to all the nations, thus becoming the source of God's peace and blessing for all people.

All four evangelists use this passage as the backdrop to Jesus' entrance into Jerusalem on Palm Sunday. Jesus' disciples linked Zechariah's vision of a humble king establishing peace for all to their understanding of Jesus' mission and ministry. For his followers, Jesus is the humble king who is the source of God's wisdom, blessings, and peace for all.

PSALM 145:1–2, 8–9, 10–11, 13–14 (SEE 1) The psalmist affirms his desire to praise God's name always and everywhere. The desire stems from the psalmist's experience of God, the Lord and king, as gracious and merciful, slow to anger, of great kindness, and always good and compassionate toward all. This creedal affirmation by Israel grounds the Jewish scriptures' understanding of God and is the basis for Jewish worship and praise.

God's love and fidelity lasts forever, is never revoked, and is all-inclusive. The repeated use of the word *all* stresses this point emphatically. God clearly manifests his love, power, and justice in his care and concern for all who are falling or bowed down. Such works are a clear manifestation of God's Kingdom and might. The all-powerful God loves and cares for all, most especially the weak and powerless. Let all praise forever the name of our king and God.

ROMANS 8:9, 11–13 Paul offers all humanity the choice of two ways or paths of living, that of the flesh or that of the spirit. Both stem from the choice we make to live either closed to God (the flesh) or open and attuned to God (the spirit). In Christ, all have been given the Spirit of God, who raised Jesus from the dead. The Spirit is always life-giving,

CONNECTIONS TO CHURCH TEACHING AND TRADITION

- "Jesus confesses the Father, acknowledges, and blesses him because he has hidden the mysteries of the Kingdom from those who think themselves learned and has revealed them to infants, the poor of the Beatitudes[1]" (CCC, 2603).

- "From the beginning, Jesus associated his disciples with his own life, revealed the mystery of the Kingdom to them, and gave them a share in his mission, joy, and sufferings[2]" (CCC, 787).

- "No one is without a family in this world: the Church is a home and family for everyone, especially those who 'labor and are heavy laden'" (FC, 85).

- "To carry out the will of the Father, Christ inaugurated the kingdom of heaven on earth and revealed his mystery to us" (LG, 3).

---

1 Cf. Matthew 11:25–27 and Luke 10:21–23.

2 Cf. Mark 1:16–20; 3:13–19; Matthew 13:10–17; Luke 10:17–20; 22:28–30.

bringing new meaning, significance, and life out of meaninglessness and death.

If we choose to cooperate with the Spirit and attune ourselves to God's ways and wisdom, then we, too, will always be with God, no matter what happens to us, including death. If, however, we choose not to cooperate with the Spirit of God, then we close ourselves off from God and life. Paul presents two paths in our relationship with God. What we choose will determine whether our lives will end in death or in life forever with God.

MATTHEW 11:25–30 In this passage, Matthew recounts Jesus' various affirmations about himself, both in his relationship to God and to his followers. The passage centers on what wisdom is and where it can be found. Matthew contrasts the wisdom found among the "wise and learned," symbolized by the scribes and Pharisees, with the wisdom that Jesus reveals to his followers, the "little ones." Jesus begins by praising God for revealing the mysteries of the Kingdom to the "little ones," and not to the wise and learned who think they know and therefore are not open to other sources of wisdom. Jesus is the source of God's wisdom because of the special relationship that Jesus has with the Father. That special relationship enables Jesus to know the Father, and in return, the fullness of God is revealed in Jesus. Anyone who is open to the person and wisdom that Jesus shares will also come to know God.

The last few verses are unique to the Gospel according to Matthew, which addresses issues important to his community. The invitation to come to know Jesus, the wisdom of God, is universal, offered to all who are willing to learn from him and follow through on the demands of discipleship. The *yoke* of discipleship calls one to live in humility and meekness, attuned to God and concerned for the other. Such a lifestyle is in contrast to the Pharisaic *yoke* that shackled and burdened people with many regulations but not much wisdom.

Jesus, the Wisdom of God, offers all, not just Jews, a yoke that is free, liberating, easy, restful, and ultimately life-giving. Humility, openness, and a willingness to enter into relationship with God in and through the person of Jesus is the key to knowing the mysteries of God's Kingdom.

- "In preaching the gospel to the nations they will proclaim with confidence the mystery of Christ whose legates they are." (AG, 24).

Fertile Ground for God's Word

ISAIAH 55:10–11 Isaiah provides an extended metaphor for the Word of God. Comparing the word of God to the rain and snow, Isaiah indicates several correlations that enable us to understand the richness of God's Word. Rain and snow are sent by God to accomplish their purpose on earth. They provide water to the ground, making it fertile and providing food for all God's creatures. Once they have accomplished their purpose, the rain and snow return to God, having fully nourished and cared for God's creation. So, too, is God's Word. It originates from God, sent to accomplish the task of attuning all to God's wishes, desires, and intentions. God ensures that it will accomplish its purpose. God's Word brings fertility, meaning, and significance to all of life. God assures us that when we attune ourselves to his Word, the Word will nourish and satisfy all our hungers.

PSALM 65:10, 11, 12–13, 14 (LUKE 8:8) While the refrain picks up the theme of the Gospel parable of the sower, the rest of the psalm itself focuses on God's rich blessing, especially during harvest time. God's blessing upon an abundant harvest is the possible backdrop to this hymn of praise and thanksgiving to God.

Picking up on the fertility of the ground brought about by the rain and snow from the First Reading, the psalm praises and thanks God for his blessing to the people exemplified by an abundant harvest. The rains that God sends provide the necessary conditions that enrich the earth for continued fertility and new life. As all creation cooperates with God, not only are humans sustained, but there also is an abundance of flocks and food to sustain all creation. The only response from humans and the rest of creation is to "shout and sing for joy" (v. 14).

ROMANS 8:18–23 Paul addresses the suffering that we experience in life, placing it within the context of future hope manifested in the Risen Lord. Paul uses Genesis as a backdrop to explain that humans suffer as a result of their refusal to attune themselves to God. In refusing to attend to God, humans not only made things more difficult for themselves, but they also brought all of creation down with them.

CONNECTIONS TO CHURCH TEACHING AND TRADITION

- "The Decalogue, the Sermon on the Mount, and the apostolic catechesis describe for us the paths that lead to the Kingdom of heaven. Sustained by the grace of the Holy Spirit, we tread them, step by step, by everyday acts. By the working of the Word of Christ, we slowly bear fruit in the Church to the glory of God!" (CCC, 1724).

- "Modern civilization itself, though not of its very nature but because it is too engrossed in the concerns of this world, can often make it harder to approach God" (GS, 19).

---

1 Cf. the parable of the sower: Matthew 13:3–23.

All nonhuman creation is unwillingly subject to futility and frustration. Because of human sin, creation cannot accomplish the purpose for which it was created—to be the means through which humans glorify and give praise to God. According to Paul, God sent Jesus to redeem and save us and all of creation. In the Risen Lord, we have the assurance of salvation and redemption. This hope, however, is still in its seedling stage. The time is coming when that hope will fully bloom. All of creation awaits this moment. Paul places the world's present sufferings in this context, as a clear indication that the long-awaited redemption is close at hand. We, along with all of creation, groan as in labor pains for the fulfillment of God's saving action, already made real in the Risen Lord.

MATTHEW 13:1–23 OR 13:1–9 Matthew 13 is a series of seven parables on the Kingdom of Heaven, situated at the center of the Gospel. The parable of the sower, which begins this chapter, is not so much focused on the sower or the seed but rather on different kinds of soil and their receptivity. Matthew is addressing a key concern of his Christian-Jewish community; namely, why some Jews accepted Jesus and other Jews rejected him and his message of the Kingdom. The parable is an attempt to explore this mystery.

In the parable, Jesus explains that some are influenced by the evil one, while others are shallow; some are too concerned with worldly affairs, while others seek riches. Those who are open and attuned to Jesus' message grow in rich soil that produces abundant fruit.

The mystery concerning acceptance or rejection of Jesus' message centers on our willingness to open ourselves to how God is present and acting in the world. It means developing ears that listen attentively and a mind that discerns thoughtfully. With God's help, this kind of soil will produce abundant fruit.

▪ "Jesus' invitation to enter his kingdom comes in the form of *parables*, a characteristic feature of his teaching.[2] Through his parables he invites people to the feast of the kingdom, but he also asks for a radical choice: to gain the kingdom, one must give everything.[3] Words are not enough; deeds are required.[4] The parables are like mirrors for man: will he be hard soil or good earth for the word?[5]" (CCC, 546).

---

2 Cf. Mark 4:33–34.
3 Cf. Matthew 13:44–45; 22:1–14.
4 Cf. Matthew 21:28–32.
5 Cf. Matthew 13:3–9.

SIXTEENTH SUNDAY IN ORDINARY TIME
The Lord Our Strength

WISDOM 12:13, 16–19 Wisdom, a late Old Testament book composed in Greek, is accepted by Catholics as inspired but is not included in either Jewish or Protestant canons. In addressing God, this passage focuses on God's supreme might and power over all things. The community asserts that "mastery over all things" enables God to be "lenient to all" (v. 16). As "master of might" God judges "with clemency, and with much lenience" (v. 18). God's power on behalf of the people has been clearly manifested in Israel's past. God's liberating power exercised on behalf of poor and oppressed slaves is the ground for hope in a God believed to hold supreme power over all. By modeling how power is to be exercised, God teaches people "that those who are just must be kind" (v. 19). God is our strength and hope because we know that whenever God's might is at work, it is always exercised with kindness, leniency, and forgiveness. Whenever we experience God's gracious and merciful touch, we experience the manner in which true power is to be exercised.

PSALM 86:5–6, 9–10, 15–16 (5A) This lament psalm manifests great trust and confidence in God who is always "good and forgiving" toward all (v. 5). Such trust is engendered through God's "kindness to all who call upon [him]" (v. 5). *Kindness* is a translation of the Hebrew word *hesed*, meaning faithful, enduring covenant love. The psalmist's confidence in God's goodness and mercy comes out of God's covenant love relationship. This covenant relationship enables the psalmist to ask God to "hearken . . . and attend to the sound of [the psalmist's] pleading" (v. 6). Because God has done great deeds on behalf of the people, not only do the people trust in God's help, but all the nations come to acknowledge and praise God. The last stanza is a traditional summary credo associated with the people's experience of God at the Exodus. Affirming key covenant attributes, the credo identifies God as "merciful and gracious, / slow to anger, abounding in kindness and fidelity" (v. 15). This strong affirmation of God's goodness and mercy propels the psalmist to ask God for mercy and for strength whenever weakness tends to overwhelm. God is our true source of strength, always ready to reach out, reconcile, and forgive.

CONNECTIONS TO CHURCH TEACHING AND TRADITION

- "Only faith can embrace the mysterious ways of God's almighty power. This faith glories in its weaknesses in order to draw to itself Christ's power[1]" (CCC, 273).

- "God is the *Father* Almighty, whose fatherhood and power shed light on one another: God reveals his fatherly omnipotence by the way he takes care of our needs; by the filial adoption that he gives us . . . finally by his infinite mercy, for he displays his power at its height by freely forgiving sins" (CCC, 270).

- "The Christian . . . should strive by works of mercy and charity, as well as by prayer and the various practices of penance, to put off completely the 'old man' and to put on the 'new man'[2]" (CCC, 1473).

---

1 Cf. 2 Corinthians 12:9; Philippians 4:13.

2 Ephesians 4:22, 24.

ROMANS 8:26–27 Continuing the theme of Psalm 86, Paul asserts that, as human beings, we are weak and fallible, resulting in our inability to pray "as we ought" (v. 26). We are prone to distraction, clouded motivations, desires and needs that pull us in various directions, and other human weaknesses. Being linked to Christ through our baptismal call, however, we are gifted with the Spirit who intercedes for us "with inexpressible groanings" (v. 26). God's Spirit comes to our aid by identifying with our weakness and helping us express to God what we often find inexpressible.

God, intimately knowing us as "the one who searches hearts" (v. 27), also intimately knows the Spirit's intention and purpose. The Spirit helps us get in touch with God's will, interceding for us even when we do not know what or how to ask. God's gracious love and mercy toward us gifts us from within with God's very presence and strength, helping and guiding us to draw more closely to God and to align ourselves with God's will. God's gracious and healing touch is ours, and we experience it every time we reach out to God in prayer.

MATTHEW 13:24–43 OR 13:24–30 Three parables are presented in this passage, highlighting the parable of the weeds and the wheat that begins and ends this selection. The parable zeroes in on the master as God. Because we are created with freedom, some will choose God and some will not. How does God deal with this reality?

Matthew's Jesus stresses that God is just and allows the wicked to live along with the good till the time of final judgment, when justice will reign. But from the psalm we learn that those exercising justice must also be kind. Therefore, God allows the wicked time to repent and turn back. Knowing our weakness, God give us time to reach out in freedom and experience God's gracious kindness and healing touch. From the Romans passage, we know that God gifts us with the Spirit who aids us in our weakness, especially when we are challenged to conform ourselves to God's will. Ultimately, for Matthew, God is good and merciful, giving us the time we need to repent and turn back. In our weakness, God is our strength and our help.

SEVENTEENTH SUNDAY IN ORDINARY TIME
An Understanding Heart

1 KINGS 3:5, 7–12 Solomon's reputation for wisdom has its source in this text. In the context of a dream, God invites Solomon, David's son and designated successor, to ask for anything and God would grant it. God's generous offer manifests God's graciousness toward the king and the people. Solomon asks for "an understanding heart to judge [God's] people and to distinguish right from wrong" (v. 9). Since reason and intellect were seen as residing in the heart in his time, Solomon asks God for a pastoral and discerning mind. His request is based on an awareness of his own inexperience, as well as the vast size of the people he is to govern.

Since Solomon has chosen well, showing concern only for God and the people, God showers Solomon not only with great wisdom but with all other good gifts besides. In biblical wisdom tradition, seeking wisdom is life's best calling, bringing with it all other goods. Such seeking aligns us with God's purposes and desires.

PSALM 119:57, 72, 76–77, 127–128, 129–130 (97A) Psalm 119, the longest psalm, is an acrostic wisdom psalm extolling the benefits of knowing God's law and relishing its delights. God's law brings with it wisdom, light, happiness, joy, peace, and direction on living rightly. God's law is not perceived as oppressive legalism, but as the gracious path that God provides. The refrain sums up well the attitude that wisdom tradition attributes to the law, "Lord, I love your commands" (v. 97a).

God's law or wisdom is more precious to the psalmist than all the world's riches. The law has its source in God's enduring covenant love, which brings comfort and delight. Love of the law and attentiveness to its demands provide sure guidance for moving forward on true paths and away from falsehood. The Lord's decrees are wonderful, shedding "light, / giving understanding to the simple" (v. 130). If one desires to gain an understanding heart, attentiveness to God's law is the surest path to gaining wisdom and establishing right relationship with all.

ROMANS 8:28–30 These beloved verses surface theological themes often misinterpreted and misused by Christians. With complete trust in God's gracious love, Paul affirms that "all things work for good for those who love God" (v. 28).

CONNECTIONS TO CHURCH TEACHING AND TRADITION

- "God has not willed to reserve to himself all exercise of power. He entrusts to every creature the functions it is capable of performing, according to the capacities of its own nature. This mode of governance ought to be followed in social life. The way God acts in governing the world, which bears witness to such great regard for human freedom, should inspire the wisdom of those who govern human communities" (CCC, 1884).

- "Human society can be neither well-ordered nor prosperous without the presence of those who, invested with legal authority, preserve its institutions and do all that is necessary to sponsor actively the interests of its members" (PT, 46).

Paul is not saying that those who love God will never have a hard time in life. Rather, Paul insists that no matter what happens in life, even in life's worst difficulties and challenges, God's love is always there, transforming times of trouble into events that are ultimately life giving.

For Paul, God's loving plan for creation existed from the beginning. God activated that plan by means of covenant love relationship and by ultimately sending Christ, the "firstborn among many brothers and sisters" (v. 29). In Christ, God's fullest outflow of love is realized as God calls all humanity to be conformed to Christ's image. This does not mean that all have to become Christian, but rather that all are to conform to the values and lifestyle that Christ modeled and manifested. In so doing, all are "justified," or saved, and at the end time, all will be "glorified" (v. 30). For Paul, God's loving plan for all humanity has been operative from the beginning to the end of time.

MATTHEW 13:44–52 OR 13:44–46 In this text, two of the three parables concerning the Kingdom of Heaven are similar while the third recalls the parable of the wheat and weeds from last Sunday. The parables of finding treasure buried in a field and a merchant seeking and finding a pearl of great price underscore the great value of being part of God's Kingdom. One is willing to sacrifice all for its sake. As we learn from Solomon and Psalm 119, gaining this wisdom is more valuable than riches.

The parable of the net catching various fish that have to be sorted once brought on board describes the diversity of God's Kingdom, along with its mixture of both good and bad. The end time judgment will sort through the differences. In the meantime, all are called and given time to conform themselves to the image of Christ, as Paul asserts in the Second Reading. The passage ends with the disciples' claim that they have understood all that Jesus has instructed them about the Kingdom of Heaven. Jesus, praising their response, confirms their role as scribes or teachers in the Kingdom of Heaven. Jesus' teaching, which they are to carry on, is a deeper reflection on and a newer understanding of the wisdom that they have inherited. Both new and old are to be used in carrying on Jesus' mission and ministry.

▪ "Pope St. Clement of Rome provides the Church's most ancient prayer for political authorities:[1] '. . . Direct, Lord, their counsel, following what is pleasing and acceptable in your sight, so that by exercising with devotion and peace and gentleness the power that you have given to them, they may find favor with you'[2]" (CCC, 1900).

---

1 Cf. as early as 1 Timothy 2:1–2.

2 St. Clement of Rome, Ad Cor. 61: SCh 167, 198–200.

Eighteenth Sunday in Ordinary Time
The Hand of the Lord Feeds Us

ISAIAH 55:1–3 As the Babylonian exile draws to a close, Isaiah invites the people to turn once again to God, who ultimately satisfies all our needs. The exile caused a rupture between God and the people, primarily owing to their lack of fidelity to the covenant relationship. Isaiah imagines God as a street vendor inviting all, both rich and poor, to a free banquet of rich food, water, grain, wine, and milk—the best of the land's bounty. Similar to the Wisdom Woman of the Book of Proverbs, God invites all to focus on what truly nourishes, as opposed to spending money on what does not. God provides not only for our material needs but also provides us with the nourishment that satisfies all our hungers. God invites the people to "listen, that you may have life" (v. 3). Isaiah wants people to know that ultimate nourishment comes from God's desire to "renew with [them] the everlasting covenant, / the benefits assured to David" (v. 3). God's covenant love is better than any riches we can imagine. All are invited to pay attention to what truly nourishes and to know that God desires nothing better than to provide us with such rich fare.

PSALM 145:8–9, 15–16, 17–18 (SEE 16) Psalm 145 is an alphabetic poem, with each verse beginning with a successive letter of the alphabet. The verses chosen for the responsorial today focus on God's care and desire to satisfy the "desire of every living thing." The first stanza is a creedal formula identifying God as "gracious and merciful, / slow to anger and of great kindness / . . . good to all / and compassionate toward all" (vv. 8–9). God's generous covenant love toward all engenders hope that God will provide for all our needs, both with food that nourishes and all that satisfies. The psalm emphasizes that God's love is for all and provides for all our needs. We believe God is "just . . . and holy" in all things (v. 17). God's right relationship with all living things assures the psalmist that the Lord is "near to all who call upon him" (v. 18). Because of God's loving relationship with us, best articulated in the Person of Jesus, we can boldly sing the response: "The hand of the Lord feeds us."

ROMANS 8:35, 37–39 For Paul, God's ultimate expression of covenant love and fidelity established with all creation is fully manifested in Christ Jesus. In Christ's suffering,

CONNECTIONS TO CHURCH TEACHING AND TRADITION

- "The miracles of the multiplication of the loaves, when the Lord says the blessing, breaks and distributes the loaves through his disciples to feed the multitude, prefigure the superabundance of this unique bread of his Eucharist'" (CCC, 1335).

- "At the heart of the Eucharistic celebration are the bread and wine that, by the words of Christ and the invocation of the Holy Spirit, become Christ's Body and Blood. . . . The signs of bread and wine . . . signify the goodness of creation. Thus in the Offertory we give thanks to the Creator for bread and wine,[2] fruit of the 'work of human hands,' but above all as 'fruit of the earth' and 'of the vine'—gifts of the Creator[3]" (CCC, 1333).

---

1 Cf. Matthew 14:13–21; 15:32–39.

2 Cf. Psalm 104:13–15.

3 Genesis 14:18; cf. *Roman Missal*, EP I (Roman Canon) 95.

Death, and Resurrection, God has bonded with us so completely that nothing can ever separate us from his love. This strong belief ruled Paul's life and, in this powerful passage from Romans, Paul desires that we be ruled by the same conviction.

Paul's Jewish upbringing would have stressed that calamities are a result of our sinfulness, separating us from God. He counters that theological tradition with the conviction that, in Christ, hardships are not God's punishment for sinfulness. Rather, in Christ, our suffering links with his suffering, bringing us into closer relationship with our life-giving God. In all these things, Paul is convinced that we "conquer overwhelmingly through him who loved us" (v. 37). In Christ, we become so united with God that neither hardships nor any power here, above, or below can ever separate us "from the love of God in Christ Jesus" (v. 39).

MATTHEW 14:13–21 The multiplication of loaves and fishes appears in all four accounts of the Gospel. All stress God's gracious love manifested in Christ as he reaches out to heal and nourish God's people. By situating Jesus and the crowd in a deserted place, Matthew is referencing God's feeding of the Israelites with manna during their desert sojourn. Seeing the crowd, Jesus is "moved with pity" (v. 14), leading him to cure the sick. As evening approaches, the disciples want to dismiss the crowd, but Jesus insists that they give them food. All they have is five loaves and two fish. Jesus asks for them, blesses them, breaks them, and gives them to the disciples to distribute. After "five thousand men, not counting women and children" are fed, the disciples pick up twelve baskets of leftover food (v. 21). Such abundance is a clear manifestation of God's love, and a sure sign that in Jesus, the Messiah has arrived. Matthew, like the other evangelists, linguistically and theologically connects this narrative with the Last Supper and the community's Eucharistic gathering. The role of Jesus' disciples in carrying on Jesus' mission and ministry of care for others is stressed as they pay attention to people's needs and, with Jesus' guidance and help, minister to them. For Matthew, Jesus clearly manifests that God does care for all and both feeds and nourishes us in all our needs.

• "God loves all his creatures[4] and takes care of each one, even the sparrow. Nevertheless, Jesus said: 'You are of more value than many sparrows,' or again: 'Of how much more value is a man than a sheep!'[5]" (CCC, 342).

---

4 Cf. Psalm 145:9.
5 Luke 12:6–7; Matthew 12:12.

NINETEENTH SUNDAY IN ORDINARY TIME
"Take Courage, It Is I"

1 KINGS 19:9A, 11–13A Fleeing Jezebel's death threats for having slaughtered all of the Baal prophets, Elijah travels for forty days to Horeb, God's mountain. Horeb, also known as Mount Sinai, is where Moses encountered the Lord during his forty-day stay. Elijah is distressed because of the people's infidelity to God's covenant and to the threats on his life. In his distress, Elijah doubts his prophetic vocation and is tempted to give up. His forty-day journey to Horeb is God's way of reassuring Elijah that the Lord is still with him.

Arriving at Horeb, Elijah waits patiently for an experience of the Lord's presence. Like Moses on Mount Sinai, Elijah experiences a strong mighty wind, an earthquake, and fire; God was not in any of these. Not experiencing God in these usual patterns, Elijah comes to know God's presence in a tiny whispering sound. Out of reverence he hides his face in his cloak and goes out to encounter the Lord. In our distress, the Lord reaches out to comfort and strengthen us. But, like Elijah, we must attune ourselves to God's presence, often in ways we least expect.

PSALM 85:9, 10, 11–12, 13–14 (8) Psalm 85 is a lament psalm in which the Israelite community seeks to experience once again God's covenant love, peace, and salvation. In the midst of distress, the community trusts in the Lord, asking that covenant love, truth, justice, peace, and God's saving ways be made evident. The psalm is an anticipatory prayer waiting upon the Lord to respond. They trust that God will respond because they are God's people, loyal to the covenant, and because they have awe and reverence for the Lord. Love, truth, justice, and peace manifest different qualities of the covenant relationship. The last stanza envisions a triumphal procession occurring as the Lord responds to the people's request for help and salvation. Justice shall walk before the Lord as a procession unfolds God's actualizing presence and qualities among the people. With the Lord in our midst, there is nothing to fear.

ROMANS 9:1–5 Paul expresses "great sorrow and constant anguish" (v. 2) over other fellow Jews who have not accepted Jesus as God's Messiah. Like Moses before him, Paul was willing to sacrifice everything for his people. He would give

CONNECTIONS TO CHURCH TEACHING AND TRADITION

- "In their 'one to one' encounters with God, the prophets draw light and strength for their mission. Their prayer is not flight from this unfaithful world, but rather attentiveness to the Word of God. At times their prayer is an argument or a complaint, but it is always an intercession that awaits and prepares for the intervention of the Savior God, the Lord of history[1]" (CCC, 2584).

- "Filial trust is put to the test when we feel that our prayer is not always heard. The Gospel invites us to ask ourselves about the conformity of our prayer to the desire of the Spirit" (CCC, 2756).

---

1 Cf. Amos 7:2, 5; Isaiah 6:5, 8, 11; Jeremiah 1:6; 15:15–18; 20:7–18.

anything, even forfeit his own connection to Christ, if they could experience God's presence and saving power that is his in Christ Jesus. Despite God's many blessings on his people, they have not come to recognize Christ Jesus as Messiah.

Paul stresses that the people have been gifted with a unique name, Israelites, and are specially favored by God. God's glory has been manifested to them and their special relationship to God has been cemented in loving covenant bonds. God gave them the Law, the path to life, guided them in worship, and always proved faithful to covenant promises. From the beginning God presented them with models of faith in the patriarchs and now, "from them according to the flesh, is the Christ" (v. 5). Paul knows that the Lord is uniquely present with us in Christ. While in distress, he waits in hope for the time when all will be one in Christ.

MATTHEW 14:22–33 Jesus' prayer on the mountain, after dismissing the crowd he had just miraculously fed by multiplying loaves and fish, connects the Elijah reading to the Gospel. When Jesus walks on water, he demonstrates his divine power. Water, while necessary for life, also exhibited powerful destructive forces, leading to its association with chaos, disorder, and evil. In the creation narrative, God's Word subordinates the watery chaos, bringing order, light, and life to the world. By walking on water, Jesus manifests similar divine attributes, showing his disciples that he is the source of order, life, and light in their chaotic world. The storm-tossed boat is symbolic of the struggle that disciples have in carrying out Jesus' mission. Approaching them on water, he soothes their fears with divine assertions and calms the storm. Jesus shows himself to be their source of strength and courage amidst life's chaos. Peter asserts faith in Jesus when at Jesus' command he ventures into the water. But doubt overtakes him and, as he begins to sink, Jesus reaches out to save him. As Jesus comes into the boat, the wind dies down as the rest of the disciples acknowledge their belief in him as the Son of God. Discipleship demands acknowledging God as our source of courage, and recognizing the Lord's presence whenever doubt and chaos overwhelm us.

- "Certain constant characteristics appear throughout the Psalms . . . the distraught situation of the believer who, in his preferential love for the Lord, is exposed to a host of enemies and temptations, but who waits upon what the faithful God will do, in the certitude of his love and in submission to his will" (CCC, 2589).

Twentieth Sunday in Ordinary Time
All Are Welcome

ISAIAH 56:1, 6–7 Isaiah 56—66, the third and last part of the prophetic book, addresses the Jewish community that has returned from the Babylonian exile. The community continues to restore the land and rebuild the temple. Building on the work the author wrote during the exile, this part of the Book of Isaiah begins with a stress on observing and doing what is right and just. Ethical living is what God requires for salvation to be revealed.

The question of acceptance or inclusion of foreigners was a major concern for the returned exiles. Some counseled exclusion and purity of race and worship. Others, like Isaiah, understood God to be accepting and inclusive. If foreigners enter into relationship with the Lord, keeping the Sabbath holy and holding to the covenant promises, then the Lord invites them to the holy mountain, the temple, and the house of prayer. Their offerings and prayers will be acceptable to the Lord, for the Lord's house is "a house of prayer for all peoples" (v. 7). God and salvation are accessible to all.

PSALM 67:2–3, 5, 6, 8 (4) Psalm 67 is a prayer of blessing to God, asking not only the Jewish community, but all nations to offer praise for God's blessings. The community asks God's face to shine upon them so that they and all the nations will come to know and bless the Lord. As God's benefits and salvation are made manifest to the Jewish people, the community prays and hopes that through them the nations will know that God guides, rules, and blesses all.

The Jewish community has consistently understood itself not only as God's Chosen People but also as a light to the nations. Their enduring hope was that, through their covenant relationship with God and fidelity to God's ways, they would become the vehicles of God's blessings upon all people. Through their faithful living, other nations would be attracted to the Lord and live according to his ways, standing in awe and giving praise to him. They would become light to the world, as we are called to be today.

ROMANS 11:13–15, 29–32 In this passage, Paul continues to grapple with the question of why most of his people have rejected the Gospel. Addressing Gentiles in Rome who have accepted the Gospel, Paul hopes that the blessings they have received by accepting the Gospel will make his people

CONNECTIONS TO CHURCH TEACHING AND TRADITION

- "The gathering together of the People of God began at the moment when sin destroyed the communion of men with God, and that of men among themselves. The gathering together of the Church is, as it were, God's reaction to the chaos provoked by sin. This reunification is achieved secretly in the heart of all peoples[1]" (CCC, 761).

- "At all times and in every nation, anyone who fears God and does what is right has been acceptable to him (see Acts 10:35). He has, however, willed to make women and men holy and to save them, not as individuals without any bond between them, but rather to make them into a people who might acknowledge him and serve him in holiness" (LG, 9).

---

1 Acts 10:35; cf. LG, 9, 13, 16.

jealous and move them toward accepting the Gospel as well. In the divine plan, Paul optimistically understands the Jewish rejection of the Gospel as the means through which the Gentiles have been reconciled to God. If rejection brings about such good results, Paul imagines that Jewish acceptance will activate the life that is ours eternally from God.

Paul stresses that the Gentiles who were distant from God have been reconciled to God because of the rejection of the Gospel by the Jews. Now, the Jews have distanced themselves from God by not accepting the Gospel. Paul's hope is that, seeing the mercy extended by God to the Gentiles, Jews will also accept the Gospel and be reconciled to God in Christ. Human disobedience and rejection of God are used by God as a means of displaying love and mercy to all. No group can claim to have cornered God's love and mercy. Being open to all people so they can know God through us is a challenge that we all face in our daily interactions with people of diverse backgrounds.

MATTHEW 15:21–28 Jesus' healing of the Canaanite woman's daughter tormented by a demon brings to the surface many issues concerning relationships between Jews and Gentiles. The consequences of breaking boundaries seem to enlighten all to the nature of God and the ministry of Jesus. Jesus crosses into Gentile territory (Tyre and Sidon) and a woman from a nation (Canaan) historically despised by Jews approaches him on behalf of her sick daughter. Both actions would have been seen as culturally negative. Yet, through the dialogue and interaction that ensues, both parties, along with the disciples and Matthew's community, learn an important lesson. Jesus displays the typical Jewish mindset that his ministry and God's salvation are exclusively for the Jews, referring to her as a dog, the common slur of Jews toward Gentiles. This closed mindset does not deter a mother's love, as the mother reminds Jesus that even the dogs are fed scraps from the children's table. Her faith overwhelms Jesus, who directly heals her daughter. Thus, we learn that Jews and Gentiles alike are part of God's family.

- "Jesus is as saddened by the 'lack of faith' of his own neighbors and the 'little faith' of his own disciples[2] as he is struck with admiration at the great faith of the Roman centurion and the Canaanite woman[3]" (CCC, 2610).

---

2 Cf. Mark 6:6; Matthew 8:26.
3 Cf. Matthew 8:10; 15:28.

Twenty-First Sunday in Ordinary Time
"Who Do You Say That I Am?"

ISAIAH 22:19–23 Isaiah the prophet addresses oracles to various nations, announcing their impending doom (chapters 3–23). Chapter 22 is an oracle against Jerusalem, the City of David. Isaiah makes the point that Jerusalem, too, was subject to God's judgment. This oracle may have been delivered when Sennacherib, the king of Assyria, launched a siege against Jerusalem. Although Jerusalem was miraculously spared, the people refused to acknowledge that their sins brought destruction near. Shebna, the steward or overseer of the house of Hezekiah, appears to have been the leader of the party that favored an alliance with Egypt against Assyria, rather than trusting in God. Shebna is the only individual against whom the prophet issued an oracle of doom. Isaiah's wrath was aroused by the wanton luxury of Shebna, especially the lavish tomb he built for himself, which the prophet predicted he would never occupy. Because of his pride, Shebna was ejected from his office and Eliakim (Hebrew: "God raises up") was given supervision over the house of David. The *key* was a symbol of power for Israel: "I will place on his shoulder the key of the house of David; he shall open, and no one shall shut; he shall shut, and no one shall open" (v. 22). Fixed in a secure place, Eliakim too would fall when he failed to put his trust in God.

PSALM 138:1–3, 6, 8 (8BC) Psalm 138 is a heartfelt prayer of thanksgiving offered by a petitioner in the Temple. Clearly, there were times when the psalmist was in danger, but he had confidence that God would rescue him. The psalmist is moved to sing of God's "steadfast love" and "faithfulness" (v. 2b): "On the day I called, you answered me" (v. 3a). The psalmist is not saved because of his virtues but because of God's fidelity. He trusts in God's continual help and prays that others might experience God's love and thereby be stirred to offer God praise.

CONNECTIONS TO CHURCH TEACHING AND TRADITION

- Christ is the head of the Church, and the Church participates in Jesus' kingly office (CCC, 908–913).

- Animated by the Holy Spirit, the Church continues to do Christ's work in the world (CCC, 542–546, 567).

- Catholics honor the authority of the pope and other bishops as being in direct line from the authority given by Jesus to Peter and the other Apostles (CCC, 851, 862).

- God continues to gift the Church by calling leaders to guide the people (CCC, 863).

ROMANS 11:33–36 Paul battled with a heartbreaking problem of his own people's rejection of Jesus Christ. He examined the question with every resource he possessed. A certain paradox existed: God gave Paul a great mind, and it was his duty to use that mind. But sometimes his human limitations were reached. The mystery of salvation could not be understood solely by the mind but by a heart that loved God. Paul says that there was nothing more to be said: "For who has known the mind of the Lord? Or who has been his counselor?" (v. 34). Paul's theology now turns to poetry; his seeking of the mind to the adoration of the heart. Paul declares that all things came from God, that all things have their being through God, and that all things end in God. Having done his best, Paul was content to accept the divine mystery of redemption.

MATTHEW 16:13–20 Jesus took his disciples to the area of Caesarea Philippi in northern Israel near Baniyas, where the Cave of Pan (identified with the Roman god of fields and forests, flocks and shepherds) stood. There may also have been a temple in this area built by Herod to honor the Emperor Augustus. In this pagan territory, Jesus asks his disciples, "Who do people say that the Son of Man is?" (v. 13b). Peter confesses his belief in Jesus as God's Son, the "Messiah" (v. 16; the "anointed one"). Jesus declares that Peter is "blessed" for announcing this revelation from God. Jesus, in turn, affirms Peter's identity and mission as the foundation, the "rock," of his Church. The Aramaic word for "rock" (*kepha*) was transliterated into Greek as "Cephas," the name Paul used for Peter in his writings (see 1 Corinthians 1:12). Matthew used the Greek masculine word *petros* (for the feminine *petra*), thus "Peter" in English. Because of Peter's new position among the Twelve, Jesus confers supreme authority on him, promising divine assistance to guide the Church. Peter received "the keys of the kingdom of heaven" (Matthew 16:19). These powers to "bind" and "loose"—that is, the power to absolve or not to absolve a person from sin—are given to the Church through Peter and his successors. The rock of Peter's faith would enable him to follow Jesus right up to his own death as a martyr.

Twenty-Second Sunday in Ordinary Time
How, Then, Shall We Live?

JEREMIAH 20:7–9 When Jeremiah was first called to be a prophet, he protested, saying he was too young: "Truly I do not know how to speak, for I am only a boy" (v. 6). With a divine touch, Jeremiah was commanded by God to speak to the people despite his age: "'Now I have put my words in your mouth" (v. 9, a good description of what it means to be a prophet; one who speaks for God). Jeremiah's career, which spanned forty years, began peacefully. Those were the days of King Josiah's reform after the book of the law was found in the Temple. But the king was fatally wounded when he tried to stop Pharaoh Neco of Egypt from aiding Assyria against Babylon. Josiah's tragic death signaled the downfall of the southern kingdom of Judah. When Jeremiah announced the forthcoming destruction of Jerusalem and the exile that would follow, he was laughed at and derided as a false prophet. Had not Sennacherib of Assyria attacked Jerusalem but was unable to destroy it? The people were lulled into false security; God would protect them because of the Temple. Like Jesus, Jeremiah lamented over Jerusalem (Luke 19:41–44).

King Zedekiah refused to listen to Jeremiah's warnings, preferring his favorite prophets, who told him what he wanted to hear. Jeremiah was close to despair. Obedience to God's Word had brought him "pain unceasing," a "wound incurable" (Jeremiah 15:18). Jeremiah even questioned why he was ever born (20:14). In one of the most personal confessions in the Bible, Jeremiah complained God had duped him (v. 7; the imagery is of sexual seduction). God proved too strong for the prophet, who vowed never to speak for the Lord again. But the prophetic word could not be contained; it was like a raging fire in him that was ready to burst forth in the coming devastation by Babylon. Amidst all the trials Jeremiah faced, God was with him, like a mighty warrior to defend the prophet against his foes.

PSALM 63:2, 3–4, 5–6, 8–9 (2B) When the psalms were put together in their final collection, many were attributed to David, the great singer of God's praises. Psalm 63 is one example, recalling David's sojourn in the wilderness as he sought refuge from King Saul, who threatened to kill him. Just as the Temple was once a place of asylum for those fleeing from their enemies, David sought God's protection in a

CONNECTIONS TO CHURCH TEACHING AND TRADITION

- Tensions of living the Christian life result from God-given freedom (CCC, 1730–1732).

- Human freedom is complicated by human passion (CCC, 1763, 1767).

- The way Christian freedom is exercised is the basis of our moral life (CCC, 1739, 1749–1756).

- Conscience is the secret core of the human person wherein God's will is discerned (CCC, 1776, 1778, 1781).

140 ORDINARY TIME

cave (1 Samuel 22:1). Like David, the psalmist was in a spiritual wilderness, longing for God's sanctuary and "steadfast love" (Psalm 63:3; Hebrew: *hesed*, "covenant love"), which is praised as being better than life.

ROMANS 12:1–2 In this final epistle of Paul, he presents an ethical exhortation (Greek: *paranesis*), teaching the Christian community how to give praise to God in their new life in Christ. Believers have received mercy from God through Christ (Romans 11:30); therefore, their loving response should be praise and worship. Because they are no longer bound by the Law, which mandated a variety of sacrifices, they can offer their own bodies as acceptable sacrifices. Christ himself set an example by offering himself on the Cross to atone for sin. Paul urges the community to imitate Jesus (see Philippians 2:5) and not conform themselves to society's standards. With minds renewed, Christians can then judge what is "good and acceptable and perfect" (Romans 12:2).

MATTHEW 16:21–27 The Church is called by God to be a new Israel, founded on "living stones" (1 Peter 2:5) of the Christian community. It is Peter, the *rock* on whom Jesus builds his Church (Matthew 16:18). When Peter recognizes Jesus as the Messiah of God (v. 16), Jesus strictly commands his followers to secrecy. Why would Jesus tell his disciples not to tell anyone? The explanation is found in the popular understanding of the Messiah in Jesus' time. The Messiah (Hebrew: *mashiyach*, usually a consecrated person such as a king, prophet, or priest, specifically the "anointed one") was expected to be a mighty ruler like David. Peter had just received the "keys of the kingdom" (v. 19), and that gave him power and authority. Peter acts on his newfound authority by objecting to Jesus' declaration that he must go to Jerusalem. Peter finds it hard to imagine that the Messiah must undergo suffering and death to achieve victory. "God forbid it, Lord!" (v. 22) Peter remonstrates. Jesus affirms that new life can come only through death. If Peter wants to be his disciple, he must get on the road leading to Calvary and follow Jesus. Anyone who follows Jesus must take up the cross. Only after the terrible events of Jesus' Passion will his disciples realize what it means to be a crucified savior.

TWENTY-THIRD SUNDAY IN ORDINARY TIME
Light, Life, and Love

EZEKIEL 33:7–9 Jeremiah's prophetic career ended during the Exile. It is believed he was martyred in Egypt, where friends took him after Jerusalem's destruction (587–597 BC). Ezekiel was another prophet of the Exile. Unlike Jeremiah, though, Ezekiel was deported to Babylon, along with King Jehoiachin and many thousands of other exiles, during the siege of Jerusalem. Ezekiel, a priest, was the only prophet to receive his call outside the Holy Land. On the banks of the river Chebar (a canal that irrigated the land around Babylon), Ezekiel had a profound experience of God's power. Ezekiel discovered that God had not abandoned the people, but went into exile with them. God appointed the prophet as a "watchman" (someone stationed on the ramparts to sound the alarm when the enemy approached; v. 7). He was given a message on a scroll and commanded to "eat" it; that is, to digest the words to speak to the "rebellious house" of Israel (2:5) and bring about their repentance. Like Jeremiah, Ezekiel's words of warning would be unheeded (3:10). The prophet's message confirmed the people's worst fears: the holy city had been destroyed, and their hopes of returning were smashed. Ezekiel declared that if they would return (Hebrew: *shub*, "to turn back, to repent") to the Lord, one day they would be able to return home. If they repented of their sins, the glory of the Lord would fill Jerusalem again.

PSALM 95:1–2, 6–7, 8–9 (8) This psalm often opens the daily office of the Church. The Latin title, *Venite Exsultemus*, "Come Joyfully," seems like another hymn of praise, but more is at stake here. The psalm is both the summons "O come, let us sing to the Lord" (v. 1) and the command "Let us kneel before the Lord, our Maker" (v. 6b). The psalmist gives a twofold invitation to worship the Lord and repent.

ROMANS 13:8–10 Paul also brought God's message. Paul asks the community to let the Gospel renew their minds to judge what is "good and acceptable and perfect" according to the will of God (12:2). Paul exhorts Christians to discern what is good for the Church (13:1–7), directing them to live in harmony with civil authority. Then he considers the good of the community itself. Christians must also live in harmony with God's law. Paul balances his own thoughts

CONNECTIONS TO CHURCH TEACHING AND TRADITION

- An essential part of our faith is that we are committed to one another (CCC, 1914).

- Each person is responsible for the good of all (CCC, 1905–1912).

- We are obliged to respect all persons (CCC, 1907) for the well-being of the community (CCC, 1908) and for peace and security (CCC, 1909).

- The Fourth through the Tenth Commandments outline our specific responsibilities (CCC, 2197–2250, 2196, 2822).

by giving the negative command "Owe no one anything" alongside the positive command "love one another" (v. 8). Jesus regarded this singular command to love (see John 13:34) as the fulfillment of the entire Law (Matthew 22:39–40). Love never wrongs the other person by acts of adultery, murder, theft, or lust for another's possessions or property. By obeying God's commands, we can live a harmonious life with one and all.

MATTHEW 18:15–20 Matthew patterns his Gospel after the five books of the Hebrew Torah. He balances each narrative—what Jesus does—with a discourse or teaching. In this fourth of five discourses, Jesus first instructs his disciples to become like children (vv. 1–4), having a child's simple attitude of faith and trust. He then warns his followers about offending their brothers and sisters, a grave offense against the community, and suggests ways to reconcile their differences. These instructions sound more like the regulations of a fully developed and organized church, which did not yet exist at the time of Jesus. Furthermore, Jesus befriends tax collectors and Gentiles, who are spoken of here as hopeless sinners. Jesus even declares that those whom the community regards as outsiders will be admitted into the Kingdom of Heaven before the self-righteous religious people of the time (see 21:31ff.).

Matthew writes at a later date (*ca.* 85 AD). His concern is how the struggling Christian community conducts itself as it awaits the fullness of God's reign. Matthew wants to help preserve the community's harmony, but not at the loss of integrity. He presents three strategies for resolving conflict. First, he advises the parties to try to settle their problems in private. In a culture in which honor and shame are the primary values, this allows each person to save face. However, if this does not work, the second tactic is for one or two witnesses to help settle the dispute. If all else fails, the final strategy is to bring the case before the *Church* (Greek: *ekklesia*, only used here and 16:18). When a single member of the Body of Christ is wronged, the whole community must be involved. But the final authority is God. "If two of you agree on earth about anything you ask" (18:19), it will be granted in heaven. The heavens rejoice when even one straying member returns to the community of faith.

The Gift of Difference

SIRACH 27:36—28:7 The Book of Sirach is also called the Book of Ecclesiasticus, meaning "church book." The early Church applied this title to the entire group of books called "Deuterocanonical" or "Second Law." Sirach is included in the Wisdom literature of the Bible. The author was a sage living in Jerusalem during the Hellenization of Palestine. His purpose in writing was to reveal the treasures of traditional Hebrew wisdom to keep Jews from dabbling in the novelties of Greek philosophy. Like the Book of Proverbs, Sirach is a collection of wise sayings.

In this passage Sirach deals with friendship and uncovers attitudes that threaten to destroy it. He speaks of anger and wrath as abominations that can devour friendship like consuming a fire. Sirach declares that the sinner prefers the cold embrace of hateful things (27:30) to the warm embrace of a friend. The next admonition regards the desire for vengeance and the unwillingness to forgive (28:1–7). This passage is a prelude to the prayer Jesus prays. In the Lord's Prayer, Jesus asks his disciples to forgive the debts of others as they wish to have their debts forgiven (Matthew 6:12).

Like Sirach (28:3), Jesus warns his followers that if they do not forgive others, neither will God forgive their sins (Matthew 6:1–15). Enmity should be set aside before death and decay come to claim the sinner. Jesus and Sirach encourage their disciples to imitate the very one who is the source of all wisdom, the most high God.

PSALM 103:1–2, 3–4, 9–10, 11–12 (8) This psalm praises divine goodness. The psalmist has recovered from an illness, proof that the author's sins are forgiven. The psalmist invites all people to join in a hymn of praise, asking for God's blessing (Hebrew: *berekah*, "to impart favor"). The mercy shown to the author is but a small portion of God's generosity to the nation. God knows human frailty well; therefore, God does not deal with the people according to their sins. God was faithful during the many rebellions of the people on their way to the Promised Land. The psalmist asks who can determine the distance between the east and west, who can measure the height or depth or width of the heavens and the earth. So, too, it is equally impossible to measure God's surpassing kindness (Hebrew: *hesed*, "loving kindness" or "covenant love").

CONNECTIONS TO CHURCH TEACHING AND TRADITION

- Justice is a cardinal virtue, a deeply ingrained habit of doing good (CCC, 1803, 1805).

- Justice is persistent work on behalf of universal rights, equity, and promotion of the common good (CCC, 1807, 1905–1912).

- Our most important social commandment is that we must work for justice (CCC, 1823, 1889, 2196).

ROMANS 14:7–9 Paul does not want Christians to enter into disputes over nonessentials, and he urges them to apply the principle of love of neighbor. One of these conflicts is over "clean" and "unclean" foods (Leviticus 11:1–23). For Paul, "nothing is unclean in itself" (Romans 14:14; see also Acts 10:13–15). Things are unclean only when people perceive them as such. Paul knows some are scrupulous in this matter and consider unclean foods as a source of moral contamination. He asks the community, "Who are you to pass judgment on servants (Greek: *diakonos*) of another?" (Romans 14:4). Jesus, the *master* (Greek: *kyrios*), will judge each, so there is no need for the servants to judge one another. We live and die as the Lord's servants and should imitate the way he lived and died.

MATTHEW 18:21–35 Jesus just finishes talking about correcting one's brothers and sisters in the community (last Sunday's Gospel, Matthew 18:15–20) when Peter asks him," Lord, if my brother sins against me, how often should I forgive? As many as seven times?" (v. 21). (In Matthew's Gospel, the word *brother* always means a member of the Christian community.) Peter thinks he is being very charitable in suggesting that he forgive seven times, for rabbinic law only required three times. Peter expects Jesus to congratulate him for his generosity, but Jesus answers that a Christian must forgive seventy times seven! In other words, there is no limit to forgiveness.

Jesus tells his followers a story of a king who forgave his servant a great debt. When the servant went out, a fellow servant, who owed a much smaller debt, approached him and begged for forgiveness. The man who had been forgiven a huge amount, literally "ten thousand talents" (a denarius was a day's wage for an unskilled laborer, and a talent was the equivalent of six thousand denarii), was merciless toward a fellow servant who owed him a mere fraction of that amount. When the king heard of this, the unforgiving servant was treated harshly. The teaching of the Lord's own prayer, "And forgive us our debts, as we also have forgiven our debtors" (6:12) shows that divine and human forgiveness go hand in hand. We have been forgiven a debt beyond paying.

Twenty-Fifth Sunday in Ordinary Time
God's Holy Ways Are beyond Our Understanding

ISAIAH 55:6–9 Seek the Lord while he may be found! Isaiah reminds the people that one cannot conjure up the divine presence. God's self-revelation occurs in God's time, not on a human timetable. Those who try to understand God on their own are doomed to failure and risk the idolatry of worshipping a god of their own making. They must rely on God for revelation, not on their own will. Those who have been unfaithful are to turn to God while there is still time.

Verses 8 and 9 reiterate the same message from a different angle. God's thoughts and ways are as different from the human point of view as the heavens are from the earth; they are beyond ordinary human understanding. Nevertheless, as the earlier verses assure us, it is absolutely possible to encounter God, just not on our own agenda.

PSALM 145:2–3, 8–9, 17–18 (18A) This psalm, among the last in the Psalter, sings God's praises. An apt response to our reading from Isaiah, it proclaims God's goodness, mercy, patience, kindness, compassion, justice, and holiness. Most of all, while Isaiah warned that one must seek God at the appropriate time—the time God has chosen—this psalm assures us that all who seek, all who call upon God in truth, will be rewarded by knowing God's presence.

PHILIPPIANS 1:20C–24, 27A In the opening lines of this reading, Paul is facing the fact that he very well may die soon. Thus, he assures his community at Philippi that no matter what happens, Christ will be glorified.

Many of us may have heard the elderly or suffering say that they would just as soon die as live on. That sort of weariness of life is not what Paul is talking about. He knows that Baptism has given him unending life. He admits that he is torn—to die would be to enjoy the fullness of union with Christ that he longs for, but to live offers him the opportunity to bring more people to Christ. What he asks of the Philippians is that they share his sense of closeness to Christ and mission. That is how they can live in a way worthy of the Gospel of Christ.

CONNECTIONS TO CHURCH TEACHING AND TRADITION

- "Catechesis is a process of formation in faith, hope and charity; it shapes the mind and touches the heart, leading the person to embrace Christ fully and completely[1]" (EIA, 69).

- "We are convinced that the Church must look with penetrating eyes within itself, ponder the mystery of its own being. . . . But it can never claim to be sufficiently investigated and understood, for it contains 'the publication of a mystery, kept hidden from the beginning of time in the all-creating mind of God'[2]" (ES, 9).

---

1 *Propositio* 10.
2 Cf. Ephesians 3:9–10.

MATTHEW 20:1–16A This parable is unique to Matthew's account of the Gospel. In some ways, it complements what Jesus taught about rewards for discipleship in 19:27–30, which ends with the same teaching as today's reading. The parable also reiterates the message of our reading from Isaiah: God's ways are not our ways.

The scene of hiring workers is familiar to anyone who lives in a town or city where there are migrants or poor people looking for work as day laborers. There are particular areas where they congregate, waiting for someone to come to hire them. When a boss shows up, many will run to the truck to be among the first to be hired. It is entirely conceivable that, if they find no work at one setting, they may move on to another where their luck may be better. As the day wears on, those still seeking work may well feel jealous of those who got hired earlier.

That is very similar to the scene Jesus described nearly two thousand years ago. The vineyard owner went out several times during the day to find workers. Interestingly, to the first group the owner promised the usual daily wage. With the second and presumably the third, he promised "what is just" (v. 4). With the five o'clock group he made no agreement, but simply sent them to the vineyard. In the end, all the workers received the same remuneration.

If we assume that the owner represents God, there are at least two potential interpretations of this. The first reflects back to the First Reading: God's ways are not our ways, and God is free to do what God will do. God's generosity cannot be limited by human expectations. The second interpretation presents a different conception of divine justice.

The owner had promised the first group the "usual daily wage" and to others he promised "what is just" (2, 4). Not surprisingly, those who had worked all day expected more reward than the others. Nevertheless, the daily wage was what one needed to survive. The owner chose to ensure the life of those he had found looking for work. No matter when they were encountered, they all needed to survive.

This parable, combined with the reading from Isaiah, invites us to stop judging by our own rules and try to understand God's perspective on what is right and just. With that in mind, we can also hear Paul's appeal that we learn to conduct ourselves in a way worthy of the Gospel of Christ.

- "By living with the mind of Christ, Christians *hasten the coming of the Reign of God*, 'a kingdom of justice, love, and peace.'[3] They do not, for all that, abandon their earthly tasks; faithful to their master, they fulfill them with uprightness, patience, and love" (CCC, 2046).

- "Economic injustice . . . keep[s] people from attaining their basic human and civil rights" (JM, 9).

3 *Roman Missal,* Preface of Christ the King.

Twenty-Sixth Sunday in Ordinary Time
Strive Humbly to Do the Will of God

EZEKIEL 18:25–28 As chapter 18 of Ezekiel began, the prophet proclaimed his doctrine of individual responsibility for sin. In today's selection, Ezekiel quotes the people's indictment of God: "The LORD's way is not fair!" (v. 25). It sounds a bit like a petulant child complaining about his or her parents' treatment of a sibling. Ezekiel has no patience for that sort of attitude. He turns his mirror back on the people and asks them whose ways are really not fair. What kind of grudges do they hold against the family of an evildoer? How willing are they to take the blame for the sin of their parents or children? Then, he explains that even sinners can repent of the evil they have done, just as the virtuous can fall into deadly sin. Ezekiel focuses on people's underlying attitudes. Are they walking in God's way, or making their own path?

PSALM 25:4–5, 6–7, 8–9 (6A) This prayer is classified as an individual lament. We begin with a proclamation of faith in the goodness of God, the God of love and truth. The verses go on with a humble plea to be shown God's way. As is typical of the psalms, the people praying remind God of the divine qualities that bolster their faith: compassion, love, kindness, and goodness. They sing the praise of their God, who shows sinners the way and guides those who are humble enough to ask for assistance. The psalm invites us to look at our own experience of seeking God's guidance and to list the divine qualities we have come to know through our own humble prayers for help.

PHILIPPIANS 2:1–11 OR 2:1–5 We hear this same reading on the Feast of the Exaltation of the Holy Cross, which occasionally is celebrated on a Sunday. On that feast, the emphasis focuses on the triumph of the Cross and Christ's exaltation, in spite of appearances to the contrary. On this Sunday, it presents us with Christ as a model of humble obedience. Before he quotes an ancient Christian hymn, Paul calls on his community to do nothing less than put on the attitude of Christ himself. This is possible only because they share in the Spirit.

The hymn that Paul cites portrays Christ as the perfect model of obedience to the will of God. When we look at Christ's life, his teaching, his miracles, and his actions, such

CONNECTIONS TO CHURCH TEACHING AND TRADITION

- "This proper way of serving others also leads to humility. The one who serves does not consider himself superior to the one served, however miserable his situation at the moment may be. Christ took the lowest place in the world—the Cross—and by this radical humility he redeemed us and constantly comes to our aid" (DCE, 35).

- "Justification is at the same time *the acceptance of God's righteousness* through faith in Jesus Christ. Righteousness (or 'justice') here means the rectitude of divine love. With justification, faith, hope, and charity are poured into our hearts, and obedience to the divine will is granted us" (CCC, 1991).

- "The first manner of humility is necessary for eternal salvation; namely, that I so lower and so humble myself . . . that in everything I obey the law of God" (The Spiritual Exercises of St. Ignatius of Loyola).

as the cleansing of the Temple and his debates with some of the officials of Israel, we might not think of him as humble. Yet, this hymn focuses on all of Jesus' teaching and life through the lens of his humble submission to the will of the Father. Just as Jesus taught about the last being first and the exalted being humbled, it was his humble submission that opened the way for God to exalt him.

MATTHEW 21:28–32 The parable of the two sons is unique to Matthew's account of the Gospel. A classic parable, it seems to indict just about everyone. We may have heard it so often that the distinction between the good son and the unfaithful son seems too obvious. Nevertheless, if we understand the parable in its cultural context, it becomes more complicated and interesting. Jesus presents the case of two sons, one who said the right words but did not obey, and the other who eventually obeyed in spite of how he had answered his father.

In Semitic cultures, respect for parents is one of the most basic and important values. The son who said yes to his father fulfilled an essential requirement of filial piety. The son who said no was guilty of an immense and disrespectful insult to his father. If we think of the characters in this parable as representing God and God's people, the one who said no was guilty of something akin to blasphemy, refusing to recognize the Father's authority. The one who did nothing was guilty of disobedience, but at least he acknowledged his father's authority. Culturally, the second was guilty of the greater sin.

If we simply ask which of the sons did the father's will, we will agree with the answer of the religious authorities: the one who did what the father asked. The son who said no seemed proud, while the other seemed hypocritical. The key to the parable is that one changed his mind. Like the sinners of Jesus' or of Ezekiel's day, the naysaying son transformed his attitude. The naysayer came to humble obedience, while the other would have allowed the father's vineyard to go to ruin while he still saved face. As Jesus said, in the end, those who are humble enough to repent, those who sooner or later follow God's path, will be the first to enter the Kingdom of God.

TWENTY-SEVENTH SUNDAY IN ORDINARY TIME
The People of God Are the Divine Vineyard

ISAIAH 5:1–7 The Song of the Lord's Vineyard gives us a rendition of the Lord's classic complaint against an unfaithful people. The song actually turns out to be something of a parable. As happens so often in the Old Testament, we hear God's complaint: what more could have been done for this people? We also hear echoes of the Good Friday reproaches: "My people, what have I done to you? / Or how have I grieved you? Answer me!"

In spite of all the divine care and effort, the people, God's vineyard, have produced "wild grapes," a phrase which could also be translated as rotten or stinking grapes (v. 4). The song actually asks the guilty to judge themselves. If they are the vineyard of God, what should God do in return for their lack of good fruit?

In the end, as is typical in the books of the prophets, God announces the ruin of the unproductive vineyard, while paradoxically still calling it a "cherished plant" (v. 7). That, too, is typical of the prophets, who tend to interpret exile and domination in terms of a learning experience for the people, an experience from which they will one day recover. The end of the song prepares us for the Gospel: the owner looked for judgment and justice, but found bloodshed and outcry.

PSALM 80:9, 12, 13–14, 15–16, 19–20 (ISAIAH 5:7A Psalm 80 is a communal lament. Following the imagery of Isaiah, it recognizes God's care for Israel and the destruction God permitted. Here, rather than playing the role of their own judges, the people cry out to the Lord to look upon them, to care for the ones who were once the privileged and chosen. They then vow to be faithful, if only God will restore them. As we pray this psalm, we are invited to remember how God has helped and saved us, to ask ourselves how we have responded, and to pray that God will remain with us as we make every effort to produce good fruit.

PHILIPPIANS 4:6–9 This reading forms part of the conclusion of Paul's Letter to the Philippians. Paul's theology of prayer in this reading is very instructive. He tells his community to present their petitions to God, not expecting a positive response to their every desire, but in order to receive the peace of God, a peace that is beyond all

CONNECTIONS TO CHURCH TEACHING AND TRADITION

- "The prophets in the Old Testament used the image of the vine to describe the chosen people. Israel is God's vine . . . the joy of his heart: 'I have planted you a choice vine';[1] 'Your mother was like a vine in a vineyard transplanted by the water, fruitful and full of branches by reason of abundant water'[2]" (CL, 8).

- "According to the Biblical image of the vineyard, the lay faithful, together with all the other members of the Church, are branches engrafted to Christ the true vine, and from him derive their life and fruitfulness" (CL, 9).

- "Life according to the Spirit, whose fruit is holiness[3] . . . requires each to follow and imitate Jesus Christ . . . in family or in community, in the hunger and thirst for justice, in the practice of the commandment of love . . . in service to the brethren, especially the least, the poor and the suffering" (CL, 16).

---

1 Jeremiah 2:21.

2 Ezekiel 19:10.

3 Cf. Romans 6:22; Galatians 5:22.

understanding (see Luke 11:9–13). It would seem that peace is central to this passage. Prayers of petition will bring the people peace, and if they live according to the teaching they have received, the God of peace will be with them.

MATTHEW 21:33–43 Today's parable follows directly on last week's parable of the two sons. Putting these parables in the context of Matthew's account of the Gospel, we will recall that we are moving toward the climax of Jesus' ministry. In chapter 21 we hear of his triumphal entry into Jerusalem, the cleansing of the Temple, healing of the sick, more than one confrontation with the religious authorities, and the cursing of the fig tree.

The parable of the tenants simultaneously looks backward to prophecies like the one we heard from Isaiah, and forward to the Passion. The difference between this parable and the one we read from Isaiah is that in Isaiah, the emphasis was on the owner. Now, it is on the workers who represent the religious authorities.

The vineyard image is familiar to the people, both because of its use in the Old Testament and because everyone who lived in the area was familiar with vineyards, absentee land owners, and tenant farmers. Like shepherds who were hired to watch the flocks of others, tenants wishing to increase their own share of the harvest could be dishonest in rendering accounts to the land owner.

In spite of that sort of common practice, these tenants committed more egregious crimes than pilfering the produce. They did not simply cheat and steal; they killed the messengers sent by the owner. Then, using insane reasoning, they told themselves that if they killed the heir, they would receive his inheritance.

As Jesus addressed this parable to the chief priests and elders, it is obvious that the tenant farmers represent those leaders. As Jesus points out in Matthew 23:4, they lay heavy burdens on the people and do not lift a finger to move them. The message Jesus communicated to the authorities was that, no matter how they retaliated for his criticism of them, the fact that they did not produce good fruit would lead to their loss of participation in the Kingdom of God. In other words, their style of religion would not succeed whether or not they got rid of Jesus.

Twenty-Eighth Sunday in Ordinary Time
We Are Invited to a Feast of Grace and Joy

ISAIAH 25:6–10A According to some scholars, this is a hymn for a feast celebrating the coronation of God as King. Yet, it is the Lord who prepares the feast for the people. Isaiah had already announced the Lord's victory (see 24:23). Now, this is the feast that celebrates it. Isaiah presents a picture of the victory of God the King that is different from any human king. Normally, the king who had vanquished an enemy would celebrate his power over the foe with a reprise of violent victories. Everyone would see how mighty and fearsome he was, thus assuring adherence to his rule.

That is not the way of the Lord. The God of Israel celebrates by serving a feast, not just for the chosen people, but for all peoples. Instead of flaunting the power of a warrior, the God of Israel appears to be more of a chef, serving fine wine and juicy, rich food. Rather than membership in a particular ethnic group or faith tradition, the only requirement for participating in this banquet is the desire to receive God's grace and participate with joy.

PSALM 23:1–3A, 3B–4, 5, 6 (6CD) We often hear this psalm at funerals, where it assures us of God's constant care and protection. In the light of our reading from Isaiah, it not only proclaims God's loving concern but repeats the banquet theme. When we read it in that light, it asks us with whom we are willing to share that banquet. Isaiah taught that the feast is for everyone from all the nations. Are we ready for that, or do we want to exclude some of the Lord's invited guests?

PHILIPPIANS 4:12–14, 19–20 With the exception of final greetings and a blessing, this is the end of Paul's Letter to the Philippians. Paul claims that he can adapt to any physical circumstances; material concerns are not important to him. He attributes his ability to adapt to anything, not to his own virtue, but to "him who strengthens me" (4:13).

Paul ends this segment assuring his community that God will care for their every need, just as God cares for his every need. Again, that does not mean that they will never be hungry, but rather that they will share in Christ's glorious riches, the divine presence that will transform them and the world.

CONNECTIONS TO CHURCH TEACHING AND TRADITION

- "The Word of God . . . was made flesh so that as perfect man he could save all women and men. . . . The Lord is the goal of human history, the focal point of the desires of history and of civilization, the center of the human race, the joy of all hearts, and the fulfillment of all aspirations[1]" (GS, 45).

- "The acclamation of the assembly following the consecration appropriately ends by expressing the eschatological thrust which marks the celebration of the Eucharist:[2] 'until you come in glory.' The Eucharist is a straining towards the goal, a foretaste of the fullness of joy promised by Christ[3]" (EE, 18).

1 Cf. Paul VI, encyclical letter *Ecclesiam Suam*, III: A AS 56 (1964).

2 Cf. 1 Corinthians 11:26.

3 Cf. John 15:11.

MATHEW 22:1–14 OR 22:1–10 Matthew's account of the Gospel is wending its way toward its climax. There is an eschatological urgency driving the writing: as many in the early Church thought, the time was short, and Christ's return was imminent. In terms of this parable, the banquet was prepared, and the time was now.

The invited guests, representing the people and leaders of Israel, made light of the banquet invitation. They had more important things to do than pay attention to the wedding of the king's son. Such an attitude was tantamount to rejecting the king himself. As we look at the details, the ones who ignored the invitation did not even express animosity; they were simply indifferent. Others did resort to violence, assaulting and murdering the servants who symbolize the prophets God had sent though Israel's history. Time and again, the rejection of God's messengers led to the destruction of the people. In act two of this parable, servants like the disciples are sent out to bring in anyone willing to come, the good and the bad alike. That riffraff, as in previous parables, represented the tax collectors and sinners who responded to Jesus' invitation. In act three of the parable, the king meets one of the latecomer guests who did not put on the wedding garment that would have been supplied for all the guests. This guest represents the one who would tag along and look for free food, but not take responsibility for the repentance necessary to participate in the kingdom feast.

In this parable, we meet the privileged, chosen ones who were not interested in what the king had to offer and the outcasts who were delighted to be invited and whose acceptance led them to conversion. It turns out that the only requirement for this banquet is the desire to receive gratefully what the king has to offer. Isaiah, the psalm, and this parable remind us that God is waiting for us, both as banquet provider and as the One who is always offering us grace and a joyous feast. We need but make the kingdom feast our priority and be willing to participate together with all those invited.

• "Jesus' invitation to enter his kingdom comes in the form of parables, a characteristic feature of his teaching.[4] Through his parables he invites people to the feast of the kingdom, but he also asks for a radical choice: to gain the kingdom, one must give everything.[5] . . . The parables are like mirrors for man" (CCC, 546).

---

4 Cf. Mark 4:33–34.

5 Cf. Matthew 13:44–45; 22:1–14.

Twenty-Ninth Sunday in Ordinary Time
God Works through Human Hands

ISAIAH 45:1, 4–6 This reading comes from Second Isaiah, someone who wrote about 150 years after First Isaiah. Writing in the name of a better-known figure is not unusual in our Scriptures. For example, a number of New Testament letters were written by an unknown author who attributes them to Paul.

Whereas First Isaiah's theology focused on the punishment God would mete out, Second Isaiah announced salvation. The passage we hear today explains that God will use Cyrus, king of Persia, to bring the people exiled in Babylonia back home to Jerusalem. Isaiah discerns God acting through human agents in history, even using foreigners for the redemption of the people. In this poetic passage we hear that God will give Cyrus victory, but all for the sake of Israel, God's Chosen People.

PSALM 96:1, 3, 4–5, 7–8, 9–10 (7B) This psalm is a fitting follow-up to Isaiah's message; it calls on the people to sing a new song to the Lord and to proclaim God's glory among all peoples. Saying that God governs the people with equity celebrates the vindication Isaiah promised. Giving God glory demands reverence (holy attire), awe (tremble), and a proclamation of God's goodness and greatness (the Lord is the King who governs the peoples with equity).

1 THESSALONIANS 1:1–5B In these days of electronic communication, many people no longer engage in or even appreciate the art of letter writing, but Paul was an expert at it, especially when writing to people he loved. In this, the oldest of Paul's extant letters, we discover his tender relationship with a community with whom he had shared the faith.

Paul and his companions address the community of Thessalonica "in God the Father and the Lord Jesus Christ." That seemingly simple statement is laden with theological meaning. It proclaims Jesus as the Son of God the Father, and the Christ, the long-awaited Messiah. Finally, the greeting "grace to you and peace" probably has its origins in the liturgical prayer they celebrated together.

As he begins, Paul expresses thanks for all that God is doing through them. As he does so, he makes the first Christian mention of what we call the "theological virtues." Paul praises the Thessalonians for their faith, which they

CONNECTIONS TO CHURCH TEACHING AND TRADITION

- "The citizen is obliged in conscience not to follow the directives of civil authorities when they are contrary to the demands of the moral order, to the fundamental rights of persons or the teachings of the Gospel" (CCC, 2242).

- "Development cannot consist only in the use, dominion over and indiscriminate possession of created things . . . but rather in subordinating the possession, dominion and use to man's divine likeness and to his vocation to immortality" (SRS, 29).

- "Jesus refuses the oppressive and despotic power wielded by the rulers of the nations. . . . In his pronouncement on the paying of taxes to Caesar (cf. Mark 12:13–17; Matthew 22:15–22; Luke 20:20–26), he affirms that we must give to God what is God's, implicitly condemning every attempt at making temporal power divine or absolute: God alone can demand everything from man" (CSDC, 379).

express in love, and for the hope that keeps them steadfast in a time of tribulation. Finally, Paul proclaims that they were chosen by God and that the Holy Spirit is working through them. In just five verses, Paul has proclaimed faith in the Trinity and reminded them that the God to whom they belong is working though their faith, hope, and love.

MATTHEW 22:15–21 There are some delightful ironies in this account of an attempt to trap Jesus. His adversaries begin in an ostensibly respectful tone, recognizing Jesus as a teacher and man of utter integrity. Finally they admit that he is not swayed by others' opinions of him. The point of their question about taxes is to force Jesus to side with either the zealots, who promoted rebellion against Rome, or with those who collaborated with the Roman rule, which some of the faithful judged to be an affront to God and the Chosen People. The questioners made up an odd partnership since the name of the Herodians implied that they were in league with political powers, while the Pharisees promoted a scrupulous compliance with the Jewish law. Jesus' ability to discredit their either-or proposition is the most obvious triumph of the incident. The fact that they were carrying coins of the realm with a forbidden graven image and an inscription about the "divine" emperor exposed the fact that they were all in unfaithful compliance with Rome.

A deeper question lies underneath the surface of this verbal skirmish. While his opponents were questioning legalities, Jesus brought them back to a question of image. The Greek word for image is *eikon*, from which we have the word icon. Jesus' response about the coin implied that it belonged to the one whose image it bore. When he spoke of God, the obvious question would be, where is God's image? Clearly, for all those who knew the creation accounts, God's image is the created person, male and female (Genesis 1:27). By using that language, Jesus trapped his adversaries far more profoundly than their question might have trapped him. In response to their supposedly scrupulous question about paying taxes, Jesus cleverly reminded them that as creatures, they owed everything to the God in whose image they were created.

EXODUS 22:20–26 Exodus 19—24 describes the covenant between God and the people whom Moses brought out of Egypt. Beginning with conversations between God and Moses (chapter 19), which is followed by the Ten Commandments (chapter 20), chapters 21–23 contain what is called the "covenant code," instructions for righteous action in accord with the covenant. In chapter 24, the people promise to fulfill their part.

Today's selection from the covenant code presents the rationale for the laws the people were to obey, assuring the people that God was not capricious, but intending to form them into a godly people. When the Lord says, "You shall not . . . oppress an alien, for you were once aliens," it is a command to imitate divine empathy. In calling for justice for widows and orphans, the people are reminded of God's attention to their cry in Egypt. They are commanded to treat the needy as God had treated them. Finally, God reminds them that lending should not be a business, but rather a way to alleviate the suffering of another person. As Leviticus 19:2 makes explicit, the Law has nothing to do with blind obedience. The Law of the Lord calls us to imitate our compassionate God.

PSALM 18:2–3, 3–4, 47, 51 (2) Psalm 18, attributed to David, gives thanks for being delivered from overwhelming danger. The whole of it proclaims God as the God of history, a God who becomes involved in the lives of the people. The response we repeat today is the motif that runs through all fifty-one verses of the psalm. That theme of love is constantly reinforced by the proclamation of God's wonderful deeds on behalf of the psalmist.

1 THESSALONIANS 1:5C–10 When Paul says, "You know what sort of people we were among you," he is claiming that he, Silvanus, and Timothy gave living witness to the Gospel they preached. He then begins to praise the Thessalonians as imitators of the apostles and the Lord, models for other churches throughout the region.

It seems that what so pleased and impressed Paul was that the members of this young church, made up largely of Gentile converts, had proven themselves to be steadfast in faith. Acts 17 describes how jealous rivals instigated a

CONNECTIONS TO CHURCH TEACHING AND TRADITION

- "Love . . . is an extraordinary force which leads people to opt for courageous and generous engagement in the field of justice and peace. It is a force that has its origin in God" (CIV, 1).

- "God is the guarantor of man's true development, inasmuch as, having created him in his image, he also establishes the transcendent dignity of men and women and feeds their innate yearning to 'be more.' Man is not a lost atom in a random universe:[1] he is God's creature" (CIV, 29).

---

1 Cf. Benedict XVI, Homily at Mass, Islinger Feld, Regensburg, 12 September 2006.

disturbance that resulted in the harassment and arrest of some of the leaders of the community of Thessalonica. Their imitation of the Lord led them to face persecution for the faith, a crisis that challenged many communities of that era. Paul proudly held up the Thessalonians as a model for others.

MATTHEW 22:34–40 The trap plotted by the Pharisees in their question about the greatest commandment was that if Jesus called one precept the greatest, they could accuse him of denigrating other commands, all of which had come from God. Jesus' reply, citing Deuteronomy 6:5, part of a prayer which pious Jews repeated every morning and evening, demonstrated his loyalty to their shared faith tradition. They could never question that premise. When he connected that prayer to Leviticus 19:18, the command to love thy neighbor, he effectively refused to prioritize commands, asserting that these two sum up all of the Law and the prophets, and thus, their entire religious tradition.

Jesus' combination of these two commandments makes them the core of Christian worship and practice. By demanding love of both God and neighbor, Jesus shows us how to avoid the traps of idolatry and oppression that can result from divorcing the two. As 1 John 4:8 says: "Whoever does not love does not know God." Believing that we can love God without loving our neighbor means that we worship an idol of our own making, not the God of Jesus. Thinking that we can love our neighbor without loving God denies that neighbor his or her deepest identity as a creature made in the image of God. Failing to respect the Creator, it is impossible to properly esteem the dignity of the created person. Ignoring God leads human persons and societies to replace the divine plan with ideologies that inevitably result in injustice. The combined command to love God and neighbor teaches us to strive for humility before our gracious God and obedient service to others, especially the poor. The more we strive for these virtues, the more we will be imitators of the Lord and models for other believers.

- "Faith should show its fruitfulness by penetrating the entire life, even the worldly activities, of those who believe, and by urging them to be loving and just, especially towards those in need. . . . What does most to show God's presence clearly is the familial love of the faithful who, being all of one mind and spirit, work together for the faith of the Gospel[2] and present themselves as a sign of unity" (GS, 21).

---

2 See Philippians 1:27.

The Great Turnaround

MALACHI 1:14B—2:2B, 8–10 Malachi deals with events after the Exile, the period between the prophet Haggai and the religious reforms of Ezra and Nehemiah. The anonymous author (*Malachi* is a Hebrew phrase meaning "my messenger," 3:1) often takes a harsh tone in delivering his message. God's prophet calls the people back to pure love of God by teaching the people what the Torah commanded. When the captives, whom Nebuchadnezzar carried away into exile, returned to the land, they rebuilt the Temple. To their dismay, it was nothing like the first Temple of Solomon (Ezra 3:12). Moreover, worship in the Temple was not up to its former standards, and the devotional life of the people was in ruins. Malachi levels sharp criticism against the rulers and religious leaders who failed to lead them. In his first oracle, Malachi indicts the leadership of the priests who offered blemished sacrifices, not only disregarding the Law of Moses (Leviticus 22:17–25), but also dishonoring God. The author foresees a day when people will offer true sacrifice to God (Malachi 1:11; the Church sees this as the sacrifice of the Mass). The prophet's second oracle is a charge against the people who ask God, "How have you loved us?" (1:2). Malachi asks in return, how have you loved God? In the third oracle, he denounces the Israelite men who divorced their wives and married pagans, a sign of their infidelity to God's covenant. The entire people of God, kings, priests, and laypeople, are called to return to God and return the love God has lavished on them.

PSALM 131:1, 2, 3 Psalm 131 is a psalm of ascent, one of the songs sung as the pilgrims ascended to the Temple atop Mount Zion. It is a hymn for individuals and the nation. When the exiles returned from Babylon, they were no longer a proud and haughty people. They did not question why such trials occurred but were content to rest in the arms of God, like weary children tired from the journey.

1 THESSALONIANS 2:7B–9, 13 God entrusted Paul with the Gospel, which he preached with power "in spite of great opposition." Paul wants the Thessalonians to know that power is available to them also. Although Paul could have insisted on his authority as an apostle of Christ, he earned his own keep while living among them, so as not to place a

CONNECTIONS TO CHURCH TEACHING AND TRADITION

- Christ continues to teach us all through the apostolic tradition in its varied forms (CCC, 74–83).

- The Church teaches in the name of Christ (CCC, 94).

- The faithful must obey the Church's teaching authority (CCC, 87, 91, 93, 892, 2037).

- We, who are always learners, are also teachers (CCC, 900, 905).

financial burden on the community (v. 9). In contrast with the harsh, authoritarian style of some preachers, Paul treated them with the gentleness of a nursing mother and the affection of a father (vv. 7, 11). Likewise, Paul exhorts the Thessalonians to conduct themselves in a manner pleasing to God.

MATTHEW 23:1–12 In Jesus' fifth and final discourse, Matthew concludes the contest between Jesus and the scribes and Pharisees who questioned his authority. (His strong criticism reflects the hostility of Matthew's community toward these religious leaders some fifty years later.) Although Jesus acknowledges that their teaching authority rests on the "chair of Moses" (the "chair of Peter'" is a similar term for Church authority), he warns his disciples not to follow their example. Jesus' adversaries, whom he calls hypocrites (*actors* is the literal interpretation of the Greek word), have laid a heavy burden on the people with their strict interpretation of the Law, which distinguished "heavy" or "light" commandments among the 613 laws of the Torah.

Jesus discourages his disciples from imitating those who competed for places of honor at social functions and grasped after honorific titles they did not deserve. (*Rabbi* was a title of honor in the first century, and it did not take on its modern meaning until the third century. *Father* was a term applied to elders and respected deceased persons and had no relationship to modern clergy. Jesus taught his followers to address God as Father [6:9].) Jesus censures the leaders who liked to call attention to excessive lengthening of the phylacteries and tassels as evidence of their piety. Phylacteries were small leather boxes containing Scripture verses attached to the forehead and hand with straps and worn by Jewish men at prayer (Deuteronomy 6:8). The tassels (adding up to 613 threads and knots) decorated the corners of the cloak (22:12) as a symbolic reminder to keep the Law of Moses. Jesus teaches his followers they are to observe the teachings of their leaders, but they are to surpass them in righteousness (Matthew 5:20).

WISDOM 6:12–16 The Book of Wisdom is one of the Deuterocanonical writings in the Catholic biblical canon. It is considered noncanonical by Jews and Protestants. The Book of Wisdom was written after 200 BC, close to the time of Christ. The author was a devout Jew living in contact and confrontation with the world of Greek philosophy. Writing in King Solomon's name, the author presents the king as the ideal devout Jew. The wisdom given to Solomon, a mortal like the rest of us (7:1), is available to all who love God and seek God's ways. The message of the book is that true wisdom (Hebrew: *hokhmah*; Greek: *sophia*) lies in entering into union with God. In Jewish tradition, wisdom is often personified in a female form (Proverbs 1:20–24; 8:1–2; 9:1–6). Wisdom is portrayed in the Book of Wisdom as a desirable woman who should be pursued by all in their spiritual quest (6:12). Wisdom invites her hearers to reject whatever is wicked and cherish what is just (1:1–15).

PSALM 63:2, 3–4, 5–6, 7–8 (2B) This psalm describes the love between God and the human soul. The soul's ardent longing for God is compared to David's hunger and thirst in the wilderness of Judah as he fled from his enemies. Though near death, David praises God: "You have been my help" (v. 7). David's needs could not be appeased by a "rich feast" (v. 5); God alone can satisfy spiritual hunger and thirst. The psalmist urges everyone to find solace and refuge in God.

1 THESSALONIANS 4:13–18 OR 4:13–14 Paul draws on biblical images to describe God's power. Trumpets, clouds, and words of command recall the scene on Mount Sinai when God revealed the Ten Commandments to Moses (Exodus 20:1–17). The images also depict God as the divine king, who proclaims justice during times of national crisis (Psalm 97:1–6). Paul uses these symbols to portray Christ's return in glory.

He offers consolation to the community as they mourn their loved ones who died before the final event. If Christ was raised from the dead, then all those who are in Christ, living or dead, will witness his triumphant return. Paul urges the community to comfort one another with this Good News.

CONNECTIONS TO CHURCH TEACHING AND TRADITION

- The Church encourages "faithful wrestling" with Scripture (CCC, 101–141).

- Christ, the great teacher, gives us important lessons to which wise readers of the Bible must pay attention (CCC, 110–119).

MATTHEW 25:1–13 In his fifth and final discourse, Jesus discusses with his disciples the last stages of history (Matthew 24–25). He warns them there will be many calamities and false prophets speaking in his name, but these are only the birth pangs of the final age (24:7–11). Because the hour of his return is unknown to them, Jesus' followers must always be prepared (24:36). Jesus compares his return to a wedding banquet, asking who is the "faithful and wise" (24:45) servant whom the master has put in charge. His answer is given in a parable of ten bridesmaids. The story is unique to Matthew, who reflects the Jewish culture of his audience. In first-century Mediterranean customs, the fathers of the bridal couple arranged the marriage. The bride, who was always under the guardianship of a male relative, was moved from the home of her father to the groom's home. Because some of the wedding guests traveled long distances, the marriage celebration lasted several days. The high point of the festivity was when the groom went to the bride's family home to escort her to his home, where the consummation took place.

Jesus' parable begins at the point of the wedding procession. Ten young women, probably sisters and cousins of the couple, await the return of the groom. Five of the women are described as wise and five as foolish (25:2). They echo the wise and foolish women making banquet preparations in the Book of Proverbs (9:1–6). In that allegory, Wisdom's feast offers her guests truth and life, whereas folly's table brings them deceit and death. In Jesus' parable the foolish maidens make no provision to obtain oil for their lamps should the groom return at night. The sensible ones are prepared for any event. When the groom comes unexpectedly, the senseless ones are caught by surprise. The banquet door is locked, and they are unable to enter. The lesson of the story is constant watchfulness. Jesus' disciples are held personally accountable and must be vigilant even if he delays his coming.

Thirty-Third Sunday in Ordinary Time
Stay Alert, Children of the Light!

PROVERBS 31:10–13, 19–20, 30–31 The Proverbs reading is grounded in words of wisdom. The image we are given of a worthy wife and mother is immersed in this metaphor about wisdom and living in fear of the Lord. Not fear as one who is frightened or paralyzed, but the wisdom of one who lives in awe of the wondrous power and majesty of God, who offers love to us. The Hebrew adjective translated "worthy" in this reading is *hayil*, and was used to describe the kind of valor and strength found in armies. That is the kind of courage it takes to enter into this kind of relationship with God. This description of a worthy wife and mother is grounded in a particular cultural time and is not meant as a rationale only for women to act in this way. Rather, it calls us to ground ourselves in this kind of awe and the courage of being in relationship with the Lord. The passage is no excuse for sexism anywhere—not in families, societies, cultures, or religions.

PSALM 128:1–2, 3, 4–5 (SEE 1A) Psalm 128 gives us another image of fear of the Lord from the Wisdom tradition. Those who walk in awe and reverence, practicing obedience in following God's ways, bring peace and prosperity not only on themselves but also on their families and God's chosen ones in the city of Jerusalem. Blessings, new life, prosperity, and peace come to the children who walk in God's ways. This *shalom* fashioned by their obedience generates harmony to all creation and right relationships with all God's people.

1 THESSALONIANS 5:1–6 Many a parent has sent a child going off to college to "remember who you are," meaning to stay centered in the way the young person had been taught to be and act. Paul gives Christians similar advice: you already know you are children of the light, so do not walk in darkness. You are children of the day. Act that way. Stay alert and sober. Do not sleepwalk through this chance to act with conviction and faith.

Paul reminds believers that they do not know when Christ will come again. It happens as stealthily as a thief in the night, or as quickly as labor pains. God does not threaten, but rather invites us to be ready to walk in the Lord's ways, as we heard in the psalm. Believers have

CONNECTIONS TO CHURCH TEACHING AND TRADITION

- "Since this mission continues and, in the course of history, unfolds the mission of Christ, who was sent to evangelize the poor, the church, urged on by the Spirit of Christ, must walk the road Christ himself walked, a way of poverty and obedience, of service and self-sacrifice even to death, a death from which he emerged victorious by his resurrection" (AG, 5).

- "Everyone is responsible for his life before God who has given it to him. It is God who remains the sovereign Master of life. We are obliged to accept life gratefully and preserve it for his honor and the salvation of our souls. We are stewards, not owners, of the life God has entrusted to us. It is not ours to dispose of" (CCC, 2280).

- "Openness to God makes us open towards our brothers and sisters and towards an understanding of life as a joyful task to be accomplished in a spirit of solidarity" (CIV, 78).

- "The Church has no other light than Christ's" (CCC, 748).

already seen the dawning of the new way of life offered to Jesus' followers. Jesus brought light to the darkness and offered it to us. Confident of our identity as children of God and children of the light of Christ, we go forward, ready.

MATTHEW 25:14–30 OR 25:14–15, 19–21 In today's Gospel, we hear another story about readiness and being prepared. The story is familiar, but it is worth paying attention to the details. A man entrusts three servants with exorbitant sums of money (some commentaries suggest one talent equaled fifteen years' worth of laborers' wages) and leaves town. He entrusts each one with abundance according to each one's ability. Two invest theirs and add to the amount, and one digs a hole and buries it. We see how the master responds to all three: there is swift affirmation and judgment, and no excuses are considered right for the third servant's inaction.

What are we to make of this parable, especially in light of Paul's admonition to walk in God's light alert and follow the ways of the Lord? The master trusts the servants, and God entrusts us with the world—everything animate and inanimate. God trusts us to be good stewards and to continue the work Jesus Christ laid out for disciples. If we wait for further instructions or for Jesus' Second Coming to be certain, we will have wasted our time—it will be the same as wasting fifteen years' wages. If we go on living as if we had one more day to act as God bids, even if we live as if we have another hour or even another minute, we do not understand the urgency of the Good News.

We are exhorted to act now, be resourceful, and use our lives and all that we have been given. We should not be hesitant about the Good News of God's loving kindness. We must tell the world the Good News of the amazing, abundant gifts we have been given. We must live freely and fully alert every moment to God's astonishing, saving love.

EZEKIEL 34:11–12, 15–17 The prophet Ezekiel was probably among the eight thousand Jewish captives exiled to Babylon in 598 BC. His writings, which continued for over twenty-five years, move from messages of doom to the consoling promise that God will bring the people back. In chapter 20, Ezekiel retold the history of Israel as a series of God's saving actions followed consistently by human rebellion. As chapter 34 opens, Ezekiel quotes the Word of the Lord, pronouncing woe on the false shepherds of Israel who have not fulfilled their mission of caring for the people. Because of the failure of religious leaders, the Lord promises: "I myself will look after them," "I myself will pasture my sheep," and "I myself will give them rest." This presents us with an image of the God who will not be thwarted by human failure, a God whose plan will be fulfilled in spite of the inadequacy of those whose vocation is to serve the flock.

What is included in the divine pastor's activity? Seeking the lost and strayed, healing the wounded, and evaluating the flock: essentially, the care of the vulnerable. The Lord warns that those who were strong enough to obtain the most for themselves, the sleek and the strong, will come to judgment, because the one who will shepherd rightly has finally arrived.

PSALM 23:1–2, 2–3, 5–6 (1) There can be no doubt why the Church chose Psalm 23 for today's celebration. It is sung by a person who has experienced God as the shepherd prophesied by Ezekiel. Praying this psalm in light of the history of our own salvation, we might gratefully remember the verdant pastures, the restful waters, and the right paths to which God has led us.

Although it is rarely emphasized, this psalm not only portrays God as a shepherd, but also as the hostess who prepares a banquet and the host or servant who anoints the guest. When we believe in a God so attentive to our need, we can wholeheartedly profess hope that we will always find goodness and kindness in the house of the Lord.

1 CORINTHIANS 15:20–26, 28 Chapter 15 of Paul's first letter to the Corinthians deals with Christ's Resurrection and its implications for believers. In our section, Paul calls Christ the "firstfruits," the tangible sign, of what is to come for all. Paul contrasts Adam, the symbol of mortal humanity, to Christ, teaching that "in Christ shall all be brought to

CONNECTIONS TO CHURCH TEACHING AND TRADITION

- "The Scriptures and the Eucharist [are] places of encounter with Christ. . . . The Gospel text concerning the final judgment (cf. Matthew 25:31–46) . . . indicates that we must not neglect a third place of encounter with Christ: 'the persons, especially the poor, with whom Christ identifies himself'[1]" (EIA, 12).

- "'Feed the hungry' (cf. Matthew 25:35, 37, 42) . . . is an ethical imperative for the universal Church. . . . Hunger is not so much dependent on lack of material things as on shortage of social resources. . . . The problem of food insecurity needs to be addressed within a long-term perspective, eliminating the structural causes that give rise to it and promoting the agricultural development of poorer countries" (CIV, 27).

---

1 *Propositio* 4.

life." The vocabulary he used in that phrase would have reminded his readers of the story of creation, thus implying that the Resurrection they awaited would bring them into the new creation.

MATTHEW 25:31–46 In the Gospel according to Matthew, the Sermon on the Mount was Jesus' inaugural public proclamation. Today's Gospel selection presents his last public teaching. The readings of the past two Sundays offered parables regarding being prepared for the coming of the Son of Man. Today's Gospel leaves no room for doubt about the behaviors that demonstrate wise preparation and the proper use of what we have been given.

Anticipating the commission to preach the Gospel to all nations (Matthew 28:16–20), today's reading proclaims that the Son of Man will judge all the nations. No one, regardless of ethnicity or creed, will be exempt from divine scrutiny. As in last week's parable, there is no middle ground: each and every person has lived as either a sheep or a goat. Interestingly, although Jesus had a preaching mission that he shared with his disciples, nothing about this judgment has to do with professions of faith or formal religious observances.

The Son of Man depicted here is the shepherd-king of the entire universe. His flock includes absolutely everyone, and his criterion of judgment has to do with nothing other than the well-being of the flock. The last judgment rights the wrongs that began in Genesis. Christ has conquered evil, and his sheep are those who continued his mission, whether or not they realize it. What the shepherd-king expects of his creatures are the simplest services possible. They involve responses to the most basic human needs: food and water, clothing and shelter, and care for the incapacitated.

Ezekiel proclaimed that the Lord himself would look after the flock. Now Jesus goes further, declaring that his concern for the vulnerable is such that he identifies intimately with them. He suffers with them and is served in them. Taken together, our readings unflinchingly remind us that if we want a share in the kingdom of the divine shepherd, we need to seek and serve him by serving those in need.

- "If we recall that Jesus came to 'preach the good news to the poor' (Matthew 11:5; Luke 7:22), how can we fail to lay greater emphasis on the Church's preferential option for the poor and the outcast?" (TMA, 51).

Holydays, Solemnities, and Feasts

Throughout the liturgical year, the Church celebrates the mysteries, events in the life of Our Lord and his Blessed Mother, events in the life of the Church, saints, angels, and all the faithful departed with solemnities, feasts, commemorations, and memorials, optional or not. A few of these days are kept as holydays of obligation, to be celebrated by all in the territories where they have been so designated. Most of these days are celebrated on their appointed dates unless they fall on a Sunday or within the Sacred Triduum or the Octave of Easter. Two, the Solemnities of the Most Holy Trinity and the Most Holy Body and Blood of Christ, are permanently affixed to the first two Sundays of Ordinary Time after Pentecost. And a few others are deemed of such importance to the life and memory of the Church that when they fall on Sundays of Ordinary Time they supersede the Sunday.

This chapter offers Scripture backgrounds for the holydays of obligation for the United States and for those feasts and solemnities that occasionally are celebrated on Sundays in Ordinary Time.

MALACHI 3:1–4 The Book of Malachi is very brief, only three chapters long. This short book covers a lot of ground, however. Malachi, whose name means "messenger," castigates the priests and Levites for their sins and for their transgressions of the laws of sacrifice. Then there are the sins of the people, which include adultery. Here in chapter 3, Malachi goes on to preach that evildoers must repent. They need to be purified and refined like gold and silver. Then, the distinction between the just and the wicked will become clear. The just are those who serve the Lord, and they will be treated with compassion. This early part of chapter 3 that we read today is a summary of the overall theme of the Book of Malachi: Prepare! Become repentant! Be compassionate! Prepare for the Lord's coming! This is the same message that is heard in the Temple in today's Gospel passage.

PSALM 24:7, 8, 9, 10 (8) Psalm 24 is a hymn of praise to the Creator in the form of a series of questions and answers: "Who is this king of glory? / The Lord of hosts; he is the king of glory" (v. 10). The portals or gates are to open so that he may come in. And these gates, like a council of elders, are bowed down and waiting for their king to come back from battle. How fitting that they are told to lift up their heads and proudly welcome the Lord. This same idea is presented in another way in today's Gospel, as this is what both Simeon and the prophetess Anna foretold about Jesus when he was presented in the Temple.

HEBREWS 2:14–18 Jesus was truly human and truly divine. This reading from Hebrews helps us believe the part that is so difficult, his true humanity. He became like his brothers and sisters in every way. Still, it was up to Jesus to free them from the power of death. Death had been brought into the world by the devil (see Wisdom 1:1–3, 2:23–24). Death meant severing relations with God. But Jesus came to face death himself, having become human. In doing so, he would free the descendants of Abraham. Becoming human in every way meant that Jesus would be tested and tempted. He must have felt especially tempted to avoid his own suffering and Death. Undertaking this for us, though, he freed us from the fear of death.

CONNECTIONS TO CHURCH TEACHING AND TRADITION

- "Taken up to heaven and glorified after he had thus fully accomplished his mission, Christ dwells on earth in his Church" (CCC, 669).

- "Inasmuch as they are creatures, these perceptible realities can become means of expressing the action of God who sanctifies men, and the action of men who offer worship to God. The same is true of signs and symbols taken from the social life of man: washing and anointing, breaking bread and sharing the cup can express the sanctifying presence of God and man's gratitude toward his Creator" (CCC, 1148).

LUKE 2:22–40 OR 2:22–32 The theological centerpiece of this part of the Gospel according to Luke is in verses 29–32, in which Simeon (whose name means "God has heard") proclaimed to God that he had seen the salvation of all peoples in this child. This is the familiar, touching, and dramatic story of Mary and Joseph taking Jesus to the Temple as their firstborn son. They were following the tradition and law to consecrate him to the Lord and to offer their own gifts. Simeon first praises and thanks God for allowing him this honor. Simeon knew that before his death he would see the Christ, and he recognized who Jesus was and who he was to become. Taking the child into his arms, Simeon told his parents of their son's destiny, and that Mary herself would experience great anguish and pain. In his own way, Simeon was telling them to prepare for the Lord's coming. The prophetess Anna, whose name means "grace" and "favor," is a symbol of those who long for the Redeemer. She waits patiently day after day in the Temple. Although Simeon is not a priest, both he and Anna embody service of God that is the heart of the Temple. The pairing of these two people corresponds to Zechariah and Elizabeth in chapter 1 of this Gospel. The Lord has come before us. We now wait to see him in our coming into heaven. While we wait we are to help others know that the Lord has come.

- "Christ is always present in his church, especially in her liturgical celebrations. He is present in the sacrifice of the Mass both in the person of his minister . . . and most of all in the eucharistic species. . . . He is present in his word since it is he himself who speaks when the holy scriptures are read in church. Lastly, he is present when the church prays and sings, for he has promised 'where two or three are gathered together in my name there am I in the midst of them'[1]" (SC, 7).

1 Matthew 18:20.

The Mystery of the Triune God

EXODUS 34:4B–6, 8–9 Throughout its history, Israel grew in knowledge of God. The God of Abraham, Isaac, and Jacob called Moses and revealed to him the name YHWH, a mysterious name indicating that no human can comprehend God (Exodus 3:14). All that we can know about God comes from God's interaction with us.

This Sunday we hear that God appeared to Moses and gave him a series of self-descriptions. After the title *Lord*, we hear that God is merciful. The Hebrew word for mercy is related to the word for womb, implying that God has a motherly love for us. That God is gracious signifies God's boundless generosity. That God is slow to anger means that God offers us ample time for repentance. Divine kindness and fidelity assure us that God will never abandon the covenant.

DANIEL 3:52, 53, 54, 55, 56 (52B) The canticle we sing this Sunday is a song of victory over persecution. In the third chapter of the Book of Daniel, we hear of Shadrach, Meshach, and Abednego, who were thrown into a fire under the orders of King Nebuchadnezzar because they refused to worship an idol. This is part of the song they sang when the angel of the Lord drove the flames out of the furnace. Its forty-eight verses call on all creation to praise the God of salvation.

2 CORINTHIANS 13:11–13 At the close of his second letter to the Corinthians, Paul gives instructions and prays what was then an exceptional blessing for the community; today we use it in our Eucharistic celebrations. It is the only explicitly Trinitarian blessing in our Scriptures, and Paul's letter predates Matthew's account of the Gospel, which calls for Baptism in the name of the Father, the Son, and the Spirit.

Paul begins his prayer, by asking for "the grace of the Lord Jesus Christ" (2 Corinthians 13:13). In Paul's writing, the Lord's grace is salvation; it includes every type of gift or blessing. Mentioning Christ first indicates that it is through him that we have come to know what we now know about God; most particularly, the revelation of God's great love expressed through Jesus. The third part of the blessing asks for companionship with the Holy Spirit, the experience of knowing God's Spirit in the community. Like his Jewish

CONNECTIONS TO CHURCH TEACHING AND TRADITION

- "The mystery of the Most Holy Trinity is the central mystery of Christian faith and life. It is the mystery of God in himself. . . . The whole history of salvation is identical with the history of the way . . . the one true God, Father, Son, and Holy Spirit, reveals himself to men[1]" (CCC, 234).

- "It pleased God, in his goodness and wisdom, to reveal himself and to make known the mystery of his will. His will was that men should have access to the Father, through Christ, the Word made flesh, in the Holy Spirit, and thus become sharers in the divine nature (see DV, 2; cf. Ephesians 1:9; 2:18; 2 Peter 1:4)" (CCC, 51).

- "During the first centuries the Church sought to clarify its Trinitarian faith. . . . This clarification was the work of the early councils, aided by the theological work of the Church Fathers and sustained by the Christian people's sense of the faith" (CCC, 250).

---

1 GCD, 47.

predecessors, Paul is reflecting knowledge of God rooted in religious experience. Only after much more reflection on that experience will the Church begin to articulate the doctrine of the Triune God.

JOHN 3:16–18 These three verses, like many Gospel citations, could be used to summarize the entire Gospel message. Verse 16 first reminds us of God's love not just for one people or nation but for the whole world. The words "gave his only Son" (v. 16) hearken back to Abraham's willingness to sacrifice his son and God's intervention to save Isaac on the third day (Genesis 22).

Verse 17 recalls God's generous love, insisting that God has no desire to condemn the world. This, too, recalls Jewish tradition expressed in passages like Ezekiel 18:23, where the Lord asks: "Do I indeed derive any pleasure from the death of the wicked. . . . Do I not rather rejoice when he turns from his evil way that he may live?" It is that same, loving God who sent the Son so that the world might be saved.

Some may read verse 18 as a contradiction to the preceding verses, but the meaning is more subtle than it first appears. Jesus is not demanding belief; he is pointing out that belief is the only path to life. The person who does not believe is comparable to people who refuse to appreciate beauty: they are not deprived by another, but rather deprive themselves of the pleasure beauty can offer. Those who refuse to believe are rejecting salvation.

In the context of the solemnity of the Most Holy Trinity, this passage, like Paul's blessing of the Corinthians, assures us of God's unfailing, immeasurable love for humanity. Our God will stop at nothing to bring us to life. Contemplating all of these readings together, we have a glimpse of God's ongoing self-revelation and the experiences that have brought us to faith in the Triune God.

DEUTERONOMY 8:2–3, 14B–16A Deuteronomy presents Moses' farewell discourse to the people as they are about to enter the Promised Land. In this passage, Moses counsels the people to remember the mighty deeds that God has done on their behalf during their desert sojourn. God promised to be with the people and was faithful to that promise by providing everything they needed. The testing in the desert was God's way of seeing how faithful the people were to their part of the covenant promises. Hunger was one of the desert afflictions that God satisfied by miraculously providing manna. This was God's way of stressing trust and dependence upon the one who satisfies all hungers. Moses repeats his advice that they are not to forget that in their nothingness, God provides for all their needs. Like them, we must seek God rather than material wealth, trusting that God will provide us with everything that we need.

PSALM 147:12–13, 14–15, 19–20 (12) Psalm 147 personifies Jerusalem as a mother gathering her children to her. All are summoned to praise the Lord in thanksgiving for his Word, which brings life and abundance. God's Word has blessed Jerusalem, strengthened her gates and walls, granted peace, and brought fertility to the fields. God has done this for no other nation. Only Israel has been so blessed, and thus is summoned to praise the Lord. The psalm stresses that God's Word brings forth all blessings. God, who gives totally and completely to satisfy all hungers, is the source of these blessings. God's Word is a dynamic reality that goes forth from God throughout the earth, accomplishing all that God commands. For this reason, all of Israel is called to praise the Lord, as we are, for the rich blessings in our lives.

1 CORINTHIANS 10:16–17 In his first letter to the Corinthians, Paul shares a significant aspect of his teaching, which concerns Christ and the community as the Body of Christ. Jumping off his cultural experience of the bonding that comes from breaking bread and sharing wine at table, Paul stresses that our share in Christ's Body and Blood intimately bonds us to Christ. Our sharing bonds us to the sacrifice of Christ's Body and Blood, which he willingly shed for all. Our communal sharing also bonds us to

CONNECTIONS TO CHURCH TEACHING AND TRADITION

- "From the beginning, Jesus associated his disciples with his own life . . . [1]And he proclaimed a mysterious and real communion between his own body and ours.[2]" (CCC, 787).

- "The *Breaking of Bread* . . . is [the] expression that the first Christians will use to designate their Eucharistic assemblies;[3] by doing so they signified that all who eat the one broken bread, Christ, enter into communion with him and form but one body in him[4]" (CCC, 1329).

- "Those who receive the Eucharist are united more closely to Christ. Through it Christ unites them to all the faithful in one body—the Church. Communion renews, strengthens, and deepens this incorporation into the Church, already achieved by Baptism" (CCC, 1396).

---

1 Cf. Mark 1:16–20; 3:13–19; Matthew 13:10–17; Luke 10:17–20; 22:28–30; John 15:4–5.

2 John 6:56.

3 Cf. Acts 2:42, 46; 20:7, 11.

4 Cf. 1 Corinthians 10:16–17.

---

one another as the Body of Christ, a community that willingly commits itself to a life of sacrifice for the sake of others, in imitation of Christ. Sharing at the Lord's table leads to a transformation of the participants into Christ, both individually and communally.

SEQUENCE: ***LAUDA SION*** This Sunday, the Church sings one of the four sequences—ancient, poetic songs that precede the singing of the Gospel Acclamation. The sequence for the Most Holy Body and Blood of Christ, *Lauda Sion*, is ascribed to St. Thomas Aquinas, who is thought to have written it at the request of Pope Urban IV. The sixth stanza of the sequence reminds us of the history of the Eucharistic feast.

JOHN 6:51–58 The context for these verses on Jesus as "the living bread that came down from heaven" (John 6:51) is the Eucharistic celebration of the early Christian communities. The Eucharist of the early communities was always aligned with the total saving event of Christ, who gave his Body and shed his Blood for our sakes. John connects the two realities when he has Jesus state that "the bread that I will give is my flesh for the life of the world" (John 6:51).

For John, God the Father, the source of all life, shares with Jesus the fullness of that life. Jesus, the living bread that came down from heaven, gives of his life for all. The phrase "flesh and blood" expresses the fullness of the life of Jesus. Those who believe, who accept and partake of the whole Jesus, the living bread, will live forever.

God's gift to Israel of the manna and of the law as true nourishment is now fulfilled in Jesus, the living bread. Those who eat of that flesh and drink of that blood abide with Jesus, and he abides with them. The manna is given new meaning in the life, Death, and Resurrection of Jesus. Jesus, the manna of God, feeds us eternally with his very self.

▪ "'The Eucharist is our daily bread. . . . Its effect is then understood as unity, so that, gathered into his Body . . . we may become what we receive'[5]" (CCC, 2837).

---

5 St. Augustine, Sermo 57.7: PL 38, 389.

JEREMIAH 1:4–10 Prophets knew they faced rejection, scorn, and suffering for their warnings. Jeremiah might be excused for his reluctance; he knew what hostility might face him if he carried the word and instruction of God to a people often stubborn and unwilling to change their ways. The promise of God to Jeremiah is that he would give him the necessary words. He simply had to be willing to be an instrument. God touches Jeremiah's mouth, giving him the words to preach and prophesize. God goes on to tell Jeremiah that, as a result of this action of giving him the words, he will be able to root up, tear down, and destroy—powerful actions signifying not Jeremiah's ability but God's power and might. Jeremiah's story tells of a faithful prophet, one in a long line of those sent by God to remind his people of their covenant. In the Gospel today we hear of another great prophet, John, the last one before Jesus himself. John, we are told by Luke, "will turn many of the children of Israel to the Lord their God" (Luke 1:17). This is the role of a prophet: to bring God's people home to God by preaching the words of his justice wherever God commands.

PSALM 71:1–2, 3–4, 5–6, 15, 17 (6B) The use of Psalm 71 for the vigil of the feast of John the Baptist's birth seems appropriate to commemorate his mission and dedication to the Messiah who was to come after him. This psalm of lament is full of strong images for God: stronghold, refuge, rock, and fortress. From the very beginning in the womb, the psalmist is confident that God is worthy of this trust and hope; God is a shelter worthy of this dependence. In the First Reading we hear a similar image of being formed by God before birth in response to Jeremiah's protest that he is too young to preach God's message. Who wants to go to hostile and unwelcoming nations to offer a message of God's promise? But Jeremiah can trust that this is his task, for it is God who does the sending. It seems an appropriate psalm to link with this feast of John the Baptist, who also experienced God in his mother Elizabeth's womb when she was greeted by Mary carrying the Son of God. John has been blessed before birth to carry the message entrusted by God. He can be certain that God will give him strength for the journey.

CONNECTIONS TO CHURCH TEACHING AND TRADITION

- "Jesus came to set this fire upon the earth, until all is ablaze in the love of God. We pray this fire will come upon us as disciples as we, led by the Spirit, carry out Christ's great commission to go and make disciples of all the nations" (GMD, 69).

- "Of her very nature, the Church is missionary. This means her members are called by God to bring the Gospel by word and deed to all peoples and to every situation of work, education, culture, and communal life in which human beings find themselves" (USCCA, 501).

- "In [John the Baptist], the Holy Spirit concludes his speaking through the prophets. John completes the cycle of prophets begun by Elijah[1]" (CCC, 719).

---

1 Cf. Mt 11:13–14.

1 PETER 1:8–12 The opening lines of the First Letter of Peter address the Gentile converts of Asia Minor. These sojourners scattered far from home are told they are a chosen race sanctified by God's grace. The spirit of Christ was preached to them by the prophets who told them of this grace of salvation. This passage seems a fitting one to celebrate John the Baptist, one of the greatest prophets the world has ever seen.

LUKE 1:5–17 The promised birth of a baby after waiting for a long time is a cause of great joy; Elizabeth and Zechariah have long waited for a child, trusting in God. There are several Old Testament stories of women who have longingly awaited a birth of a child: Sarah (Genesis 15:3; 16:1); Rebekah (Genesis 25:21); Rachel (Genesis 29:31; 30:1); the mother of Samson (Judges 13:2–3); and Hannah (1 Samuel 1:2). With this image, Luke connects the story of John the Baptist to a long heritage of Old Testament figures who have played a role in Israel's history. This child, Zechariah is told, is no ordinary child, for he will not only be a source of joy to them but "will be filled with the Holy Spirit even from his mother's womb, and he will turn many of the children of Israel to the Lord their God" (Luke 1:15–17). He will be a prophet, the last before the coming Messiah, who will prepare the people for the coming of the Lord. In Luke's account of the Gospel, John the Baptist prepares himself in the desert until he comes forward to announce the coming of the Lord. But as Luke recounts in chapter 3 of his Gospel account, John constantly points the way to the coming Messiah. John baptizes, urging repentance and a change of heart to prepare for the Messiah, who will baptize with the Holy Spirit and fire. John fulfills the promise of his birth by preaching to the people what God commands as he prepares the way for the Lord.

ISAIAH 49:1–6 Even though his people still languished in exile, the prophet referred to as Second Isaiah saw visions of a restored Israel. In the center of these visions stood a figure the prophet called the servant of the Lord. To celebrate this servant, Isaiah wrote four songs. The first song (Isaiah 42:1–4) pictured the servant as a great leader who will lead Israel out of exile and into a new era of justice and mercy. In the second song, which today's reading is drawn from, the servant is identified with Israel itself. God's people, who seem to have failed miserably in fulfilling their calling, now receive an even more important task: to be a "light to the nations." Israel is the channel through which the people of the world will come to know the glory of God.

Isaiah's words foreshadow the ministry of John the Baptist. Like the servant, John called people to return to God and pointed them to the glory of God yet to come. These are our tasks as well; according to Isaiah, the servant's ministry is the ministry of us all.

PSALM 139:1–3, 13–15 Psalm 139 is a prayer for deliverance. Tradition attributes the psalm to King David, who had many enemies and often prayed to be delivered from them. The psalm begins with a long preamble praising God as all-knowing. To God the psalmist's life is like an open book, revealing the psalmist before he was even born.

The life of John the Baptist is again foreshadowed. Like the psalmist, John was known and called by God from his mother's womb (Luke 1). He was also aware of how God searches the heart. While the psalmist sought the defeat of his enemies, John called enemy and friend alike to repentance.

CONNECTIONS TO CHURCH TEACHING AND TRADITION

- John the Baptist prefigured what the Holy Spirit will achieve in and with Christ (CCC, 720).

- John bore witness to Christ in his preaching, his baptism of repentance, and his martyrdom (CCC, glossary).

- God knows and calls us even before the beginning of our being (CCC, 381). All life is sacred to God (CCC, 2258).

- Over the centuries Christian people organized the days, weeks, months, and seasons into a liturgical year or calendar (CCC, 1168–1171).

ACTS 13:22–26 Like Peter before him, Paul places Jesus in the history of the Jewish people. Beginning with the Exodus from Egypt, Paul traces that history through the conquest of Canaan up to the establishment of the Davidic monarchy. Paul reminds his listeners of God's promise to David that out of his descendants would one day come a Savior who would redeem Israel. That Savior, Paul says, is Jesus. To emphasize his point, Paul even quotes John the Baptist, whom many thought was the promised Savior. Paul explains that John is not the Savior but the Savior's forerunner. That is why John was born to prepare people for Jesus' coming.

Although our part in God's plan may not be as pivotal as that of John, each of us does have a part. We, too, are here for a reason, however insignificant that reason might seem.

LUKE 1:57–66, 80 Luke recounts the births of both Jesus and John the Baptist. This is no mere coincidence; in Luke's mind John is a crucial, although secondary, figure in God's plan for the salvation of the world. Like that of Jesus, the importance of John's birth is underscored by angelic visitations, miraculous signs, and songs of praise.

The townspeople wonder what kind of man this child will grow up to be. Some may even wonder if he is the promised Messiah. His parents, however, already know their son is not. He is instead the Messiah's advance man, a prophet "with the power and spirit of Elijah [who] will make ready a people prepared for the Lord" (v. 17).

While the other passages today emphasize the hand of God in John's birth, this passage shows us the role of his parents as well. God called John before he was born, but the faith of his pious parents, even in such a simple matter as what to name their son, led John onto the right path. Through Elizabeth and Zechariah, God prepared John for the work ahead of him.

ACTS 3:1–10 The account of Peter's healing the crippled man comes immediately after the idyllic description of the life of the early community in Jerusalem. They shared all they had, met to pray in the Temple area, and broke the bread in their homes as more and more joined them. Given that they shared everything in common, it is not surprising that Peter and John would tell the crippled man that they had neither silver nor gold. In a way, we might consider them the precursors of the Franciscans, holding nothing of their own, but putting all their goods at the service of the community and especially the poor. In addition, we might infer that the two disciples were dressed rather shabbily as all they had to say to the lame man was "Look at us" and Peter explained "I have neither silver nor gold, but what I do have I give you" (vv. 4, 6). Then, declaring from whence came his power he healed the man "in the name of Jesus Christ the Nazarene" (v. 6).

The healing gave Peter an audience so that he could preach his message about Jesus, the second Person of the Trinity. Peter's speech is replete with allusions to the Old Testament. As a result of that preaching, Peter and John were arrested and sent before the religious authorities, the very ones who were threatened by their success. When the authorities ordered the Apostles to cease their preaching, their reply was "Whether it is right in the sight of God for us to obey you rather than God, you be the judges" (4:19). Acting in the name of Jesus is both powerful and dangerous. This reading and what follows invite us to ask ourselves what we are willing to risk to act in Christ's name.

PSALM 19:2–3, 4–5 (5A) This short response is aimed at helping us appreciate the work of the disciples, whose message has gone through all the earth and across the ages. It also reminds us that, for those who do not hear the preaching of the Gospel, nature itself, the heavens, the earth, and day and night, reveal their Creator.

CONNECTIONS TO CHURCH TEACHING AND TRADITION

- "In reality it was Christ's own love, free and unsolicited, which gave rise to his question to Peter and to his act of entrusting 'his' sheep to Peter. Therefore, every ministerial action— while it leads to loving and serving the Church —provides an incentive to grow in ever greater love and service of Jesus Christ the head" (PDV, 25).

- "Our pastoral service . . . requires proclaiming Jesus Christ and the Good News . . . denouncing sinful situations, structures of death . . . and fostering intercultural, interreligious and ecumenical dialogue" (*Aparecida*, 95).

- "You go too. The call is a concern not only of Pastors, clergy, and men and women religious. The call is addressed to everyone: lay people as well are personally called by the Lord, from whom they receive a mission on behalf of the Church and the world" (CL, 2).

GALATIANS 1:11–20 As Paul began this letter, he upbraided the Galatians for falling into the clutches of those who would pervert the pure Gospel message with the insistence that the people also follow the Jewish law. This was a major hurdle for the early church to overcome; and the solution was worked out at what some call "The Council of Jerusalem" which probably took place around AD 49 (see Acts 15:1–29).

After Paul leveled his first critique of the community he launched into his autobiography. He responded to the critique that he never knew Jesus in the flesh with the statement that the Gospel he preached was not of human origins. He owns up to his former way of life as a persecutor of the Christians. Nevertheless, he claims that God set him apart from his mother's womb (see Jeremiah 1:4–5; Isaiah 49:1).

Paul says that after receiving the revelation of the Son of God and being baptized by Ananias he still did not consult human beings, implying that for three years he continued in intimate prayer and learning from the Risen Christ and from the Father (see Acts 9:1–19; 22:3–16; 26:2–18). His claim comes down to the assertion that all that he did was learned, planned, and carried out in the name of Jesus.

Along with telling us more about Paul, the reading invites us to ask ourselves how often we plan our own lives based on discernment of God's will, and how much we simply make our own expedient decisions or allow others to direct us.

JOHN 21:15–19 Just as we tend to remember Thomas more for the doubt he expressed on one day than for his long-term discipleship and mission activity, we can easily remember Peter primarily for his threefold denial of Christ. Today's Gospel presents the scene in which Jesus thoroughly rehabilitates him. "Do you love me? Do you love me? Do you love me?" Peter responds three times in the affirmative, but words are not enough. Jesus gives him the vocation to be a good shepherd to his people. Prayers and verbal testimony are fine, but they only carry weight when we, like Peter, allow our dedication to Jesus' mission to lead us where we would not otherwise go—even to death.

ACTS 12:1–11 As we celebrate the Solemnity of Sts. Peter and Paul, we begin with a scene from Peter's colorful career, one of his prison escapes—or, better said, rescues. In a highly symbolic statement, we are told that Herod Agrippa, the grandson of Herod the Great, had Peter arrested "on the feast of Unleavened Bread" (v. 3). This happened after Herod had ordered the martyrdom of James the brother of John. (Note the echoes of the death of John the Baptist and Jesus' arrest.) Peter was well chained and guarded while the community was gathered in prayer in the home of Mary, the mother of John Mark. Presumably, both Peter and the gathered community were praying for his safety. Unexpectedly, an angel miraculously freed him and then disappeared when they were clear of the jail and the guards.

What today's reading does not include is the comic result of all of this. Peter hastened to the place where the community was gathered in prayer, the home of Mary. When Mary's maid heard his voice outside the gate, she got so excited that she ran upstairs to tell the community, leaving Peter stranded on the street. He eventually got in and explained all that had happened and then left for another place to preserve their safety as well as his own.

This is an interesting piece of the biography of Peter. He escaped from prison more than once (see Acts 5:17), and as time went on he grew in his role as the shepherd who risked everything and eventually lost his life for the Gospel.

PSALM 34:2–3, 4–5, 6–7, 8–9 (5B) Peter could well have prayed this psalm after his rescue. It is particularly appropriate in light of the visit of the angel. One line well worth our meditation is verse 5: "I sought the LORD, and he answered me / and delivered me from all my fears." The person praying is delivered not from danger and persecution, but from fear. As we pray this, we are invited to look to the Lord for help. When we experience God's help, whether we are rescued from danger or from fear, we will be radiant, forgetting all our worry and shame.

2 TIMOTHY 4:6–8, 17–18 In writing to his dearest protégé, Paul is handing on his legacy as well as facing the inevitable in his future. He says he is being poured out like a libation, a sacrifice offered to God. Although he knows he is facing

CONNECTIONS TO CHURCH TEACHING AND TRADITION

- "A first essential setting for learning hope is prayer. When no one listens to me anymore, God still listens to me. When I can no longer talk to anyone . . . I can always talk to God. When there is no longer anyone to help me . . . he can help me" (SS, 32).

- "During thirteen years in jail, in a situation of seemingly utter hopelessness, the fact that [Cardinal Nguyen Van Thuan] could listen and speak to God became for him an increasing power of hope, which enabled him, after his release, to become for people all over the world a witness to hope—to that great hope which does not wane even in the nights of solitude" (SS, 32).

martyrdom, Paul's focus is on being with the Lord. He can say that the Lord will rescue him from every threat, knowing all the while that such a rescue implies eternal life, not an escape from any further suffering. Thus, he can end his letter glorifying the God he hopes to meet soon.

MATTHEW 16:13–19 This segment of Matthew's account of the Gospel is a defining moment in the Gospel. Jesus has never called himself the Messiah, but Matthew has hinted at that identity (see 1:1, 16:18). Before this event, the group of disciples had proclaimed Jesus as Son of God (14:33). Now, Peter's proclamation of Jesus as Messiah brings a special commendation. As we move through the Gospel, we will see that Peter's commission to bind and loose is not exclusive: in Matthew 18:18 Jesus addresses the same statement to the entire group of disciples. Nevertheless, it was Peter who spoke in the name of the group, calling Jesus the Messiah (Christ), the Son of the living God.

Following Peter's proclamation, Jesus forbade the group to reveal what they knew to anyone and he began to teach them about his coming suffering. Hearing that, Peter rebuked him, saying that they would never allow that to happen. But Jesus replied that Peter was thinking like human beings, not like God (16:20b–23).

It is easy to be like Peter and say the right words. What is difficult is to begin to accept the meaning of those words as God understands them, not as we do. Peter had the vocabulary; he just did not grasp the fullness of Jesus' meaning.

In the scriptural depictions of Peter we hear at the vigil for this solemnity, he appears to be a much more mature man. He had learned what Jesus had taught and was ready to follow the crucified and Risen Messiah. He had begun to understand from God's point of view.

Taken together, we see Peter in his imprisoned poverty, freed by an angel of the God to whom he and the community prayed. He was the poor one who called out and was—at least this time—rescued. Peter and Paul had become poor for the sake of the Gospel, and in spite of their past denials and persecutions—had learned to call upon the Lord and to follow where he led.

• Therefore, all the disciples of Christ, persevering in prayer and praising God,[1] should present themselves as a living sacrifice. . . . They should everywhere on earth bear witness to Christ and give an answer to everyone who asks a reason for their hope of eternal life[2]" (LG, 10).

1 Cf. Acts 2:42–47.
2 Cf. 1 Peter 3:15.

DANIEL 7:9–10, 13–14 At about the time that Daniel was written, the Jewish people lived under the rule of Antiochus Epiphanes. Antiochus wanted to impose Greek culture and religion on his Jewish subjects. The dreams and visions described in chapters 7–12 are addressed to persecuted people, particularly those persecuted by Antiochus. In the verses that precede the reading, four mythical beasts emerge from an abyss. These beasts can be identified as empires that ruled over the people of Israel: Assyria, Babylon, Persia, and Greece. These beasts terrorize and destroy people (7:5). Amid this destruction comes "an Ancient One" (v. 9), taking his throne of fiery flames. God appears and judges the beasts, in particular a beast's horn that represented Antiochus. The horn is destroyed (v. 11), and on the horizon a new vision arises. A being in human form appears before the Ancient One and receives authority over the world for eternity (vv. 13–14). For the people undergoing persecution, this vision promises that God, not human rulers, reigns over the world and throughout history.

The Book of Daniel promises that faith will triumph: the good and righteous will be saved and the wicked destroyed. Later Christians interpreted the one given authority to be Jesus Christ, whose power comes from God and whose rule is eternal.

PSALM 97:1–2, 5–6, 9 (1A, 9A) Psalm 97 celebrates the reign of God over Israel. The people experience God as a mysterious force, like "clouds and thick darkness" (v. 2). God's reign is founded on justice (v. 2), and God's power is overwhelming. The highest points on earth dissolve in the presence of the mighty one (v. 5). The psalm proclaims that no god is greater than the God of Israel (v. 9).

CONNECTIONS TO CHURCH TEACHING AND TRADITION

- In the Transfiguration Jesus' real nature is revealed to his followers and to us (CCC, 464–469, 480–482).

- Face-to-face with the mystery of Christ's dual nature, the apostles respond in wonder (CCC, 554–556, 568).

- The Transfiguration is a preview of God's glory, visible only with the eyes of faith (CCC, 2809).

2 PETER 1:16–19 The early Christians, who once believed that Christ would return momentarily, became confused as the years progressed. Some people began to teach that belief in Christ's return was one of several clever "myths" (v. 16). In the Second Letter of Peter, someone writing in his name addressed these false teachers.

The passage defends belief in Christ's return with an appeal to the Apostles' experience of the Transfiguration. According to the author, the experience of Jesus' transformation and the words spoken from heaven revealed him to be the one from God. The Transfiguration is like a window offering a view into the reality to come. Present time is compared to darkness, but Christ's reappearance will mark the dawn of a new day. Until then, believers must stand firm in their faith founded on the Apostles' witness.

MATTHEW 17:1–9 The Transfiguration is a mysterious event that revealed Jesus' divine nature and the glory that would be his after the Resurrection and exaltation into heaven. Peter, James, and John, the same disciples who accompany Jesus to the garden at Gethsemane, are led to a mountain to see Jesus transform into a being of light. Two great leaders, Elijah and Moses, also appear. Moses and Elijah both experienced the glory of the Lord on a high mountain: Moses received the Law (Exodus 19–34) and Elijah heard the voice of God (1 Kings 19:8–14). They may represent the law and the prophets that Jesus has fulfilled.

In all three Gospel accounts, the Transfiguration immediately follows Jesus telling his followers that discipleship involves denying oneself and taking up the cross (Mark 8:34–38). The Gospels teach that if the disciples persevere through suffering and trial, they will also share a glorious encounter with God.

Sometimes God comes to us with light and glory, but God usually comes to us at the deepest levels of our ordinary experiences: in the beauty of a flower, in the love of a child, in a creative project. The memory of these meetings with God provides strength in the deep valleys of life and gives us hope that one day we will reach the final mountain we call heaven.

Victory through Christ

1 CHRONICLES 15:3–4, 15–16; 16:1–2 This reading recounts the transfer of the ark from the Judean hillsides to Jerusalem, the city that David had established as his royal city. David calls together all of Israel, along with those who exercised ritual functions, the Levites, the sons of Aaron, and the chanters, to be intimately involved in the transfer. Once the ark is established in its new dwelling place, David and the Levites make burnt offerings to God and David concludes the service by blessing "the people in the name of the Lord" (16:2).

The ark of the covenant is an ancient symbol for Mary, the Mother of the Lord. The ark held within it the Law, the path of life, which God had given to the people through Moses. The Law was revered because it brought people closer to God and manifested God's intimate presence with the people. The vessel containing it was venerated simply because of its precious cargo. Christians link Mary with the ark, she who freely chose to be the vessel for bringing Christ, God-with-us, into the world. Today's vigil feast celebrates the special gift God has given to Mary, and to us, in desiring to be one of us, and in granting us victory through Christ.

PSALM 132:6–7, 9–10, 13–14 (8) This royal psalm celebrates the transfer of the ark of the covenant from Jaar, a location in Judea near Jerusalem, to Jerusalem itself, David's royal city. The name Ephrathah refers to Bethlehem, the city of David's birth, establishing David's lineage to the ark and Jerusalem, the city that God has chosen as a dwelling place. The rest of the psalm is a celebratory procession of the ark to its dwelling place. Because of God's dwelling among us, represented by the ark, justice is to clothe the priests and people, as prayers are offered for a just rule by the Davidic king, God's anointed. All this is possible because God has favored the people by choosing Zion, Jerusalem, as a dwelling place, preferring her "forever" (132:14). Christians link the psalm's Zion to Mary, chosen by God as a dwelling place from whom the son of justice would come forth to reside with all God's people. In Christ, the Son of justice dwelling among us, all have been blessed and given victory.

CONNECTIONS TO CHURCH TEACHING AND TRADITION

- "Christ, 'the first-born from the dead,'[1] is the principle of our own resurrection, even now by the justification of our souls,[2] and one day by the new life he will impart to our bodies[3]" (CCC, 658).

- "Only faith can embrace the mysterious ways of God's almighty power. This faith glories in its weaknesses in order to draw to itself Christ's power.[4] The Virgin Mary is the supreme model of this faith, for she believed that 'nothing will be impossible with God,' and was able to magnify the Lord: 'For he who is mighty has done great things for me, and holy is his name'[5]" (CCC, 273).

1 Colossians 1:18.
2 Cf. Romans 6:4.
3 Cf. Romans 8:11.
4 Cf. 2 Corinthians 12:9; Philippians 4:13.
5 Luke 1:37, 49.

1 CORINTHIANS 15:54B–57 Paul brings his reflections on death and resurrection to a conclusion in this passage from chapter 15 of his first letter to the Corinthians. At the end time, all believers who have died and all who live will be clothed with immortality. Combining Isaiah 28:8 and Hosea 13:14, Paul shows how God desires us to overcome death, the one thing that prevents us from full union with God. Paul claims that through Christ's Passion, Death, and Resurrection, God has "swallowed up" death (15:54), completely removed its sting, and clothed us with immortality. From Paul's perspective, sin, choosing self over others, results in "the sting of death" (15:56) separating us from God eternally. The law contributes to death by facilitating blind obedience rather than the exercise of freedom by the children of God. Paul thanks God for the victory over death that has been given to us "through our Lord Jesus Christ" (15:57). The vigil of the Assumption prepares us to fully celebrate the effects on Mary of Christ's victory over death. By extension, we are also celebrating the profound realization that in Christ, the same victory over death is fully ours as well.

LUKE 11:27–28 In this episode, unique to the Gospel according to Luke, a woman in the crowd to which Jesus is speaking praises his Mother, saying, "Blessed is the womb that carried you and the breasts at which you nursed" (11:27). Jesus, while not denying his Mother's singular and unique blessedness, expands and specifies it further by blessing all "those who hear the word of God and observe it" (11:28). For Luke, Mary is the first disciple of Jesus who not only hears God's Word, but brings the Word to life in her, and shares him with all humanity. Mary willingly cooperates in God's plan to bring Christ into the world. God's Word takes flesh in Mary, the vessel through whom God becomes Emmanuel, God-with-us. In Jesus' birth, Mary offers Christ to the world, enabling God to accomplish victory over sin and death through Christ Jesus. Mary's life is spent reflecting on these events, and their meaning for her and for all humanity.

In Mary, we have the ultimate model of discipleship, one who hears God's Word and observes it. Through Christ, we and Mary experience many blessings culminating in victory over death and in eternal union with God forever.

- "Mary's function as mother of humankind in no way obscures or diminishes this unique mediation of Christ, but rather shows its power. All the Blessed Virgin's salutary influence on men and women originates not in any inner necessity but in the disposition of God. It flows forth from the superabundance of the merits of Christ, rests on his mediation, depends entirely on it and draws all its power from it. It does not hinder in any way the immediate union of the faithful with Christ but on the contrary fosters it" (LG, 60).

REVELATION 11:19A; 12:1–6A, 10AB This end-time vision of God's anointed initiating an era that will result in the defeat of evil powers is filled with apocalyptic and mythological images. The vision begins with the heavenly temple opened for all to see the ark of the covenant. Both temple and ark are images indicating God's presence among the people. The vision switches to a pregnant "woman clothed with the sun" (12:1) who is laboring to give birth. A destructive dragon, symbolic of evil, stands ready to devour the pregnant woman's child. The woman gives birth to a son, "destined to rule all nations with an iron rod" (12:5). Through God's intervention, both mother and child are rescued from the dragon, while a voice loudly proclaims that "now have salvation and power come / . . . the Kingdom of God / and the authority of his Anointed One" (12:10).

The woman is often interpreted as God's people, Israel, and by extension both Mary and the Church. The dragon represents all evil powers out to destroy God's anointed. God's intention both now and at the end-time is that Christ, God's anointed, reigns among us with salvation and power, destroying evil and establishing God's eternal kingdom of peace. Today we celebrate Mary, the first among us to experience fully the effects of God's saving actions, which are intended for all humanity.

PSALM 45:10, 11, 12, 16 (10BC) This psalm is a wedding song celebrating a royal marriage, possibly that of King Ahab and Jezebel, who was a princess of Tyre and Sidon as referenced in verse 13. The refrain and first verse chosen for this feast focus on the honor rendered to the king by having such a beautiful and richly adorned queen stand at his right hand. The other verses chosen speak directly to the queen, advising her to forget her people and give all her attention to the king, who is now her lord. The last verse recounts the bridal procession of queen and maids entering the king's palace "with gladness and joy" (45:16).

The Solemnity of the Assumption celebrates Mary being welcomed, body and soul, into God's royal abode. Standing at God's right hand, she is crowned Queen of Heaven. The psalm's wedding song images speak to this event in Mary's life, which is nowhere in Scripture but has been traditionally held by Catholic Christians. With Mary, we honor and

CONNECTIONS TO CHURCH TEACHING AND TRADITION

- "The Assumption of the Blessed Virgin is a singular participation in her Son's Resurrection and an anticipation of the resurrection of other Christians" (CCC, 966).

- "The Virgin Mary . . . is acknowledged and honored as truly the Mother of God and of the Redeemer. . . . But, being of the race of Adam, she is at the same time also united to all those who are to be saved. . . . Therefore she is hailed as a preeminent and as a wholly unique member of the church, and as its exemplar and outstanding model in faith and charity" (LG, 53).

sing praises to God who, through Christ Jesus, has enabled both Mary and us to be so richly blessed.

1 CORINTHIANS 15:20–27 Paul sings God's praises for having raised Christ from the dead, "the firstfruits of those who have fallen asleep" (15:20). Since death entered through humanity's (Adam's) sinfulness, so too in Christ, a human like us, all humanity "shall . . . be brought to life" (v. 22). Paul articulates an apocalyptic process and time frame for these events. Upon Christ's return, all who belong to Christ will rise. Next comes the end of time, in which Christ will defeat all forces contrary to God. Death is the "last enemy to be destroyed" (v. 26), at which time Christ will hand over all to the Father who commissioned him for this purpose.

With Mary's Assumption, we sing praises to God for bringing Mary to life and allowing her full entrance into the heavenly kingdom. We, too, live in hope that through Christ's defeat of death, we will be brought to life and join Mary and all the saints in God's heavenly kingdom to sing God's praises forever.

LUKE 1:39–56 Two women form the frame in this Lucan painting. Elizabeth, the barren one, and Mary, the virgin, are both pregnant. Together they honor one another, as they sing praises to God's mercy and care for all the people. John, Elizabeth's child, begins his ministry of preparing the Messiah's path by jumping for joy in his mother's womb, at the recognition of the child in Mary's womb. Elizabeth honors and praises Mary for God's gift to her, for believing God's Word, and for being willing to cooperate with God's merciful plan of salvation.

Mary honors Elizabeth with her visit and her assistance during her pregnancy while she praises God's greatness in the Magnificat. Her song of praise is an affirmation of God's ways in contrast to human patterns of thinking and acting. The song speaks of God's graciousness in reversing expectations by choosing the lowly, the hungry, and the poor as vehicles through whom God's work of salvation is accomplished. In and through Mary, God's lowly hand-maid, salvation has come. With Mary, all we can do is rejoice and sing God's praises for the Almighty has done great things for all of us.

- "In countless hymns and antiphons expressing [Marian] prayer, two movements usually alternate with one another: the first 'magnifies' the Lord for the 'great things' he did for his lowly servant and through her for all human beings;[1] the second entrusts the supplications and praises of the children of God to the Mother of Jesus, because she now knows the humanity which, in her, the Son of God espoused" (CCC, 2675).

---

1 Cf. Luke 1:46–55.

NUMBERS 21:4B–9 The Book of Numbers (Greek: *arithmoi*) is a combination of law and history. It derives its name from two censuses taken of the Hebrew people, one at the end of their encampment at Mount Sinai and the other at the arrival at the borders the Promised Land. The censuses were taken to determine if Israel had sufficient numbers to possess the Land. Chapter 11 begins a series of complaints and rebellions on the part of the people. The common pattern is as follows: (1) the people complain; (2) God expresses wrath; (3) Moses is asked to intercede; and (4) the Israelites are punished for their rebellion.

Although the people win their battle over the Canaanite King Arad (21:1–3), in today's reading, they complain to Moses that they have no food or water, asking, "Why have you brought us up out of Egypt to die in the wilderness?" (v. 5). As punishment for their lack of trust, God sends "seraph serpents" (a species of snake whose fiery venom was poisonous) to bite them, and many people die. They call on Moses to plead to God on their behalf. In his prayer for the people, Moses receives instructions from the Lord to make a bronze serpent, mount it on a pole, and elevate it for all to see. Moses faithfully follows these instructions. Then, by gazing on the object of death, the Israelites recover and live. Thus, through the Lord, death has now turned into life.

PSALM 78:1–2, 34–35, 36–37, 38 (SEE 7B) This psalm narrates the infidelity of the people of the Northern Kingdom of Israel, which led to their ruin. The people were disloyal to God, as were their ancestors in the wilderness: "Their heart was not steadfast toward him; they were not true to his covenant" (Psalm 78:37). Would the Southern Kingdom of Judah be as faithless as Israel? Although the Israelites tested God again and again, he "forgave their iniquity, and did not destroy them" (v. 38). We, like the Israelites, are to remember the merciful works of the Lord.

PHILIPPIANS 2:6–11 Paul writes from prison, making a plea for unity, exhorting the Philippians to humbly "regard others as better than yourselves" (Philippians 2:3). He urges, "Let the same mind [Greek: *phroneo*, "like-mindedness"] be in you that was in Christ Jesus" (v. 5). Paul quotes an early Christian hymn, which the Philippian community would

CONNECTIONS TO CHURCH TEACHING AND TRADITION

- The Cross of Jesus is the Paschal sacrifice (CCC, 612–623).

- In the mystery of God's plan through the Cross (CCC, 549, 620), Jesus was made to be sin "who knew no sin, so that in him we might become the righteousness of God" (CCC, 602–603), and was exalted to the Father's right hand (CCC, 662).

- Through the unique sacrifice of Christ on the Cross, we have the possibility of being made partners in the Paschal Mystery (CCC, 618).

- The Paschal Mystery includes both the Death of Christ and his Resurrection (CCC, 654).

have known. The hymn begins with the preexistent Christ, who, "though he was in the form [Greek: *morphe*; v. 6] of God," did not grasp at equality with God. Christ was like God in his being or form; he was divine. Taking the form of a slave, he was obedient to the point of death on the Cross (vv. 7–8). Because of this, God exalted him, giving him the "name that is above every name" (v. 9): *Lord*. Thus, Jesus remains forever exalted and every tongue is to confess that he "is Lord, to the glory of God the Father" (v. 11).

JOHN 3:13–17 Israel's history shows how merciful and compassionate God is despite the people's sinfulness. For Christians, his definitive and everlasting love is expressed in the coming of Christ. In the Gospel proclaimed today, we hear: "For God so loved the world that he gave his only Son, so that everyone who believes in him may not perish but may have eternal life" (3:16). Nicodemus, a member of the Sanhedrin, the Jewish council, is curious about Jesus, but is afraid to come to him in broad daylight. Jesus tells him that it is not enough to claim membership in the Chosen People. To become a child of God, one must be "born from above" (v. 3) and to enter the Kingdom of God, one must be "born of water and Spirit" (v. 6).

John views the Cross as the triumphant beginning of Christ's return to glory. When Jesus teaches Nicodemus about salvation, he connects the saving power of the Cross with the story of the bronze serpent in the desert, heard in today's First Reading. Just as life came to the Israelites through the bronzed serpent, new life now comes through the Cross. Jesus' sacrifice on the Cross, however, surpasses the life the Israelites received. Through the Cross, eternal life—salvation—is available to all. Through the Cross, Jesus fulfills the promise of life in the Old Testament. All who look with faith on the Cross are healed. As the serpent that brought death had to be lifted up by Moses, so it was necessary that the Son of Man be lifted up and exalted on the Cross. Eternal life could be offered in no other way than for Christ to obediently experience suffering and death.

REVELATION 7:2–4, 9–14 Revelation is a New Testament book that is described as "apocalyptic," from the Greek word that means "revelation." The author of this book, a Jewish Christian prophet named John, describes visions of future events as he issues warnings about current behaviors. Revelation is a richly symbolic book that was never intended to be taken literally, but it does reveal certain truths.

In today's reading, there are two visions. The first is a brief message from an angel of God to protect the land until a huge group of people representing all the tribes of Israel is sealed as God's servant. The second is a vision of an even greater multitude of "every nation, race, people and tongue" that has been saved by the blood of the Lamb. The people of this multitude carry palm branches as a sign of the victory and don white robes to symbolize the new life won by this ultimate sacrifice. As the early Christian community is suffering persecution by Roman authorities, Revelation's author focuses on a message of hope. The suffering of the present time was indeed great, but it was not an end. There is hope, for Christ the Lamb has won salvation and eternal life.

PSALM 24:1–2, 3–4, 5–6 (SEE 6) This psalm of praise was sung by the Hebrew people in celebration of God's creation of the earth. For out of chaos, God "founded it upon the seas / and established it upon the rivers." With abundant praise, the psalmist celebrates the awesome power of God and simultaneously encourages all believers who yearn to be counted among God's faithful to follow these instructions: remain clean of heart, hold to what is right, and thus "receive a blessing from the Lord."

1 JOHN 3:1–3 When the First Letter of John was written around the end of the first century, the author had two purposes in mind. One purpose was theological in nature, responding to challenges in the early community about the nature of Jesus' humanity and divinity. What we now accept as the language of doctrine was in the process of being formulated in those early times. The writer of this First Letter of John was intent on making it clear that Jesus was both fully human and fully divine.

CONNECTIONS TO CHURCH TEACHING AND TRADITION

- "The followers of Christ, called by God . . . must therefore hold on to and perfect in their lives that holiness which they have received from God. They are told by the apostle to live 'as is fitting among saints' (Ephesians 5:3)" (LG, 40).

- "The teaching and spreading of her social doctrine are part of the Church's evangelizing mission. . . . It [this doctrine] consequently gives rise to a 'commitment to justice,' according to each individual's role, vocation and circumstances" (SRS, 41).

- "Lay people share in Christ's priesthood . . . and so fulfill the call to holiness addressed to all the baptized" (CCC, 941).

- "The social order requires constant improvement: it must be founded in truth, built on justice, and enlivened by love" (GS, 26).

The second purpose of the letter is to be an instruction on love. Its significant wisdom is "love is of God; everyone who loves is begotten by God and knows God" (1 John 4:7). John writes that this great and generous love has made all people children of God, bound together as one family. Immersed in divine love, the children of God find their guidelines for all of life. Though the mystery of God's great love will never be fully understood on this side of life, if love guides and shapes each day, the promise will be fulfilled when "we see him as he is."

MATTHEW 5:1–12A On the solemnity of All Saints, we remember all those who have gone before us in faith and who we trust now live forever in God's heavenly love. It is also a feast of recommitment for those of us who, inspired by their lives, are encouraged to imitate them. Though most of us will never be officially recognized by the Church as saints, our baptismal call to this goal is no less ours. Today's passage from the Gospel, Matthew's account of the Sermon on the Mount, provides guidelines for attaining that goal.

In the passage, Jesus walks among a great crowd and finds a place to sit where he delivers intentional teachings, not an offhand set of remarks. These teachings are at the core at his ministry and the life of those who choose to follow him. The eight "blessed" statements are no less a challenge to us today than they were then. Perhaps that is why Jesus sat down, as if to say, "Pay attention to these directions; they will lead to eternal life."

Faithfulness and justice are the central themes of these blessed statements. The "poor in spirit" are those who consider wealth unimportant because they live simply, either by choice or situation. They are blessed not because they are morally better than others, but because God has a special care for them. Blessed are the meek, not because they are quiet souls who fade into the woodwork, but because they are gentle and avoid revenge. Blessed are the merciful because they imitate God's great capacity to forgive without giving up. The clean of heart are those who have a great love of justice. Similarly, the peacemakers are those who stand for righteousness. These are challenging words; nonetheless, they are the guidelines for faithful living.

2 WISDOM 3:1–9 OR WISDOM 4:7–15 OR ISAIAH 25:6–9 *This reflection focuses on the reading from Isaiah.* This Sunday's reading from Isaiah comes from the Apocalypse of Isaiah found in chapters 24–27. Believing that God's action in human history would someday eliminate the suffering and death that began in the Genesis story, the prophet proclaimed the future time when God's people would die no more. God's people needed to practice patience and trust in God's action. Isaiah's images give a hope-filled sense of this future certainty: the Lord will provide, the veil of death will be destroyed, tears will be wiped away, and reproach will be removed. God will save, and all God's people will rejoice. Today is the day when we remind ourselves of the mercy of God upon all who have died, and this message from Isaiah is fitting. Those who have died will rise in new life. God's mercy endures forever. Death has no power. Along with Isaiah's listeners, we proclaim: "Let us rejoice and be glad that he has saved us!" (25:9).

PSALM 23:1–3A, 3B–4, 5, 6 (1) (4AB) OR PSALM 25:6 AND 7B, 17–18, 20–21 OR PSALM 27:1, 4, 7, 8B, 9A, 13–14 *This reflection focuses on Psalm 27.* The possible readings for the celebration of All Souls are also those that may be used for Masses for the Dead, including Psalm 27. This psalm offers hope even at the most desperate of times. All that we need is God. With God as an anchor, whom should we fear?

In the psalm, the singer takes an active role: I seek, I gaze at God, I contemplate, I wait with courage, I believe, I ask. I do all these things because God is my light and my salvation. Recognizing the power of this light over darkness, destruction, terror, sin, and even death, the believer trusts that God's presence is enough. As we look through the eyes of the New Testament and the stories of Jesus in the Gospel, we know that God dwelt among us. It gives special power to our desire to seek God's face and find an eternal dwelling place with God.

CONNECTIONS TO CHURCH TEACHING AND TRADITION

- "All are called to this union with Christ, who is the light of the world, from whom we come, through whom we live, and towards whom we direct our lives" (LG, 3).

- "The Christian vision of death receives privileged expression in the liturgy of the Church:[1] 'Lord, for your faithful people life is changed, not ended. When the body of our earthly dwelling lies in death we gain an everlasting dwelling place in heaven'[2]" (CCC, 1012).

- "Jesus portrays his own path, which leads through the Cross to the Resurrection: the path of the grain of wheat that falls to the ground and dies, and in this way bears much fruit" (DCE, 6).

---

1 Cf. 1 Thessalonians 4:13–14.
2 *Roman Missal*, Preface of Christian Death I.

ROMANS 5:5–11 OR ROMANS 5:17–21 OR ROMANS 6:3–9 OR ROMANS 8:14–23 OR ROMANS 8:31B–35, 37–39 OR ROMANS 14:7–9, 10C–12 OR 1 CORINTHIANS 15:20–28 OR 1 CORINTHIANS 15:51–57 OR 2 CORINTHIANS 4:14—5:1 OR 2 CORINTHIANS 5:1, 6–10 OR PHILIPPIANS 3:20–21 OR 1 THESSALONIANS 4:13–18 OR 2 TIMOTHY 2:8–13 *This reflection focuses on 2 Corinthians 5:1, 6–10.* Paul's image to the Corinthians of "our earthly dwelling, a tent" (2 Corinthians 5:1) is a reference to our earthly body, which Paul understood to be temporary until we dwelt with God in heaven. Paul gives believers a reason to wait for the Lord to come: God will replace our earthly body and give us a new body. Earth is a temporary place for all, and death comes to everyone, even to God's own beloved Son. Jesus' own passage through death to new life gives all humans the authentic path to come to dwell in God's house, the way to follow for eternal life. Trust in God as Jesus did, and do the Father's bidding. If we live this way of faith and discipleship then we will be ready, Paul says, to go home to God.

MATTHEW 5:1–12A OR MATTHEW 11:25–30 OR MATTHEW 25:31–46 OR LUKE 7:11–17 OR LUKE 23:44–46, 50, 52–53; 24:1–6A OR LUKE 24:13–16, 28–35 OR JOHN 5:24–29 OR JOHN 6:37–40 OR JOHN 6:51–59 OR JOHN 11:17–27 OR JOHN 11:32–45 OR JOHN 14:1–6 *This reflection focuses on Luke 7:11–17.* Today's reading from the Gospel according to Luke consoles us as we remember those who have gone before us. They shall be told to arise and will be given new life. Those who mourn will be comforted, and God will be praised and glorified. In Luke's story, Jesus is moved with pity, or compassion, for a widow whose only son died. In his culture the loss of a husband and son, who would have provided for her, meant that her protection was gone. Jesus knew that this could mean that she might be homeless with no one to care for her. He demonstrates his belief that God's presence eliminates all fear and mourning in his invitation to the young man to arise. This is how it will be in God's reign: death has no power and there will be no more distress or pain. Everything that Jesus did continually pointed to the day when God's reign would cover the whole earth. The crowd not only recognizes Jesus as a prophet, but also sees that this miracle expresses the intimate presence of God among them. God does indeed visit his people.

- "Those who die in God's grace and friendship and are perfectly purified live for ever with Christ" (CCC, 1023).

- "The Spirit is truly the dwelling of the saints and the saints are for the Spirit a place where he dwells as in his own home, since they offer themselves as a dwelling place for God and are called his temple[3]" (CCC, 2684).

3 St. Basil, *De Spiritu Sancto*, 26, 62: PG 32, 184.

EZEKIEL 47:1–2, 8–9, 12 Ezekiel paints an astounding vision of God's dwelling with his people, which demonstrates God's very real presence with his people. Like the images in the psalm, it has the overtones of the creation story. The Temple, water, the east, and living creatures all act as symbols in Ezekiel's vision. The Israelites believed that God was with them in a concrete way in the temple. Ezekiel paints a picture of the living water that flows from this Temple, from God, toward the east, the place where the new dawn would rise. Salvation is promised like a new day. The living water continues until it reaches the salt water of the sea and, in an astounding way, turns salt water into fresh water so that living creatures flourish and fish multiply. It is the wonderful image of the abundance of creation where all life springs from God's actions.

Along the banks of this living river, the trees bear fruit, and there is food and medicine in abundance. God's actions bring forth new life that dwells in God's people, who are called to be living fruit to one another and to the earth. Called to replenish ourselves at the waters of new life, we go forth and make God's dwelling known to the world. God's people now become the holy temples of God and live lives of praise and gratitude echoing the psalm response: "The waters of the river gladden the city of God, / the holy dwelling of the Most High" (46:5). Refreshed, we offer the fruits of our labor so that all may behold the amazing power of God's wondrous deeds.

PSALM 46:3, 4, 5–6, 8, 11 (5) Though this psalm is not proclaimed on any Sunday of the year, the strong images are familiar to us and inspired the hymn by Martin Luther, "A Mighty Fortress Is Our God." The verses we hear on this feast offer various titles as well as images for God: Most High, Lord of Hosts, God of Jacob and our refuge, strength, help in distress, our stronghold. It gives a glimpse of God's creative power and glory and seems an appropriate image to celebrate not only a church structure, but the Church as God's people.

CONNECTIONS TO CHURCH TEACHING AND TRADITION

- "As often as the sacrifice of the cross by which 'Christ our Pasch is sacrificed' is celebrated on the altar, the work of our redemption is carried on. Likewise, in the sacrament of the Eucharistic bread, the unity of all believers, who form one body in Christ,[1] is both expressed and achieved" (LG, 3).

- "The worship 'in Spirit and in truth'[2] of the New Covenant is not tied exclusively to any one place. The whole earth is sacred and entrusted to the children of men. What matters above all is that, when the faithful assemble in the same place, they are the 'living stones,' gathered to be 'built into a spiritual house.'[3] For the Body of the risen Christ is the spiritual temple from which the source of living water springs forth" (CCC, 1179).

---

1 Cf. 1 Corinthians 10:17.
2 John 4:24.
3 1 Peter 2:4–5.

The psalm begins with a picture of chaos, yet in the midst of this there is refuge and safety in God. This is God's holy dwelling place, and nothing can overcome God's power. Though the mountains and the earth quake, God is in control of all creation. Nothing can overcome the strength of God. God does astounding things in this sacred place and is always victorious over forces of chaos and evil. God's mighty deeds unfold before our very eyes, revealing the holy dwelling place of God here on earth with his people.

1 CORINTHIANS 3:9C–11, 16–17 Once again in today's readings we hear images of buildings: "like a wise master builder I laid a foundation," "each one must be careful how he builds upon it," and "the temple of God, which you are, is holy" (3:10, 17). Paul's message to the Corinthians is clear: they are to be and act like the manifestation of God in the world. Christ is the foundation, and they are each a temple built upon that foundation. Again, the Second Reading underscores that today's feast is not just a celebration of a physical church structure, but the very living and holy temples of God. Faced with these words of Paul, faithful believers, like the Corinthians, recognize this manner of living as both a privilege and a challenge. We, too, are offered the opportunity to build our lives on the foundation that is Christ.

JOHN 2:13–22 On this Feast of the Dedication of the Lateran Basilica in Rome, we celebrate not only our identity with the mother church of all Roman Catholic churches, but even more our identity as the Body of Christ. In John's sobering account of Jesus' cleansing of the Temple in Jerusalem, we hear Jesus claim his role as the new temple: "'Destroy this temple and in three days I will raise it up' . . . he was speaking about the temple of his body" (John 2:19, 21). His Body, raised from the dead by his Father, is the new temple, and by our Baptism we are identified with him as Christians and members of this Body. The central celebration of this feast is then not solely about the physical structure of a church, but about believers who are united in Christ's Body and who celebrate this union at every Eucharistic feast.

- "The church is not truly established and does not fully live, nor is a perfect sign of Christ unless there is a genuine laity existing and working alongside the hierarchy" (AG, 21).

GENESIS 3:9–15, 20 This passage begins at the point of encounter between Adam and God, following the Fall. It bears typical characteristics of the J (Yahwist) tradition. God is presented anthropomorphically, and Adam's sin is portrayed in all its brash stupidity. Though Adam initially speaks, the key characters are Eve and the serpent. She is tempted by the serpent and falls victim to his wiles. God addresses him first with the divine curse.

Adam and Eve had previously held mastery over animals, but their sin has subverted this order. Now there will be hostility between humans and animals, continuing throughout time. Christian tradition has read these verses as the protoevangelium, a first announcement of the Gospel, asserting the eventual conquest of evil by Christ, offspring of Mary.

The closing line, naming Eve as "the mother of all the living" (Genesis 3:20), has a connection with the Gospel for the solemnity of the Immaculate Conception. In contrast with Eve's negative response to God's command, Mary responds with obedient faith. Through Mary's response, the tide of human history turns.

PSALM 98:1, 2–3, 3–4 (1A) Psalm 98 belongs to a collection within the Book of Psalms known as Hymns of the Lord's Kingship, or Enthronement Psalms (Psalms 95—99). These psalms tell of the Lord's kingship over Israel and the whole world. The "right hand and holy arm" (Psalm 98:1) of the Lord has brought about victory for God's people, accomplishing wondrous deeds. The opening call to "sing to the Lord a new song" (Psalm 98:1) suggests that this marvelous, divine feat calls for a concomitant response that offers to God something new, distinct, creative, and wonderful.

In the context of this solemnity honoring Mary's Immaculate Conception, the antiphon opening the psalm presents a call both to Mary and to all who celebrate this day. When Mary is called to bear the Son of the Most High, she is invited to sing a new song to the Lord for what God is about to accomplish in her, and through her, for the world. Mary's yes overturns the avalanche of sin that has followed Eve's no to God. A new day dawns in the history of salvation, and the community of believers lifts up praise to God

CONNECTIONS TO CHURCH TEACHING AND TRADITION

- "The Solemnity of December 8 . . . is a joint celebration of the Immaculate Conception of Mary, of the basic preparation (cf. Isaiah 11:1, 10) for the coming of the Savior and of the happy beginning of the Church without spot or wrinkle" (MC, 3).

- "In order for Mary to be able to give the free assent of her faith to the announcement of her vocation, it was necessary that she be wholly borne by God's grace. . . . By the grace of God Mary remained free of every personal sin her whole life long" (CCC, 490, 493).

- "When we read that the messenger addresses Mary as 'full of grace,' the Gospel context . . . enables us to understand that among all the 'spiritual blessings in Christ' this is a special 'blessing.' . . . In an entirely special and exceptional way Mary is united to Christ. . . . As the Council teaches, Mary 'stands out among the poor and humble of the Lord, who confidently await and receive salvation from him'" (RM, 8).

for what has been accomplished in Mary for the world's redemption.

EPHESIANS 1:3–6, 11–12 Here we are given what is believed to be an early Christian hymn for the liturgy, extolling the ineffable plan of God to bring redemption to the world through Jesus Christ. The text praises God for the election offered to the human race, to be made "holy and without blemish before him" (Ephesians 1:4). Though we know ourselves to fall painfully short of the grace and blessing offered us, the fact of our own inadequacy pales beside the gift of God's love bestowed upon us.

When Paul declares that "in love he destined us for adoption to himself through Jesus Christ" (Ephesians 1:5), he affirms that God's will for our salvation flows forth in divine love. One element of this surpassing love of God may be discerned in the singular grace bestowed on Mary, from the moment of her conception, to be free of original sin. It is important for us to note that even this grace comes to her through Christ, who brings all of us up into the fullness of divine life.

LUKE 1:26–38 Two important themes converge in this passage from the Gospel according to Luke: the moment of the turning of the ages and Mary's faith-filled response. Recalling 2 Samuel 7, where God promises that the Messiah is to come from the house of David, we see that this passage brings that prophesied salvific moment to full reality. It is presented in contrasting terms of utter fragility (the young and inexperienced maiden) and divine strength ("you shall name him Jesus" [the Lord saves] "and of his Kingdom there will be no end") (vv. 31–33).

Mary is immediately addressed as "favored" (full of grace). She already possesses grace from God, which sets her apart, and though she initially demurs from the angel's announcement, saying, "How can this be?" (v. 34), she listens to the continuing explanation of a plan quite different from her own. In the end, her wholehearted response, "May it be done to me according to your word" (v. 38), quietly, and with profound nobility, sets off the turn of the ages.

Key to Abbreviations for Church Documents

The following documents are referenced under the Connections to Church Teaching and Tradition sections that appear for each date. The full document texts can be found in LTP's four-volume *Liturgy Documents* series; in *Vatican Council II: Constitutions, Decrees, Declarations; The Basic 16 Documents* translated by Austin Flannery, OP, published by Liturgical Press; on the Vatican website (www.vatican.va); on the United States Conference of Catholic Bishops website (www.usccb.org); or in other online locations, which can be located by searching the English, Latin, or Spanish title.

AA	*Apostolicam actuositatem*
AG	*Ad gentes divinitus*
Aparecida	*Documento Conclusivo de Aparecida*, Fifth General Conference of Latin Bishops (CELAM)
CCC	*Catechism of the Catholic Church*
CSDC	*Compendium of the Social Doctrine of the Church*
CI	*Christian Initiation*, General Introduction
CIV	*Caritas in veritate*
CL	*Christifideles laici*
DCE	*Deus caritas est*
EE	*Ecclesia de Eucharistia*
EG	*Evangelii gaudium*
EIA	*Ecclesia in America*
EN	*Evangelii nuntiandi*
ES	*Ecclesiam suam*
FC	*Familiaris consortio*
GDC	*General Directory for Catechesis*
GIRM	*General Instruction of the Roman Missal*
GMD	*Go and Make Disciples: A National Plan and Strategy for Catholic Evangelization in the United States*
GS	*Gaudium et spes*
JM	*Justitia in mundo*
LG	*Lumen gentium*

LH	*Liturgy of the Hours*
MC	*Marialis cultus*
MD	*Mulieris dignitatem*
NDC	*National Directory for Catechesis*
PDV	*Pastores dabo vobis*
PP	*Princeps pastorum*
PT	*Pacem in terris*
RCIA	*Rite of Christian Initiation of Adults*
RH	*Redemptor hominis*
RM	*Redemptoris mater*
RMI	*Redemptoris missio*
SC	*Sacrosanctum concilium*
SCA	*Sacramentum caritatis*
SRS	*Sollicitudo rei socialis*
SS	*Spe salvi*
TMA	*Tertio millennio adveniente*
USCCA	*United States Catholic Catechism for Adults*
VD	*Verbum Domini*